Fair Shares

Fair Shares

The Future of Shareholder Power and Responsibility

JONATHAN CHARKHAM AND ANNE SIMPSON

OXFORD

UNIVERSITY PRESS

OXFORD

UNIVERSITY PRESS

Great Clarendon Street, Oxford OX2 6DP

Oxford University Press is a department of the Univerity of Oxford.
It furthers the University's objective of excellence in research, scholarship,
and education by publishing worldwide in

Oxford New York

Athens Auckland Bangkok Bogotá Buenos Aires Calcutta
Cape Town Chennai Dar es Salaam Delhi Florence Hong Kong Istanbul
Karachi Kuala Lumpur Madrid Melbourne Mexico City Mumbai
Nairobi Paris São Paulo Singapore Taipei Tokyo Toronto Warsaw

with associated companies in Berlin Ibadan

Oxford is a registered trade mark of Oxford University Press
in the UK and in certain other countries

Published in the United States
by Oxford University Press Inc., New York

© Jonathan Charkham and Anne Simpson 1999

The moral rights of the author have been asserted
Database right Oxford University Press (maker)

First published 1999

British Library Cataloguing in Publication Data
Data available

Library of Congress Cataloging in Publication Data
Data available

ISBN 0–19–829214–7

10 9 8 7 6 5 4 3 2 1

Typeset in Utopia
by J&L Composition Ltd, Filey, North Yorkshire
Printed in Great Britain on acid-free paper by
Bookcraft Ltd, Midsomer Norton, Somerset

Acknowledgements

WE would like to acknowledge the contributions of the many company directors and executives, investment managers, trustees of both public and private sector funds, and shareholders who have provided the essential subject matter for this book over many years. Also, our colleagues and associates in their work, writings, and conversations with us have provided comment, material, and a healthy degree of constructive criticism! Among many others in the UK some deserve special mention, including Sir Adrian Cadbury, John Plender, Victoria Younghusband, Mark Sheldon, David Freeman, Alan MacDougall, Stuart Bell, and Janice Hayward, and, for their international perspective on a British problem, Ira Millstein, Bob Monks, Nell Minow, Carolyn Brancato, Holly Gregory, Bill Patterson, Sarah Teslik, Sophie L'Helias, and Mats Isaksson. Kit Bingham and Matthew Gaved both made contributions to particular chapters, for which many thanks. It should be noted that despite our various professional associations, we both write in a personal capacity. We would also like to thank David Musson, who as editor has always been thoughtful and informed in his contributions. Finally, the patience of friends, colleagues, and family over the many months' drafting deserve our thanks and appreciation, as well as those whose opinion and comment have helped shape our proposals.

J.C.
A.S.
November 1998

Contents

Abbreviations

ABI	Association of British Insurers
AIMA	Australian Investment Managers' Association
CBI	Confederation of British Industry
CII	Council of Institutional Investors
DOL	Department of Labor (USA)
DTI	Department of Trade and Industry
ERISA	Employee Retirement Income Securities Act
FSA	Financial Services Authority
GDP	Gross Domestic Product
IFMA	Institutional Fund Managers' Association
IMRO	Investment Managers' Regulatory Organization
IOD	Institute of Directors
ISC	Institutional Shareholders' Committee
LAPFF	Local Authority Pension Fund Forum
LSE	London Stock Exchange
NAPF	National Association of Pension Funds
NED	non-executive director
OECD	Organization for Economic Cooperation and Development
OFT	Office of Fair Trading
PIRC	Pensions & Investment Research Consultants Ltd.
RSA	Royal Society of Arts, Manufacture and Commerce
SEC	Securities and Exchange Commission
UKSHA	UK Shareholders' Association

Introduction

Why a Book about Shareholders?

THIS is a book about the shareholders of companies listed on the stock market—who they are, what they own, and why their role matters to us all. It argues that for shareholders, as with others in a democratic system, power confers responsibility, and sets out a programme of reform to ensure this. The costs, conflicts of interest, and inefficiencies of the current system make it rational for many shareholders to avoid the responsibilities of ownership. This is neither in their own long-term interest as investors, nor in that of others who depend upon the prosperity of these companies for investment returns, employment, the provision of goods and services, or even their contribution of tax to the public purse. Shareholder passivity may be individually rational, but is collectively to the detriment of UK PLC.

In considering the role of shareholders we trace the origins of the joint stock company and the different parts played by shareholders of various types in the UK system. Along the way we review the legal and regulatory framework and look at practical examples of shareholder efforts to make the system work. The reforms we propose address the antique legal and regulatory framework of the UK, and present practical ideas for updating our corporate governance system. In the debate on reform of the financial system internationally, the position of shareholders in one of the largest and oldest capital markets provides an instructive case study.

Since starting this book two years ago, much has been published on corporate governance. There have also been some dramatic changes in the role shareholders play. More needs to be done to make active ownership the rule, rather than the exception.

Despite the implicit importance of their role shareholders have too often played a bit part in corporate governance debates. They crop up in the academic text amidst the theory and new jargon of corporate governance: in discussions of 'principals' and 'agents', tensions with 'stakeholders', as players in the 'nexus of contracts'. Shareholders may appear in the somewhat bewildering charts that now seem to be a requirement in academic tracts on the subject, with two-way arrows and Venn diagrams describing their relationships with auditors, government, directors, management, and even employees. Their role and responsibilities are left largely unexamined. Shareholders are in principle acknowledged to have a key role, but one which is rarely explored in practical terms.

This is not to say they have been entirely ignored. Shareholders feature in codes and guidance notes, and are referred to in solemn, but scanty, terms in pronouncements on best practice. They are described as the 'owners of companies' or even the 'guardians' of corporate accountability. How this is to be ensured, and the barriers to its practical achievement, have been generally left unexplored. The patent virtues of shareholder responsibility are viewed as sufficient to ensure its realization.

POWER WITHOUT RESPONSIBILITY

Under the current legal and regulatory framework UK shareholders have no responsibilities, other than a modest requirement to disclose any holding over 3 per cent, and to abide by the Takeover Code's provisions. By contrast that same framework has provided shareholders with what look like formidable powers over companies—to appoint and remove directors, similarly auditors, submit resolutions, convene meetings; and their permission must be sought for alterations to the company's constitution and share capital. Uniquely among the various groups concerned with how companies perform (employees, the state, communities, lenders, and customers among them) it is only shareholders who formally have the power to hold directors accountable for their stewardship of the company. For that reason, their role cannot be ignored, and if we seek more effective corporate governance then their influence needs to be marshalled.

The law has been designed (and is maintained) with the view that shareholders are a single body. They may be equal in the eyes of the law, but shareholders are not a homogeneous group. There have been profound shifts in the pattern of ownership in the UK as elsewhere. This book examines the consequences. The pattern of shareholdings in the economic landscape has dramatically altered. In the space of thirty years, the ownership of companies has been transformed from dominance by private investors to institutional shareholdings formed from the public's savings. The potential for responsible and active share ownership has been transformed in the process. No longer are listed companies owned by fragmented individual holdings or family stakes; the collective saving vehicles of the nation's pension funds, insurance savings, and unit trusts are the new owners of companies. With the concentration of ownership and professional resources such investors bring to the market, it is not only desirable, but necessary, to review the role of institutions who have command of the nation's capital. How that influence is exercised (or not), and how it could be exercised, is the subject of this book.

PRIVATE COMPANIES, PUBLIC SAVINGS

The economy has seen another dramatic development, which is linked to the phenomenal rise of institutional share ownership: the growth in the UK equity market. The liabilities of pension funds are long term and require investments which outpace wage inflation. Equity investment over the long term has provided the returns which can meet such liabilities. Investment in the shares of companies has become the largest asset in the portfolios of pension funds (and of growing importance to insurers). Governments' intentions to expand funded pensions provision by establishment of Stakeholder Pensions will also contribute to the trend towards capital accumulation via equity investment. The source of industrial and commercial capital is therefore based on funds whose liabilities require real growth over decades not years.

There are various reasons, such as the lack of alternative sources of finance for companies in the UK capital markets, which explain why a stock market listing is the route chosen by so many. To this has been added the grand experiment of privatization and, more recently, the incorporation of mutual societies to swell the ranks of listed companies. The upshot is that the UK is ending the century with a GDP worth less than the value of listed companies on the stock market. Others have written at length about the paucity of venture capital and dearth of long-term debt financing for the UK's small and medium-sized companies. The result is that the UK depends upon listed companies for goods, services, and investment returns to finance retirement and even housing provision, to an extent almost unknown elsewhere in the developed economies. The success or failure—both relative and absolute—of listed companies is hence of paramount importance. The role of share-holders to whom the directors of these companies are accountable is thereby of public interest. For other economies making a similar shift in the development of their capital markets, the same questions will need to be addressed.

FROM STATE TO SHARE OWNERSHIP: THE MYTH OF 'SID'

With the retreat of the state, part ideological, part pragmatic, shareholders have been put into the role of owner for large swathes of routine, but essential, economic activity. It is easy to forget that until recently services such as water, lighting, and heat were owned by the state, as were key industries like defence, telecoms, and coal. Even basic infrastructure was clearly in the public domain. The journey to work by bus or train, and even aeroplane, meant being a customer of a government-owned business.

Privatization has changed all that. However, the new owners of industry are not the private investors promoted by Mrs Thatcher in her vision of a share-owning democracy. We are not a nation of 'Sids'—the eponymous individuals dreamed up by the advertising agency promoting the sale of shares in British Gas to the public. Private investors may have grown in number, but their role has dwindled, as institutions have become the dominant shareholders. The tax advantages put in place by government have fostered the growth of collective savings via pension funds and mortgage endowment policies, resulting in the virtual eclipse of the private shareholder. Thirty years ago private investors owned two-thirds of the stock market; today they hold less than one-fifth.

The rise of the institutional shareholder means that companies are no longer owned by family groups (though these still exist even in some large listed companies) or even highly fragmented private investments. It is not institutional ownership *per se* which is important, but the concentration of ownership this has brought about through the restructuring of the investment service industry during the 1980s. Following 'Big Bang' a wave of takeovers and mergers has resulted in concentration of ownership among investment managers who have the majority of institutional funds as clients. Typically, half of a UK company's share capital will be in the hands of thirty or forty investment managers. The need for accountability by this influential group is a key theme in this book.

The very size and economic influence wielded by the institutions in our society, both at home and abroad, means their role merits attention. This book, however, is not simply a narrative account of who does what and when. We are concerned with the weaknesses in the current system, flaws and conflicts of interest which have led to inefficiencies and a lack of accountability.

LACK OF SHAREHOLDER OVERSIGHT

A raw example of the problems shareholders face in exerting effective oversight is the continuing controversy over executive pay. Shareholders may foot the bill, and have formal power to intervene, but even where they have had misgivings or objections to apparently extravagant executive compensation they have not succeeded in stopping pay abuse. A rare example of shareholder resolutions on executive remuneration policy is the British Gas AGM of 1995. Elsewhere shareholders have begun to vote against remuneration committee members, such as at Granada in 1998, and share option schemes such as GEC in 1997. Despite these brave efforts, overall, shareholders have proved unable to stem the rising costs of pay or calm the public controversy.

LOSING IT ALL—CORPORATE COLLAPSES

It is not just single issues such as pay which warrant a rethink on the role of shareholders. The series of corporate collapses which prompted formation of the Cadbury Committee focused attention upon the integrity of financial statements, internal controls, and audit committees, but also the role of the shareholders in approving directors, auditors, and financial statements. The ability of shareholders to protect their interests will be tested during the next economic downturn. In the meantime, internal control failures such as the losses at NatWest in mispricing of derivatives, the collapse and sale of Barings, the hefty compensation paid to advertisers at Reed Elsevier over inaccurate circulation figures, and accounting errors at Wickes, have provided a steady stream of reminders that all is not for the best, in the best of all possible worlds. Corporate governance is an essential part of risk management for shareholders.

COMPETITIVENESS—THE NATIONAL INTEREST

A further issue is competitiveness. The 'long tail of underperforming companies' has attracted the attention and concern of academics and government. Improving the performance of these companies would generate an improved tax base, a stimulus to growth, expansion in employment, and the associated economic and social benefits. Shareholders would clearly benefit too. There is a new and growing interest in governance and performance by institutional shareholders. With honourable exceptions, until recently shareholders have either sold or lain low when there are problems, hoping perhaps to be rescued from underperforming or incompetent boards by a takeover. Even then, the costs can be high, as the overhang from board problems means sluggish performance. Shareholders often appear willing to suffer the pain of extortionate transaction costs in order to be bought out of trouble by a willing bidder. Prior to the bid from Granada, the board of Forte had attracted some criticism but chairman Rocco Forte claimed that not one institutional shareholder had sought to meet and discuss board problems. If a problem relates to the board why not replace it, instead of taking the far more costly option of changing ownership when the remedy lies in changing the directors?

IRRATIONAL SHAREHOLDERS?

Is this irrational behaviour by shareholders? Or perhaps it is that practical barriers, conflicts of interest, or lack of coordination, impede the exercise of effective influence. What is perhaps individually rational for one shareholder (time, cost, effort, commercial conflicts of interest, the hassle factor) leads to collective inefficiencies in the market.

A common explanation for investor passivity is that shareholders do not have the skill, resources, or interest to assume the responsibilities of ownership. It is also argued that shareholders are not in a position to coordinate their activity, or play an effective role due to 'free rider' problems. However, if it is clearly in their self-interest (and the public interest) that shareholders play a more active role, then we need to examine closely why it is not happening in a systematic fashion.

Greatness may have been thrust upon them, but it is not clear that most shareholders are willing or able to discharge the responsibilities of collective ownership for listed companies which will ensure that a number of objectives are met: that the economy improves its competitive position; that the public interest in these companies is properly considered; and that the legitimate concerns of other groups contributing to and dependent upon the company have been dealt with.

That aside, why is it in shareholders' own interest to become active? The answer is: performance. There is a growing body of research examining the relationship between shareholder activism, board dynamics, and corporate performance. This has mainly been commissioned by activist shareholders in the United States who want to check on the returns to their investment in activism *per se* (Gordon Group, Wilshire Associates, Department of Labor). New studies are being published in the UK (PIRC 1998*c*) and Continental Europe (ProxInvest 1997) which are building some evidence on the issue.

A major study by Professor Paul MacAvoy of Yale and Ira Millstein concludes there is a positive relationship between economic value added and 'the dynamic board' (*Columbia Law Review*, June 1998). It has been clear for some time that the presence of an 'active' shareholder or public threats to put pressure on poorly performing companies has generated returns for the shareholder. Others have also benefited from the effect. Part, however, seems to be related to an immediate increase in share price, as the US market *anticipates* future financial improvement. In other words, Wall Street believes in it, so shareholder activism is rewarded. UK sentiment may not react as quickly in this helpful way, so that activists may have to be patient and wait for the underlying improvements in performance and prospects to be recognized by the market.

THE LINE OF LEAST RESISTANCE: SELL

The highly prized liquidity of the UK stock market has offered most shareholders an alternative to the challenging, expensive, and sometimes fraught business of tackling poorly performing directors. The line of least resistance is to sell. This is deceptively easy. For the institutions, the very size of the assets accumulated in their portfolios means that, for the most part, trading out of trouble can be an awkward and expensive solution. The size of their holdings means that the counterparty is likely to be another institution. It is a game of 'pass the parcel' played at the expense of the beneficiaries and to the advantage of the intermediaries. To compound this, there has been a rapid growth in indexation, where an investor holds a selection of shares which replicate the market (or some part of it). The portfolio of shares is held 'passively', and the small amount of trade which is done is only to ensure that as the composition of the market changes (through takeovers of new listings) so too does the investment fund. The growth of such funds has brought down the average trading figures for large pension funds (though the number of 'bargains' overall in the market continues to rise).

SHAREHOLDER ACTION

Despite these secular shifts in the pattern of ownership, the majority of shareholders are still largely inactive in the exercise of their voting rights. There are honourable exceptions, and their approach is examined later in the book as providing practical examples of the potential for reform. However, for the most part, to date UK shareholders have not used their voting rights to pursue improvements in corporate performance. This is despite much advice to the contrary. The Cadbury Committee saw clearly that these formal powers were important to the effective monitoring of corporate governance standards: in a brief, though weighty, section of the report devoted to the role of shareholders, it advised in 1992 that

Given the weight of their votes, the way in which institutional shareholders use their power to influence the standards of corporate governance is of fundamental importance. Their readiness to do this turns on the degree to which they see it as their responsibility as owners, and in the interest of those whose money they are investing, to bring about changes in companies when necessary, rather than selling their shares . . . Voting rights can be regarded as an asset, and the use or otherwise of those rights by institutional shareholders is a subject of legitimate interest to those on whose behalf they invest. *We recommend* that institutional investors should disclose their policies on the use of voting rights. (Committee on the Financial Aspects of Corporate Governance 1992: s. 6)

Has this advice had any impact? Perhaps not as much as would be hoped for. The six years since the Cadbury Report was published have seen only a marginal rise in voting activity. Furthermore, among those voting some have stated they follow the advice of the directors on how to vote, expressed as 'it is our policy to support the board'. It would no longer be fair to characterize institutional votes as rubber stamping proposals either from a misplaced sense of loyalty to the board or else from lack of suitable alternative research and advice upon which to base a decision. It would not be right to be complacent. There is little evidence of shareholders challenging the board in an informed and constructive way even when the circumstances suggest this would be to the long-term advantage of the company. In short they sit on their hands too often. However, the practice of 'discretionary' voting, where the chairman makes the decision on behalf of the shareholder, can be viewed either as a touching display of trust or abdication of judgement on the issues. The senior partner at a leading law firm candidly admitted that one of their services to companies was to scrutinize the votes which came in from shareholders, and chase up those who had voted against the advice of the directors. The purpose of this was to allow a call from the chairman which might persuade them of the error of their ways. Such tales may not be typical, but they illustrate the arcane nature of much of what passes for a shareholder democracy. The episode also raises the question of confidentiality in the voting process. Without a requirement for policies on voting to be declared by institutions, and disclosure of proxy votes at company meetings, confidence in the system will remain at a low ebb.

A SCLEROTIC SHAREHOLDER DEMOCRACY

The figures on shareholder voting are not impressive. A four-year survey of proxy voting trends culled from company registrars at the top 350 companies shows an increase in voting from 36 per cent to 38 per cent. By 1998 this had risen to around 45 per cent (PIRC 1998*d*). This is against a backdrop of institutional ownership of over 80 per cent (if overseas investors are included). Similarly the average vote in favour (including discretionary votes provided to the chairman) on average declined only marginally from 99.3 per cent to 98.6 per cent (PIRC 1997*a*). There are notable exceptions, and later we look at the efforts of some institutions to become active owners and exercise their formal powers responsibly.

This lack of critical scrutiny by the majority is puzzling when considered against the long list of issues for shareholders to tackle: expensive losses suffered by shareholders through failures of internal control (from the collapses of the late 1980s typified by the Polly Peck and Maxwell disasters to blue chip disasters such as Barings); the loss to public reputation suffered by companies and shareholders in the controversy on executive remuneration; growing public concern regarding corporate citizenship, over environmental and social policy (for example at Shell and BP); set against a backdrop of decline in investment relative to competitors, which has inspired White Papers on a regular basis under governments of both complexions.

At worst, the lack of shareholder attention is an abdication of responsibility—to the companies they own shares in, and thereby to the beneficiaries on whose behalf they invest. The lost potential is immense. The DTI's own assessment of this missed opportunity put in simple financial terms is that if UK companies could be pulled up to the level of US competitiveness, GDP could be boosted by £60bn. The point is that shareholders (unlike other stakeholders) are in a position to do something to improve their lot. The responsibility for a company's performance rests squarely on the shoulders of its directors; shareholders have the practical option of appointing, monitoring, and, if necessary, removing those who are not delivering the goods.

If the traditional role of trading shares for most shareholders is now no longer practical due to their size (and one would also hope consideration of their long-term liabilities as pension funds and insurance companies), what are the alternatives to corporate governance activity? There is the traditional view that the UK market for corporate control does the job for them. It is argued that the market solution of takeovers to tackle underperforming companies should be relied upon. The evidence is not compelling. Unless fundamental to industrial restructuring, hostile takeovers have proved at best an uncertain solution, and overall the transaction costs are rarely recouped via improved performance in the merged enterprise (LSE Centre for Economic Performance 1996; University of Essex 1997). Proponents of this solution to underperformance in companies also have to consider whether the threat of takeover leads to an overly nervous concern with short-term share price movements by the directors, rather than the long-term strategy upon which the institutions' returns will best be secured. Although it is viewed as passé to discuss 'short termism' in the UK market, there was a steady stream of complaint from manufacturers to the Trade and Industry Select Committee inquiry into competitiveness in 1994 that long-term funds could not be raised. Other research and comment reflect the view that many institutional investors lack real interest. Extel's annual survey of company attitudes to the City has highlighted that company directors considered the shareholders who visited them did not know what to ask, had not prepared an agenda, and had a narrow range of short-term interests (Extel 1997). The exceptions to this were ranked in a special award (won that year by insurance company Standard Life, one of the few to publish a corporate governance policy).

Few institutions are forthcoming about their policies on corporate governance. Despite the Cadbury Report's advice that institutions should make these known to those 'with a legitimate interest', of the 150 institutions surveyed regarding their corporate governance policies, 80 per cent stated that they were not for public consumption. For a significant group, even the companies in which they held shares were not entitled to a copy (PIRC 1997b). This is surely taking the virtue of discretion too far.

PRIVATE INTEREST AND PUBLIC INTEREST

The dominance of listed companies has put their institutional shareholders into a prime position of responsibility in the economy. Both in the UK and overseas, beyond their direct financial interest (which is considerable) in ensuring that companies perform, there is the wider public interest. With the retreat of the state and lack of credible alternatives to monitor performance, shareholders will have to accept the greatness that has been thrust upon them. This book is about how this situation has emerged and what reforms we consider are needed to allow (and where necessary require) institutional share- holders to behave like owners of companies, rather than traders of shares.

INTERNATIONAL TRENDS: GOVERNANCE ESPERANTO?

In the era of global capital markets, the issue of the shareholders' role is of international importance. To facilitate the free flow of capital across borders there will have to be a convergence in minimum standards of accounting disclosure, information, and protection for external suppliers of capital. Not- withstanding this, the accepted role of shareholders varies across the major markets, reflecting not only the particular economic and social history of nations, but the associated values attached to the role of different stakeholders, and shareholders in particular, and even the purpose of the company. The tension between harmonization of standards to allow capital raising in global markets and domestic variations on the corporate governance theme means there will be no bland international standard. The challenge of promoting enterprise *and* accountability is common to all markets. The corporate govern- ance world cannot be neatly divided into two camps as some have proposed. (For example, the Anglo model in which investors operate in a liquid trading market and the Rhine model in which investors hold long-term stakes and use their influence to effect changes.) The differences between markets within these two camps, such as the UK and USA, merit special attention. To place Germany, France, and Japan into the same group conceals as much as it illuminates.

The growing literature on shareholders published in the USA does not therefore serve as a short cut to examining the British situation in detail. Although the countries have a common heritage, the differences are as important as the similarities in the corporate governance system. Both countries are examples of democratic politics; but the US constitutional arrangements differ from those of the UK; so too with corporate governance. The regulatory and legal framework, the rights and duties of shareholders, and individual corporate charters are extremely different. In the European debate on corporate governance, an understanding of weaknesses as well as strengths of the UK system is essential in debating the integration of capital markets, even within the confines of EU convergence. In considering the need for reform at international level we need first a clear grasp of how particular systems work.

SHAREHOLDERS AND OTHER PLAYERS

Despite their neglected role, we accept that shareholders are only one part of a corporate governance system. Even so it is potentially of such importance that it should be understood by all parties. This includes: the directors and senior managers of companies and those who advise them on investor relations and the markets; shareholders of all kinds, and their intermediaries and advisers, including stockbrokers, trustees, fund managers, and merchant bankers; policy-makers across the political spectrum; employees; all the regulatory agencies; and last, but not least, the academic world, for which corporate governance is approaching the status of a fashionable discipline in its own right. This book is written with a view to those with a practical, particular, or even academic interest in the subject, and other onlookers who wonder about the prosperity of the nation's companies and their 'absentee landlords'. The authors fully realize the crucial importance of smaller and unquoted companies. Many of the things written in this book apply to them with equal force, simply because the principles of good corporate governance apply to them as well. But there are important differences, and for reasons of clarity we concentrate on companies whose shares are quoted on a stock exchange. Readers will know that under UK law a company may be a PLC but not be quoted; on the other hand it must be a PLC if it wants a quote. Throughout the book it is quoted companies to which we refer, unless we say otherwise.

A PRACTITIONER APPROACH

The book is organized in a series of chapters which are not of the same length, and we have not tried to achieve a discussion of equal parts simply to provide a suitable number of pages. Some chapters are quite short, because the matter has been dealt with briefly. On other subjects, we take more time, because we view it as relevant to the overall thrust of the argument and conclusions.

In setting the scene for reform, we need to understand the status quo, and how it came to be. For that reason we spend some time delving into the history of the joint stock company. The essential framework elaborated in the nineteenth century has not been overhauled in the last 100 years. This is for pragmatic reasons, but the British preference for voluntary codes and pseudo-legislation has led to a tangled undergrowth of rules. At times there is overlap and some contradiction between the requirements of statute (in the Companies Acts) and regulations (in the form of listing rules) and codes of practice (from Cadbury, Greenbury, and more recently Hampel to guidelines from august bodies such as the Institutional Shareholders' Committee). Companies can be forgiven for feeling confused.

Some aspects of the law are patently outmoded. One small but important example is the quaint tradition of taking business at the AGM on a show of hands when most vote by proxies which are then unused. Shareholders may seek a poll, which is usually viewed as disruptive, though the results can show occasional surprises.

There is recognition of the need for reform, for instance in the Department of Trade and Industry review of shareholder resolutions, which was left to gather dust in the run up to an election (DTI 1996). This followed House of Commons Select Committee hearings after the uproar at the British Gas AGM the same year. Similarly, committees, such as that chaired by Paul Myners of fund manager firm Gartmore's, gave some good advice on how to improve matters. The Hampel Committee, which is the successor to Cadbury and Greenbury, sought views on how to improve the process but was not minded to recommend legal reforms. These are piecemeal responses. It is our view that a thorough review is long overdue. During the later stages of the preparation of this book the government announced its review of company law. We welcome this initiative.

A PRACTITIONER VIEW

This is not intended as an academic book. It has not been produced to hone theory, but to reflect on practical experience which between the two of us not only spans many years thinking about and working in the field, but encompasses both corporate, shareholder, and regulatory experience.

Jonathan Charkham spent some years running the family manufacturing firm, and later in the civil service headed the Whitehall Public Appointments Unit which provides a service to ministers for the appointments they make. Later at the Bank of England he had close involvement with corporate governance issues, as adviser to the Governor, and via the establishment of PRO NED, where he was seconded as director. Whilst at the Bank he made a series of comparative studies on other countries' corporate governance systems (Charkham 1994). As a member of the Cadbury Committee he has participated in the debates on reform, and is now a non-executive director of a number of listed companies. He is a visiting professor of the City University Business School.

Anne Simpson is joint managing director of PIRC, the UK's leading independent adviser to shareholders on corporate governance and corporate responsibility issues, and is a corporate representative regulated by the Investment Managers' Regulatory Organization. She joined PIRC at its foundation in 1986; it now counts among its clients fund managers and public and private sector pension funds with assets over £150bn. in value. PIRC has coordinated negotiations and formal shareholder initiatives at a wide range of companies—including the first successful transatlantic shareholder proxy at Hanson, and resolutions at both British Gas, and Shell Transport and Trading. PIRC has conducted primary research on corporate governance issues from corporate responses, to the various codes of conduct, to executive pay, and more recently to explore the relationship between governance and performance. She is a member of the Egon Zehnder Institutional Investor Advisory Group and the Ad Hoc Task Force on Corporate Governance convened by the OECD. Prior to joining PIRC she had a varied career working in journalism, banking and finance research, and for the development agency OXFAM.

In short, this is a practitioners' contribution to the debate. We conclude that the active role of shareholders is key to effective corporate governance, and thereby to competitiveness of the economy, accountability of the firm, and the cohesion of wider society. The current system is riddled with practical inefficiencies and outmoded rules, and dogged by conflicts of interest which prevent effective oversight by institutional shareholders, who are in turn not required to be accountable to those on whose behalf they invest. In a bygone age of classical education the Latin title for this book would of course have been *Quis ipsos custodies custodiet?*—who is guarding the guards?

We consider that government has a role to ensure a clear framework for the statutory and regulatory undergrowth that impedes the efficient working of the system. We also consider that new responsibilities have been inherited, but are not generally recognized, by the majority of institutions, whose role in the economy has a wider impact on us all.

To sum up, we consider that power confers responsibility for shareholders as with any other body in society. We set out an approach to ensuring a fiduciary investor has a responsibility, and that other large investors should be given an incentive to exercise their votes. We have dubbed this 'the obligations of significant ownership'.

We also argue that companies have a broader purpose than to promote shareholder value. Providing rent on capital is essential, but companies are economic organizations which serve a variety of functions. It is critical that shareholders recognize the complex social and economic relations that underpin wealth creation.

We also conclude that without protections and better organization promotion of individual share ownership has of itself little merit. The experiment of promoting privatized industry shares to the public has produced millions of individual investors who have little power and ability to protect their interests, or to act as monitors of corporate abuse. Those trampled underfoot at Eurotunnel (mainly in France) are one example, and despite the fine efforts of groups such as Yorkshire Water Watch it is uphill elsewhere. Private investors are still vulnerable.

In examining the current role of shareholders, describing the legal framework, and setting out proposals for reform, we have also delved into history. The company we see on the stock market is governed constitutionally by a legal framework that was not chosen for its marked superiority over other models, or even subject to a recent overhaul considering the need for improvements. It has its origins in an evolution of law in response to practical developments in the economy—from the South Sea Bubble to the need to raise capital for the early railways system or trading of Empire. It is time to recognize that the economy cannot be run from the legal equivalent of the Victorian parlour and consider a new framework fit for the next century, not the previous era.

At the heart is disclosure. Much of the current system of corporate governance (and in particular shareholder activity) is shadowy and poorly understood. There is much to be gained from allowing daylight to shine in. At present, outside the relatively small circle of investment managers and advisers who control the UK's leading shares, little is known. What passes in private may be of genuine commercial sensitivity and properly remain confidential. There is also the question of insider dealing rules to be considered (which we address also in the proposed reforms). The institutions are and will be instrumental in encouraging openness and accountability in the companies in which they invest; at the same time their own practices will bear scrutiny.

1

The Purpose of the Company

WE all rely on many kinds of business to produce the goods and services we need in our daily lives including nowadays such basic services as water, light, and heat. Some of these are small family firms, but in the UK many are companies or subsidiaries of companies that are quoted on the Stock Exchange. We may not even realize that the product we are buying is just one of a hundred lines produced by a great multinational company because it looks to all intents and purposes as if it were made by a separate 'stand alone' business; nor should we neglect the service sector of which much the same is true. Is our local restaurant or pub separate or part of a chain? Probably the latter. The concentration of corporate ownership in the UK is almost unique among OECD economies, and we are virtually alone in having a GDP worth less than the collective value of companies listed on our stock market. What happens to those companies, how they are controlled, and in whose interests they are run affects us all. With the significant assets held by these institutions overseas, their role in global as well as domestic markets is of prime concern.

We all have an interest in their success, not just because we use their products and services, but also because they are the blocks of which our economy is constructed. They are the source of revenue; from the taxes they, their employees, shareholders, and customers pay come the resources for all the things society deems good—health services, education, infrastructure, public endowment for the arts, and defence. It is these businesses which provide much of our employment, directly and via suppliers indirectly also. In one calculation, Demb and Neubauer estimated that between 17 and 21 million people worldwide were directly or indirectly dependent upon the activities of the largest ten global companies. They comment, 'Add to this the employees, families and dependents of their direct suppliers and customers and the number would easily double' (Demb and Neubauer 1992). They argue that 'Fewer than 200 directors bear the ultimate responsibility for resources of the ten largest corporate employers.' In practical terms, perhaps, but to whom are *they* accountable? The shareholders, who are rarely seen, and rarely heard.

LEFT AND RIGHT ON CORPORATE GOVERNANCE

Once there was a simple distinction to be made. On the one hand there were those who considered the state had a key role, via directly owning key industries, or at the least regulating them. Balancing powers within the company would ensure not only state control but employee representation via trade unions. On the other side were the fans of the free market, in which simply ensuring the state kept well out of it was all that mattered. The disciplines of market rigour, by competition, takeover, and the pressure of share price, would ensure that companies throve and failures were cast aside. We are now at a juncture where state control is viewed, not just by the right, but by much of the political left, as inefficient and outmoded. So too, the market experiment has thrown up evident inefficiencies, not least in the privatization of natural monopolies like water, in which government must retain a regulatory role in the absence of competition to protect the public interest.

LISTED COMPANIES AND THE REST

In this book we are looking at listed companies. This is because they are so dominant within the UK economy and increasingly important to capital markets internationally. Investors can also hold shares in a variety of unlisted companies, such as family holdings, unquoted investments, or venture capital portfolios. The role of shareholders in these circumstances requires another book.

What distinguishes listed companies from others is that shares have been issued publicly in return for capital from investors, and the purpose of the market listing is to allow those shares to be traded. Simple though this point is, from this flow profound consequences for the relationship between company and shareholder which marks out the investor's role in corporate governance.

The existence of a market in shares makes it possible for a wide range of people directly or indirectly (through collective savings) to participate in the prosperity of the economy. Although all those connected with a business ultimately matter to it—customers, employees, suppliers, bankers, local communities—the shareholders matter both to it and to the community at large because under UK law they are invested with powers in relation to the company which others do not possess. They are not only the providers of capital in the first place, but in so far as continuity can be ensured—and there is never a guarantee of this—they have an important part to play. It is in this sense that they are the ultimate guardians of continuity—on which prosperity depends.

Table 1. Numbers of companies and market capitalization

	Number of companies	Market capitalization in ECU million
London	1,745	1,038,818
Paris	710	389,380
Germany	678	438,638
Madrid	362	148,676
Italy	250	163,701

Source: European Stock Exchange Statistics (1995).

OWNERSHIP AND CONTROL

The high-water mark of communism is now long past, as is state ownership and control in Western economies; privatization has become fashionable. One of the failures of state control is the inability of the state to play an appropriate role as owner. This problem is revisited in the form of shareholders. The shareholder may be substituted for the state via private ownership, but the real problem is not who owns what, but what is done with the influence and power that ownership confers. There are academic debates in corporate governance regarding the distinctions between ownership of shares and ownership of other forms of property. We return to this issue later. John Kay revisited the issue to conclude that ownership of an umbrella was not the same as ownership of BT shares (*Financial Times*, 28 Feb. 1997). We agree. The owner of the umbrella does not have any responsibilities towards it. The owner of a company's shares may well have responsibilities, as control over the equity confers influence over an economic and social organization from which the shareholder draws a rent on his or her capital.

There are many fascinating aspects to this discussion, but for practical purposes it is control not ownership, which we view as key to the corporate governance debate (see Chapter 8 below). Shareholders are the owners of the company's equity; strictly they are not owners of the company, which cannot be reduced to being considered nothing more than a collection of share certificates. Ownership of shares confers control, not ownership of the company in legal, practical, or moral form. There are other claims on the company (creditors for example), and employees have partial recognition under UK law via the duty for the directors to protect their interests under the Companies Act.

Privatization transfers the dilemmas of ownership and accountability; it does not automatically solve them. Shareholders may make a better fist of it than government, but there are still problems to address. Chronic abuse in private ownership of some industries (such as coal) or the need for a national strategy (as with railways) led directly to public ownership via nationalization in the first place.

THE STATE VERSUS SHAREHOLDERS

Before turning to discuss the challenges faced by shareholders it is worth remembering the dilemmas which face government in attempting to act as the owner of companies. Notwithstanding the original reasons (largely in the public interest) for nationalizing some industries, government as entrepreneur or even guardian of the public interest has been a mixed success.

Regardless of the problems in the command economies of the former communist bloc, a succession of UK governments of both parties—with ministers of ability and integrity—could not solve the problem of how to run the nationalized industries, precisely because they could never decide what the role of the government as owner should be. They would have liked to operate at arm's length, in accordance with Morrisonian doctrine formulated in the post-war Attlee administration of 1945–50. In reality they found themselves faced with an ineluctable conflict of interest. If an industry was a net user of taxpayers' money they felt they had some duty to consider its use. Even if it was not, they found themselves impelled to interfere on matters like prices, investment, and salaries in the greater good—often to set an example. The famous example of civil servants briefing ministers regarding the type of plastic ashtray to be installed in cars by Leyland is a case in point.

The result was to produce in the nationalized industries a hybrid organization that lacked the clear public service ethos (so evident in the civil service, National Health Service, and education), but did not sit easily with private sector mores either. Imagine a situation in which the board of directors at the nationalized industry is free to fix executive salaries, but the pay of executives on the board is controlled externally at levels below those of their colleagues not on the board. It happened, because the Treasury for a while required it: there were not in that period many candidates for promotion to the board! Furthermore, the levels were so uncompetitive that there was great difficulty in recruiting from outside where this was necessary. As consumers no doubt we were pleased when the government of the day held prices down in those inflationary times. But this too created a distortion, affecting everything but particularly investment. The governments of the day insisted on particular locations for investment in plant on social grounds (famously for ICI after the war to ease unemployment in particular areas). This is a perfectly worthy objective, but sometimes in conflict with long-term competitive pressures that ultimately affect the economic viability of those industries.

There were many motives for privatization, political as well as economic. It certainly relieved the government of the responsibilities—and benefits—of ownership. Those responsibilities were not extinguished, but transferred, initially to the millions of new shareholders who took the opportunity to make an investment at an advantageous price. In the course of time institutional shareholders increased their holdings, but even today the denationalized industries are in a very different position from many large companies as they have many more small shareholders, and in some cases a regulator. And the problem of effective accountability endures.

THE GLOBAL INVESTMENT VILLAGE

The issue of share ownership cannot be viewed even here from the perspective of a little Englander. UK pension funds (as the largest group of shareholders in our economy) invest almost one-quarter of their assets overseas. In turn, nearly 20 per cent of the UK stock market is owned by foreign investors. London is not alone. France now finds that 30 per cent of its bourse is owned by overseas shareholders.

One of the pressures driving new activity by shareholders is globalization of the capital markets. On the one hand there can be no economic isolation, so competition from any and every quarter can be expected to be relentless; on the other, there can be no prospect of any state blinding its citizens to the progress being made elsewhere or concealing from them their own relative deprivation. The UK has a permanent struggle on its hands to keep its businesses efficient and competitive, and this applies wherever their seat of control may be.

The prosperity of any country may well be affected by the way in which the systems of corporate governance work somewhere else, perhaps on the other side of the globe. The control of car plants in the UK for instance lies ultimately in Japan, and we know that the network of accountability, now under intense pressure, is quite different from ours, including the shareholders' role (Charkham 1994). Globalization does not demand uniformity. Corporate governance systems have emerged from distinct national and regional cultures, which are reflected in the legal and economic framework within which companies operate. By turn the rights and responsibilities of shareholders are fashioned according to the values expressed in these laws. No country can now impose burdens on shareholders, if it needs to attract footloose international capital. Each nation is in competition to offer the global shareholder a good deal, and the pressure to harmonize accounting standards, disclosure of information, and even shareholder rights of redress stems directly from this, rather than a crude effort to appease the Anglo-Americans who are familiar with a different regime at home (OECD 1997a).

An intertwined theme is the emergence of the global corporation, alongside the global investor. Transnational companies are those which, although domiciled in one (or perhaps two) host countries, having trading and investment activities that span many jurisdictions. The concentration of resources held by these corporations poses new questions of accountability. Fewer than half of the largest economic organizations in the world are nation states; their GDP is less than the turnover of the biggest transnational corporations.

ETHICS AND GOVERNANCE

The global village has also raised the expectation of minimum standards. Whilst sensitivity surrounds the notion of local cultural standards in the global economy (such as the role of women, employment of children, balancing of environmental and economic goals), the pressure is on global companies to ensure they operate to international standards. How these are defined, and by whom, is a moot point. But shareholder activism around these issues has been prominent—from the International Brotherhood of Teamsters in the USA persuading Levi jeans to limit production from mainland China in order to avoid the use of prison labour, to pension funds filing a resolution at Shell on environmental standards and human rights. These examples show that investor concerns are not narrowly financial or confined to their home territory. Those with a long-term view are clear that companies operate within, not separate from, society, and the bedrock of commercial success is ethical standards of the highest order. These shareholders are redefining Milton Friedman's famous maxim that, in the long term, the only social responsibility of business is to make a profit. They consider that the only businesses to make a profit will be those which are socially responsible (Simpson 1991).

   As we near the end of the century, even in our own region, we can see in Europe prosperity emerging after the catastrophe of the two wars and depression. Change has been rapid. Even in the most ravaged countries there were many survivors among the populace and among businesses, although few companies escaped unscathed. Competition, technological developments, macroeconomic management, or political upheaval all put profound pressure upon companies. Other regions grapple with the impact of restructuring which is no less painful. Sound corporate governance systems play an indispensable role in helping companies grapple with such problems and survive in the medium term. In economies like the UK—where ownership of companies is traded freely—the role of shareholders will be critical in shaping a framework for prosperity.

THE ROLE OF GOVERNMENT

Shareholders cannot operate in a legal, social, or regulatory vacuum. We sympathize with those who reject excessive regulation but nevertheless consider there is a continuing vital role for the state, and one that requires international liaison. Under democracy governments are elected to represent the public interest and to provide the conditions within which economic progress can be made to meet the aspirations of the nation. Within this, the system of corporate governance is vital, not just in ensuring prosperity but in ensuring accountability for the exercise of power. The role of those responsible for the company—managers and executive directors, boards, shareholders, and employees—needs to be considered by government to ensure that the system is running efficiently and balances the legitimate interests of those dependent upon the company.

In this, we consider the shareholder role has been neglected. In a period of rapid change—where the landscape of share ownership has been transformed from private holdings to institutional ownership—little has been said. Much has been written on the role of directors and boards, but comparatively little attention in the UK has been paid to shareholders. We concentrate on their critical role because of its attendant impact and responsibility.

We do not therefore shy away from examining the government's broader role. It has for instance found it necessary to protect the consumer against producers' cartels and monopoly; the public against private spoliation of the environment; potential investors against those who seek to take advantage of the unsophisticated; employees against oppressive employers. The arguments against EC legislation to limit the working week are distant cousins of those that once maintained that our coal industry would be ruined if child labour could no longer be employed in the mines. The pure milk of competition has been watered down, not least because its logical conclusion is monopoly. The economic price for perfect competition may be to tear the fabric of society in an unacceptable way.

UK governments have been reluctant in recent times to check up on the effectiveness of the statutory framework within which companies operate. They have left the matter to committees or informal initiatives which have considered the dilemmas of the shareholder role. Despite this, there has been an unwillingness on governments' part to accept the logic of the *laisser-faire* creed which both Conservative and Labour politicians now claim as their own. Politicians to whom free markets are an article of faith are nevertheless often—and sensibly—unwilling to let major enterprises fail. That is why there is banking supervision; no one will risk systemic failure and the resulting economic chaos. Companies may become too big to fail. The kiss of life was given to Lockheed and Chrysler; to Air France and Crédit Lyonnais. If national pride or defence procurement is affected the bitter pill of intervention seems easily swallowed. Fokker was left to fail but would any German government let Daimler Benz collapse? The UK government stood back whilst Barings went under, though few admired this unflinching commitment to the free market principle.

Governments have a delicate path to tread. The free market economic creed states that Darwinian processes of the commercial world must be allowed to work; only in this way will real progress be made. But these processes do not mean that accidental as well as economic causes should determine survival. The failure of many companies or whole industries becomes inevitable in the wake of technological progress. There is no special external reason why the UK does not now run a single car manufacturer of any size; the reasons are various—and internal. Success and failure seem inevitable only in retrospect. It is the role of governments not to abrogate the laws of the economic jungle but to ensure that they work in a way which is in total not harmful to their community. That is why their responsibility for the legal framework of corporate governance is one which they must never repudiate or pretend to ignore. For that reason, the UK government's review of company law is of vital national importance and of international interest.

WHAT ARE COMPANIES FOR?

Companies are creatures of statute, not nature. The history of the development of the legislation is traced in outline in the next chapters. The present laws exist to serve various purposes. Although the enrichment of proprietors was a legitimate object (and indeed a necessary one if the system was to work), it was not the main purpose, far less the sole purpose. It follows that the answer to the question 'What are companies for?' is not simply 'To make money'.

Sir Adrian Cadbury in the 1993 Ernest Sykes memorial lecture put the contrast between the Anglo-American and Continental view of companies in the following terms:

'In the European context, however, it is important to point out that the Anglo-American view of the nature of a company differs from that which is held by the majority of Continental countries. The accepted view in this country is that a company is a capitalistic enterprise. It owes its origins to the funds subscribed by the shareholders and, therefore, the relationship on which the company is founded and which governs its actions is that between owners and managers. Hence the importance of such matters as property rights and agency costs in the British and American debates on corporate governance.

The Continental view is much more along the lines of a company being a social institution, which is based on a coalition of interests between those who run the business and those who work in it. The key relationship is accordingly that between managers and the employees as a whole. The Continental approach to governance, therefore, accords a place to employees and the community which the Anglo-American governance model, formally at least, does not. There is less recognition of the rights of shareholders on the Continent, offset by a greater recognition of the rights of other elements in society.'

The Hampel Committee argued that the overriding objective shared by all companies is to provide shareholder value. Economic life is not so simple.

The report of the Business Sector Advisory Group on Corporate Governance to the OECD in April 1998, paras. 40 and 41, squares the circle:

The Primary Corporate Objective

40. Most industrialised societies recognise that generating long-term economic profit (a measure based on net revenues that takes into account the cost of capital) is the corporation's primary objective. In the long run, the generation of economic profit to enhance shareholder value, through the pursuit of sustained competitive advantage, is necessary to attract the capital required for prudent growth and perpetuation.

41. However, 'generation of long-term economic profit to enhance shareholder value' is an overly simple description of the task facing corporations. Corporations must succeed in complex and unusually competitive global markets—competing not only in selling goods and services, but also in attracting capital and human resources.

* In the production of goods and services, corporations serve as an efficient instrument of cooperation among all the required resource providers, such as suppliers of capital, labour, intellectual property and various professional skills.

* By hosting relatively durable relations, corporations also form social networks. Long-term cooperation and resulting mutual dependencies among owners, managers, employees, suppliers, consumers, local communities, etc, create loyalties, expectations and understandings that go beyond pure market interaction.

* Corporations also serve wider national objectives. They mobilise the economic resources of a country across different regions and segments of society; they generate employment, income and training for citizens; they secure domestic supplies of goods, technologies and services; they provide tax income, foreign currency, etc.

We ourselves consider that the purpose of the company can be expressed as 'to provide ethically and profitably the goods and services people need or want.' Of course, profit is crucial. In a world always hungry for capital no unprofitable company will long attract the investment it needs to survive and expand. Very properly people will not risk their hard-gotten savings in enterprises that will waste them. Besides, over time profits are a useful yardstick of success. They tell the world something about how well a company is satisfying customers' needs compared with competitors. In the short term profits can of course be misleading, as they may reflect windfalls of fortuitous success, and particular though isolated misjudgements and mistakes. The evolution of accounting standards has taken up many of these issues, and accountants (and auditors) know all too well the limitations of the accounts in expressing the value of a company.

Our formula about the purpose of companies recognizes implicitly the question of time—a critical factor in international competition—from many angles. How quickly can investors expect a 'satisfactory' return on their money? How quickly can new products be brought on stream? Some societies are more patient than ours in seeking returns on investment, and when they are, the UK firms in competition with them will be handicapped. The capital markets are now mostly free so that investment should logically flow to where it can get the best, i.e. biggest and quickest, returns having taken risks into account (of all sorts, political as well as economic): but logic is tempered by social or political considerations and loyalties.

The market is not some invisible process—or even an invisible hand as Adam Smith would have it. It is the collection of decisions made by people. A company that does not put their interests first will ultimately itself pay the price. And this is true even of companies which by luck, aggression, or efficiency find themselves monopolists—or near so. If they leave behind unsatisfied needs or wants others will arise to meet them.

We do not believe in predestination in economics (or anything else). The 'market' is not a force of nature. All economic life is a maelstrom of individual and collective decisions made by ordinary and extraordinary men and women with differing motives, means, and knowledge. Each of us to an extent chooses our own fate, however uncomfortable it is to admit it.

In the debate on corporate purpose, ethics and economics have been viewed as alternatives, as competing issues. We disagree. Companies operate within, not apart from, society. A somewhat sterile debate has ensued between those stuck in 1980s economic neo-liberalism whose mantra is 'shareholder value' and those centring on the softer 1990s who speak of 'stakeholders'. It is clear to both sides that one cannot survive without the other. Stakeholders rely upon shareholders to provide capital and ultimately to ensure accountability by the board. In the UK shareholders are drawn from other stakeholder groups. Pension funds are the largest group of shareholders, yet their assets are drawn from the savings of half the workforce and invested to provide retirement income when this group becomes pensioners. Similarly, insurers, as the next large group, rely upon the endowment policies taken out by home owners who represent the majority of the adult population. Even the private shareholders promoted through privatization are not just investors in their local utility or regulated industry. The small shareholder in BT is probably a customer, whose pension and insurance savings are perhaps also invested in the company.

Ethical behaviour is in the long run the bedrock on which modern Western capitalism stands. It is not only morally unacceptable, but business folly, for companies to behave as environmental hooligans; or to neglect their employees; or to bear down on suppliers by not honouring their bargains in the knowledge that the power of their position will inhibit the weak from claiming what is due when it is due. Despite the legal framework in the UK in which shareholders (and, in dire circumstances, creditors) have powers over the company, it is arrogant for shareholders to claim that the end for which companies exist is solely profit. Rent on capital must be paid, but shareholders' needs should be balanced by the directors, whose duty is to the company, not any group of investors who happen to hold shares at one point.

Professor Charles Handy has expressed the notion elegantly. In the *Journal of the Royal Society of Arts* (139/5416 (Mar. 1991): 231 f.), he wrote:

The principal purpose of a company is not to make a profit—full stop. It is to make a profit in order to continue to do things or make things, and to do so even better and more abundantly. Late in the sixties Jim Slater came to talk to the students at the new London Business School. He was at the height of his fortunes and he was happy to explain his secret to the young men and women. 'I am the only person in British business', was his message, 'who is interested in making money. That makes it easy for me to look at assets and investment decisions in a totally uncluttered way.' Three years later his business was finished. I never got to ask him if he still felt that way.

For these reasons, we do not consider it necessary to impale ourselves on the barbed wire of the stakeholder versus shareholder argument. There are many who have put the point eloquently (Plender 1997, Hutton 1996). They provide a compelling argument that a stakeholder perspective is vital, even to serve the interests of investors.

The advantage of the framework of the present British law is that in principle the lines of accountability are clear. The stakeholder concept is based on the vision of 'the company in society', and that is in reality how companies should operate—indeed shareholders we consider have a role in ensuring that companies fulfil this role. What shareholders can perform, which no other group can, is to ensure a system of effective accountability. The directors must be responsible for relations with stakeholders, but accountable to the shareholders.

Other legal models provide a role for stakeholders within the board structure familiar to the UK—in Germany and other Continental European economies, the two-tier board has half of its representatives elected from the workforce. Similarly, banks have a seat at the top table. In the UK some companies have experimented with developing more formal involvement for stakeholders, such as NFC which allowed for a director elected by employee shareholders for some years and the John Lewis Partnership which is a thriving example of collective endeavour and reward in a commercially successful organization. There are new pressures on British companies finally to abandon the traditional narrow approach to management of people and responsiveness to customers. It is notable that even whilst the Conservative administration had provided a convenient 'opt out' on Social Chapter rules for UK companies operating in Europe, many established works councils and other forms of staff consultation in recognition that it would be divisive and unproductive to try and prevent new forms of employee involvement.

SHAREHOLDERS AS GUARDIANS

This raises a critical question: can shareholders be trusted to put the long-term interests of the enterprise first? This is an issue to which we will return, and as Continental and Asian companies feel the bracing winds of change from active shareholders in the USA the question of the company's purpose is to the forefront of international debates. Shareholders are not inherently wise or well informed. They are not even by definition long term. Arbitrageurs can have more success moving markets than the most dedicated proxy voter. How shareholders can care for their goose, rather than simply demand a quicker supply of golden eggs, requires thought and care. Self-interest may not produce the common interest, and some regulation is in order to ensure that legitimate interests are protected.

The issue of competitiveness runs throughout this book. The UK for many centuries has been a trading nation and there is a critical requirement that proposals to improve corporate governance improve competitiveness. In many fields—environment and ethical standards among them—international standards, properly observed, are the only way forward if we are to avoid a Gresham's Law of deteriorating practices—where bad practices will drive out good ones under pressure of competitive cost-cutting.

The Role of Shareholders in the UK

CORPORATE governance is an awkward phrase and there are many definitions. For simplicity and brevity the definition in the Cadbury Report cannot be beaten: 'Corporate Governance is the system by which companies are directed and controlled' (Committee on the Financial Aspects of Corporate Governance 1992).

The first thing to notice about this definition is that it talks about systems (not minutiae or individual items) and specifically addresses direction (the board) and control (shareholders) rather than management. This is the division that has created the corporate governance industry. This should not be taken to mean that any less importance attaches to good management than it did, or that there is a great divide between corporate governance and management in practice. Good business will be well managed, well directed, and well controlled. Indeed one of the functions of good corporate governance is to help ensure that good management is in place. Nevertheless, some of the most conspicuous failures in recent years have stemmed from a failure of the control function or from poor direction.

INTERNATIONAL VARIETY

All systems of corporate governance have to be considered against the social, economic, legal, and political background of the country in which they developed. In the next chapter we trace some of the most important historical elements. A study of the relevant laws governing corporations will not reveal enough in any country; we have to understand attitudes and patterns of behaviour too if we are to make sense of them. The company laws of Japan and the UK are not too dissimilar in structure, but the results are poles apart. When we examine remuneration we find a marked difference in approach between the USA and Germany, where exorbitant share schemes have in the one become common and barely exist in the other. The impact upon competitiveness appears irrelevant. Other differences abound. We find that banks play a much larger part in Germany and Japan, not because of any deliberate policy, but because their economies happened to develop in ways in which this occurred; by the same token the stock market has a bigger role in the UK and USA. Reforms on both sides show that no system is immune to pressure for change, be it domestic or international.

Companies do not live for ever. Some wither away because the drive that created them has weakened, some because a new technology which they lack the skills to acquire has overwhelmed them, some because they have been undercut by new entrants to the market—or there can be any combination of these factors. When we look back on the companies that have disappeared we can usually see clearly enough what the causes of decline were. Hindsight needs no telephoto lens.

We can also see that in the short run many systems of governance appear to work, so long as management knows where it is trying to go and keeps its eye firmly on the fundamentals, including investment, cash flow, personnel, design, and marketing skills. The commercial scene is however littered with the wrecks of businesses which failed to live up to their early promise. One purpose of good corporate governance is to reduce this accident rate, because unnecessary collapse is so damaging to all concerned; and where it occurs in a major company may be catastrophic. A bad mistake may destroy a company: better-funded companies survive but even a much loved and respected company can falter in its ventures. Another purpose is to encourage management to seize opportunities, and we can only speculate on how many have not been taken in the UK over the years. Corporate governance as a subject therefore is as broad as life itself, because it touches upon fundamental elements in the economy and society at large. Put simply,

a system of corporate governance is as important to a nation as any other part of its institutional framework, because on it depends a good portion of the nation's prosperity; it contributes to social cohesion in a way too little recognised. A proper framework for the exercise of power is an economic necessity, and a moral imperative. (Charkham 1994)

That is why all governments should be concerned about corporate governance, seeking to encourage the effective operation of the system in use in their particular country and keeping it under review. Fifteen years ago no one spoke of corporate governance and even now no one knows how this term came into general use. It has survived because a more convenient term has not been found for a portmanteau of issues which are increasingly regarded as important. Corporate governance has gained a reputation for being the penicillin of the commercial world, a sort of managerial antibiotic capable of curing all ills if taken in the correct dosage. It is not. There are those like Sir Stanley Kalms of Dixons PLC who go on the record as opponents of what they regard as a substitution of bureaucratic process for initiative. Of course, if this is what takes place they are right to object. But this kind of inversion can only occur when there is a misunderstanding of the proper principles.

Almost every major economy now has a code or guidance note on corporate governance. Take as a sample the following:

- Cadbury Report—UK—1992;
- King Report—South Africa—1994;
- Toronto Stock Exchange Report—Canada—1994;
- Jenkins Report—USA—1994;
- Australian Investment Managers' Association Report—Australia—1996;
- Greenbury Report—UK—1995;
- National Association of Corporate Directors Report—USA—1996;
- Hampel Report—UK—1998;
- Vienot Report—France—1995;
- Peters Report—the Netherlands—1996;
- EASDAQ Rules—Europe—1996.

More recently, even India and Japan have joined trends towards codes and guidance notes, and the OECD is considering the value of international guidance.

TWIN PRINCIPLES: ENTERPRISE AND ACCOUNTABILITY

'Good' corporate governance is not a particular formula or process; there are many ways of achieving it as international comparisons demonstrate, providing that two basic principles are followed:

1. *That management should be free to drive the enterprise forward with the minimum interference and maximum motivation.* Interference may come from outside the company in the form of government pressure or diktat, from excessive litigation or the fear of it, or from undue pressure from the market, associated with a fear of takeover.
2. *That management should be accountable for the effective and efficient use of this freedom.* There are two levels of accountability, from management to the board and from the board to shareholders. In certain countries the board is divided into two tiers to facilitate the first part of this process. Where this is not so, the 'unitary' board contains executive and non-executive directors (UK/USA). There are variants of both: the unitary board in the UK comprises usually a majority of executives; in the USA it is invariably dominated by non-executives, with only the CEO on the board. Similarly with two-tier boards, the Netherlands, Denmark, Germany, and France have home-grown varieties. The second level of accountability—of the board to the shareholders—is the subject of this book.

ENTERPRISE AND ACCOUNTABILITY

These two principles are common to the different forms of corporate governance operating across the OECD member states. Implementing them requires the effective operation of the structures and processes within the business (internal) and those outside it (external). The main task is to ensure the continued competence of management, for without adequate and effective drive any business is soon doomed to decline. The point of accountability is not to make executive directors sit exams, but to ensure the maintenance of high standards of competence. Nell Minow of the Lens Fund in the USA provides a vivid image to explain why shareholder attention improves performance. She notes wryly that 'Directors are like sub-atomic particles; their behaviour changes under observation.'

We would argue along similar lines, that there is a parallel with the human resource 'experiments' undertaken many years ago at a US manufacturing plant to identify scientifically what would contribute to increased production among the workforce. The scientists duly arrived at the plant with clip boards and questionnaires, and their intention was to vary the physical conditions of work, to identify whether variations in heat, light, or even speed of the production line had an impact on productivity. Productivity rose each time. The experiment was a failure in its stated task. Each variation in conditions was met with a rise in productivity: the lights were dimmed, the lights were raised, the production line was slowed, it was speeded up; the heating was on; and then it was off. The conclusion from this study was that the workforce improved its performance because it was being monitored, not just in a managerial form of observation, but also through the interest and involvement from the staff in the 'productivity' question which was raised by the research team's arrival. Although the team did not answer the question they had come to answer, which was 'how can we vary the physical environment to improve productivity?', they had stumbled upon something just as useful: 'How can the attention of an observer affect productivity?' The impact of observation upon human behaviour was dubbed the 'Hawthorne Effect'. The team concluded that close attention affects the behaviour of those to whom it is directed. In corporate governance terms this attention lands up ultimately with the shareholders, but just as in the Hawthorne study, it is benign. Their instruments are attention and encouragement, remedial action a last resort.

Shareholders are not the only route to this oversight. We have discussed earlier the problems faced by government in being the overseer of industry via state ownership (regulation is another matter). There are various ways in which accountability can be organized. Looking towards the Continent of Europe we can see how important the banks are both internally through membership of boards, and externally through the relationships they form and the obligations—and privileges—that go with them. They play an important part in making sure that accountability means something—though even so every country we know has its share of commercial disasters. For various legal and historical reasons the banks in the USA and UK play little part in the corporate governance of their commercial clients. This is in contrast to Germany where banks often have a far more complex relationship with a company and are correspondingly better informed about it. In Germany for example banks often hold shares both on their own account and as depositary agents for others—and they often have a seat on the supervisory board: this multiplicity of connections makes it possible for them to have a fruitful relationship with the firms of which they are the *Hausbank* and it is one which both parties appreciate. The effectiveness of the German system is under scrutiny, and reform is in hand.

A natural reaction to such emphasis on accountability is to ask why matters cannot be left to executive management itself, which stands to lose so much if the company is unsuccessful. Sadly, motivation does not ensure competence (as is proved by the huge number of devoted private entrepreneurs and family businesses that fail every year). So in most countries the board structure is designed to improve process within the company by including non-management people, whether on a unitary board or as a separate supervisory tier.

THE SHAREHOLDER ROLE: THE LIMITS

In discussing the role of shareholders, the limits as well as possibilities of their position need to be acknowledged. Shareholders are provided with various powers at law. Their role is potentially wide-ranging, and some have claimed that being an active owner means crossing the floor and becoming a substitute for the directors. We are quite clear that it is never the shareholders' job to micromanage the company; that path leads to uncertainty and confusion. The division of labour between shareholders and directors is clear. The key role for shareholders is to ensure that the board is performing effectively in its role of overseeing management and driving the company forward. Shareholders by their careful scrutiny of board appointments should have made sure that the board has a complement of directors well equipped to bring an objective mind to bear in the collegiate atmosphere of good board discussions. If the shareholders do not like what is going on they have the power under UK law to introduce resolutions at general meetings, which may be approved or rejected by other shareholders. An ordinary resolution has advisory status only. A special resolution (which requires a 75 per cent vote in favour) can instruct the directors in a course of action. These resolutions will only be successful if they win the broad support of others. This in itself is a useful discipline. However, the threat is rarely made.

The shareholders' role, *in extremis*, is to intervene by removing those who are failing. Generally, though, shareholders will depend upon the board, which can get to grips with the detail and provide a solution. The board may however be divided. It follows therefore that the more routine task of the shareholders is to monitor board performance not only in relation to financial performance but also in the way it ensures the company will continue by serving the interests of its customers, motivating the employees, and retaining the respect and support of local communities.

It is of course impossible for shareholders to judge a board's dynamics, that is to say how the people on it work together. What they *can* do is take an active interest in the nominations process which determines the selection of candidates for the board, and when these candidates are proposed give proper consideration to the voting opportunity. This process is frustrated when companies provide little information regarding the person concerned. The law requires no disclosure, and the Stock Exchange only asks for 'brief biographical details' for the non-executives. Hampel has made a partial improvement by asking that this be provided for any director facing election.

Shareholders have other powers, such as annually appointing auditors, and approving various alterations to the capital structure or articles of association. As we have noted, their main and most important function is to ensure that the company's board is satisfactory, in other words, approving the 'government' of the company. Politics are a poor comparison for many reasons, but there is a parallel with the democratic process. The electorate seldom considers separate issues through referenda, though these may be important on constitutional issues (such as devolution), or major economic decisions (such as entry into the European Union). Other jurisdictions make more use of this form of democracy. For the British, the main way of expressing disapproval is by voting a government out at a general election. Some constitutions, such as the USA's, force the electorate to rethink, by limiting the period for which one person may hold office. No president there can serve for more than two terms consecutively. Some US academics have argued that no CEO should serve in that capacity in any one company for much longer than that, though this is probably too bureaucratic an approach.

Shareholders, however, have a much easier task than electors since the latter have to weigh up effectiveness in so many different fields. A country may have a poor macroeconomic policy, but be quite soundly governed in many other respects; or, and more probably, the reverse. Shareholders by contrast should not look further than the company's prospects of survival and prosperity. For if they are unsatisfactory, nothing else is of much consequence. The caring philanthropic company that fails renders worse service to them and to the community in general terms than its better-focused competitor which by its success continues to provide employment. There are outstanding examples of enlightenment and competitive toughness going hand in hand, and some of them like Lever Brothers (now Unilever) and Cadbury go back to the last century or beyond.

Comparisons between government and the governance of companies cannot be pressed too far. Many a company for instance has been saved by retrenchment and the people concerned have been acclaimed for doing it. The authors cannot think of a single statue to a politician whose fame rested on saving the taxpayers' money! The political electorate has the advantage of a campaign with an opposition (though loyal to the Crown). By contrast, shareholders are usually presented with the directors' slate, and must take it or leave it. There is only a rare example of a serious challenger and shareholder champion (such as Bob Monks at Sears in the USA or Diana Scott at Yorkshire Water).

BOARD ASSESSMENT

Key to the shareholder role therefore is making an assessment of whether a board's stewardship is adequate. It is a difficult judgement in some cases. There are always examples from both ends of the spectrum—of companies run superbly or dreadfully. Between these extremes there is a wide band of mediocrity and it is difficult for outsiders (and sometimes insiders) to plot a company's position. How can shareholders tell? The obvious pointers are absolute and relative performance (by reference to the sector) over a reasonable period; to which should be added the level of current investment and the past record of making new investment pay. Industries with long time horizons present a special problem as the market does not often ride them comfortably. Besides, nothing stands still; the decline of the most talented may be so gradual as to be virtually imperceptible. By contrast, there are companies today still run by yesterday's genius whose gradual decline in effectiveness is manifest to everyone but himself. So somehow shareholders have got to acquire and weigh the evidence and form a judgement on it. There may be important non-financial indicators, but no human beings, including directors, can be reduced to a set of numbers that can be accurately assessed without judgement. And among the elements to be considered is the company's internal monitoring process, since it is axiomatic that the better this is, the less shareholders will need to intervene.

That is why adherence to guidelines on board process is so important. The Cadbury Report's recommendations on nomination committees are one example, which defines a set of procedures which cannot guarantee success, but at least give shareholders some assurance that a professional process is at work, which allows them to make a judgement. Nomination committees have been the poor relation among the governance committees. They deserve greater prominence and status, as the Hampel Committee implied. Directors should report on their procedures for recruitment, retirement, and succession on the board as a matter of course.

Shareholders now have the advantage of being able to look at what a board does (and how it is constituted) in relation to a set of guidelines, but guide-lines are not the answer in themselves. They are only useful to the extent they provide comparable information, to allow judgement by shareholders. Their other purpose is to spur a change in practice at a company. This is not guaranteed. If conformity is real and effective, shareholders should have little to do. The trouble is that this is difficult to tell from the outside. Companies can tick every line of the code, and yet not conform in spirit; or they can conform and yet be poorly run. They can indeed be relatively well run and yet fail to conform. In fact, shareholders should care, because bottom lines in companies with poor accountability tend to plunge sooner or later. So shareholders need to know about corporate governance issues, but they need to get to the heart of things and the due diligence of assessment in line with guidelines is the starting point. This is not box ticking for its own sake, but as the starting point for further enquiries.

This is an extraordinarily difficult area since boards themselves do not always have properly considered ways of checking not only the performance of the executives, but also their own performance individually as directors and of the board as a whole. Are such assessments conducted regularly and thoroughly and if so by whom? Are there still many directors whose con-tribution is marginal? If so, quite apart from the expense, their presence may well confuse, giving as it does, especially if they are eminent, an illusion of authority. The issue has been flagged up by Hampel, but there is very little work available in a UK context to guide shareholders on the issue and it is vital that more thinking is done on the subject.

As we noted earlier, shareholders ought to be reassured that a proper selection process is in place, starting with a careful analysis of what the balance of the board most requires, and a thorough combing of the market for candidates who meet the specification. Too often the process starts the wrong way round with the candidate identified first and the specification written later! Getting the process of selection right is the main reason for having a nomination committee—but it also helps to bring in candidates with the right attitude; loyalty to the company as a whole rather than any particular personality within it.

What are shareholders to make of the list of names put before them? Of course they are right to have a degree of confidence in what the board proposes, but this should not amount to total confidence because the board's recommendations may reflect:

- limited vision due to the horizons of present members;
- the wishes of a powerful or dominant chairman/chief executive (reflected in a complaisant board);
- the line of least resistance (how can we get rid of old Charlie?);
- poor standards of judgement;
- the obligations of patronage;
- the chairman paying off an old debt.

So they are entitled to ask themselves two series of questions:

- Does the board look as if it is the right size and balance? A board of 24 of whom 20 are executives, dominated by a powerful chairman/CEO, is obviously suspect. It is too large and badly balanced between executives and non-executives.
- Do the individuals match up to the job? Generally shareholders will be content to leave the choice of executive directors to the chairman/chief executive though they do need to know what their responsibilities are and what their careers have been. In respect of the NEDs they will be concerned about:
- experience and calibre;
- age;
- independence;
- length of service;
- availability.

All the relevant facts should be supplied to help shareholders understand the board's recommendations. Some points are controversial. Take age for instance. We all know people who are spent at 55 and others who are sharp at 75. Boards need people who are still involved: it may seem cruel to deprive a pleasant person of their last directorship, but unless they are still in the swim, it is usually necessary when they are past 70. There are always exceptions to every sound rule and that includes both age and length of service, where we agree with the PRO NED view, that however good a person is, after a certain time there is a danger of objectivity diminishing (though they would be the last to know it); eight to ten years is certainly long enough. Independence likewise may diminish even though the people themselves do not realize it. Where does their allegiance lie? What subtle connections are there? Good NEDs can always find new companies where their independence is not suspect. Why keep them as independents if it is? (They can perfectly well stay aboard, but not classified as independents.) Availability speaks for itself: the point is as old as the hills—and still not sufficiently recognized. Companies should publish the attendance records of their directors even though it would only tell part of the story, as their assiduous interest is needed even when they are not at meetings.

These are not new concerns. The following extract from a contemporary tract on choosing directors for the Bank of England in 1695 makes the point neatly:

Thus having forewarned you of some you are to avoid, I may be the briefer in characterising those you should choose.

(1) Choose men of known integrity, honesty and probity; that are truly sincere: this is the only true foundation; for whatever other characters men may have, yet if sincerity be wanting, they are not men fit for your service.

(2) Men of good ability; versed in affairs of all sorts both at home and abroad; some

in affairs of one kind and some in another, so that the choice be not confined to one sort of men, but that there be a mixture of divers ranks, as gentlemen, merchants, citizens, and traders.

(3) Men of industry and assiduity, that are not of idle tempers, but addicted to labour, to whom employment is not a toil or burden, but rather a diversion and delight; that can and will take pains, and that without regret.

(4) Men of opportunity, that have time and leisure from the crowd of other affairs; for if a person cannot give his attendance he will be but useless to you, therefore being needful qualification, care should specially be taken that men have reasonable leisure. . . .

The right to vote periodically on the election of directors is one of the main parts of the shareholders' role. They are justified in being jealous of any provisions in a company's articles that 'insulate' directors, i.e. exempt them from re-election; or which restrict their power to re-elect in another way.

The irritation that companies express, often in intemperate terms, tells us that patronage is a sensitive issue, and that any criticism is bound to pro-voke. We have seen overreaction from respectable companies to mild criti-cism of the composition of the board. This suggests it is a matter of power and therefore jealously guarded. Vituperation is never justified. If a criticism is unreasonable it can be dealt with without shouting; if there is substance in it, there is nothing to shout about. Overreaction generally suggests that a sensitive target has been hit.

Shareholders come in all shapes and sizes, from the individual with a ha'porth to the insurance company with 3 per cent of the company or more. Their skills differ. Their power differs. But they have a common interest. For as long as they hold the shares they want the company to succeed, so as to improve their income and the value of their capital. Shorting funds, which seek out the weaklings of the pack and sell the shares short, are not an exception as they are not shareholders. All shareholders have some-thing else in common—the ability to sell in the market place sooner or later. (The 3 per cent holders must go slowly if they are not to ruin the market.)

The original framers of the statutes which created the familiar company structure with limited liability were clearly mindful of the need to facilitate the aggregation of capital. People could thus risk some of their savings without endangering the rest. At the same time they realized that compa-nies were not commodities but a collection of individuals engaged together in an enterprise; that being so the individuals might change, prove dis-appointing, or require replacement. So the shareholder was given the means of addressing this problem. It was a right, but not a duty. It was, from the shareholders' point of view, unnecessary to go further in regard to quoted companies, because they could sell in the market if they lost con-fidence in the company's governance. Had it been turned into a duty they might very well have not been willing to assume the obligation or buy shares in the first place. There is a limit on the extent of the obligations that can be imposed on shareholders, if they are not to be deterred from investing. We shall return to this point and what is meant by ownership and control in Chapter 8.

The reality is that although the shareholders have a common role, which we have described, it is entirely up to the interest and acumen of the private shareholder to decide what to do about it. We discuss later what course of action is open to them (and we argue that if they have substantial holdings they *ought* to accept the responsibility of ownership).

TRUSTEES

The most important group here, because of the size of their assets, is pension funds. The formal responsibility for these issues lies with the trustees who generally engage fund managers to invest on behalf of their beneficiaries. Trustees of these funds owe their duty to the beneficiaries, although conflicts of interest can also run through the system. Companies often make one or more of the directors trustees of the pension fund, thus recognizing their interest in its effective management, since the company will have to make up shortfalls, and may, if there is a surplus, be able to take a contributions holiday and claw some back. Employees may also be among the trustees, and some of the pension funds of formerly nationalized industries specifically allow for this. The Pensions Act requires companies to consult their employees and if agreed to permit one-third of the trustees to be elected by members of the fund. Some companies go further. ICI, for instance, permits half the trustees to be drawn from among the members. We consider that the duty to exercise effective shareholder oversight should rest with the trustees, and discuss the issue in more detail later. However, if trustees are to take a more active role, they need training, not just to master the fundamentals (which would naturally include diversification, turnover, and the cost of trading; and voting), but also because it is essential to have the confidence to face 'professionals' and distinguish between sound argument and jargon-ridden flannel. It is not easy, as anyone who has tried to do it will confirm.

FROM FRAMEWORK TO DYNAMICS

It is not sufficient to examine the problems of UK industry and commerce, particularly those associated with their shareholders and the financial world in terms of structure. We have to look just as carefully at the motivational forces at work. The market economy model assumes that all participants are driven mainly by self-interest, and a powerful dynamic it has proved to be; none more so. It is in no way a reproach therefore to say that businessmen, fund managers, consultants, and stockbrokers act in what they perceive to be their own self-interest. At the same time they cannot reasonably object if others say that the total sum of their self-interest as they perceive it does not necessarily add up to what is best for the nation—or even what is best for themselves in the longer term. It is at least arguable that decline in British industry, which affects everyone's standard of living, is a direct result of the pursuance by all parties of policies which seemed at the time to be in their own immediate interests. A more enlightened self-interest would have produced a better-trained and motivated workforce; investors with long time horizons; and governments capable of putting country above party to stabilize macroeconomic conditions.

In investment the sum total of self-interest, as it applies to companies and their shareholders, is not yielding the best results for any of the parties or for the country. Yet the *danse macabre* continues. We do not lose sight of the fact that, however it is dressed up, what we are discussing is the exercise of power, and therefore likely to be bitterly contested.

SHAREHOLDERS AND THE MARKET

Until quite recently there would have been a widely held view that in practice the shareholders' role was marginal. For lack of interest or organization they barely had one (unless a company wanted to raise more capital). What is more it did not matter, as the stock market did all that was needed. It sent signals to management via the rating of the shares and in extreme cases of underperformance this would open the way (since 1958 at least) to hostile takeover bids largely financed in the City of London. This view is not always the case. Share prices may reflect other things than performance. There are many cases of companies collapsing even when their share price gave no indication of impending doom.

This is not an attack on markets, but simply a statement that price movements reflect many other things besides a company's propensity to fail, likelihood of survival, imminent prosperity, or more distant prospects of success; if they hold a mirror up to management it is a distorting one in which can be seen not the perfect conclusions of a myriad of Socratic philosophers working with the most perspicacious judgement on the basis of perfect information, but rather the trading decisions of a large number of self-interested operators who despite their best endeavours may interpret incorrectly the incomplete data on which they have to work. Markets imperfectly price all the available information, which is why transparency is so critical. The simple point is that stock prices cannot be taken for more than they are, the temporary expression of the delicate balance between buyers and sellers on any given day, of whom nearly half will soon find they were on the wrong side of their last transaction. Unless they disagreed there would be no market! Stock markets too often provide the perfect expression of Oscar Wilde's definition of a cynic—they know the price of everything and the value of nothing.

The market performs a useful function but it was not designed to provide the mechanisms for ensuring good governance. The system cannot depend upon it to do so. In a UK context it is the shareholders who are the ultimate guardians of the balance between dynamism and accountability in the corporate governance framework of any company.

To set out propositions in regard to all the shareholders as if they were a single entity is to ignore the central fact that they are not, as Berle and Means (1932) saw sixty years ago. Writing in the United States in the 1930s they saw an immense concentration of corporate power, with no countervailing influence from shareholders, who were small, fragmented, and dispersed. Whilst this was so, the task of arranging concerted action was thought insuperable. Now, however, the concentration of shareholdings in the hands of the institutions has produced (potentially) a radical change. Most companies could now be controlled by a group of shareholders small enough in size to fit into any decent-sized smoke-filled room: a vote of 20 per cent or 30 per cent would be quite enough to settle most issues. One thing seems certain: shareholders in the next century will have a bigger part to play for their own sake and for society's too. In due course we shall look at who they are, what they now do, and then at what in our view the future should hold. First, however, we should look briefly at how we got to where we are. Most countries are to some extent imprisoned by their history, and the UK, whose institutions have survived much longer than most, is sometimes deeply incarcerated.

CHAPTER

3

···

The World of Regulation

Society has long made a rather curious distinction. To steal a purse, or to pilfer from a shop, is regarded as a crime worthy of retribution, including, even today, imprisonment. Contrast this with the financial world. Here it is regarded as part of the rough and tumble of investment. Fraud is viewed, if not indulgently, then certainly with less retribution, even though it may amount to a worse robbery than picking a man's pocket. True, the rules about fraud have tightened and some of the more egregious scams are now technically barred, but it does not stop dealers legally taking advantage of their counterparties wherever they can do so within the law or without fear of being found out. It is still not unknown to puff shares disguising one's firm's long position.

There is nothing more appetizing to the unscrupulous 'financier' than parting people from their money in any way that the law does not debar, whatever the morals of it. The people who present them with the most pleasing prospects are the greedy, the uncaring, the ignorant, and the gamblers. Perhaps it is because the victims contribute so much to their own misery that society has been rather reluctant to interfere. In our own day we have seen the debacle at Lloyd's of London illustrate all the old points. Hopeful but ignorant investors; unscrupulous or incompetent operators; bad luck—or rather a misjudgement of how much good luck could be expected. All the constituents of a con-trick were there including a period of satisfactory trading to lull the greedy into a sense of security, and operators who, not necessarily wicked, nevertheless became infected by unwarranted complacency. It is no consolation to Names on the Open Years to distinguish between losses caused by a fool or a knave.

The state has to hold the ring between the various contending forces in society. It is quite properly reluctant to interfere. It cannot protect everyone's interest against their own greed or stupidity. One would think that whenever a pound was offered for 90 pence, people would instantly realize there was a catch in it; or whenever the interest rate offered was above the norm, there was a greater risk attached to it. The state's attitude in commercial dealings was the rule of commerce that said 'Buyer beware' (*caveat emptor*).

In the non-financial world in former days any reasonably experienced person was assumed to be able to understand what was being purchased and form a judgement on it. As time went on and objects became more complex and latent defects more difficult to discover, buyers were no longer assumed to be able to form a sound judgement, however diligent they were, so we find by the end of the last century Parliament intervening to afford them some protection, for instance in the Sale of Goods Act 1893.

In the world of companies and shareholders, which is our concern, there have long been two distinct types of chicanery, those affecting the primary and secondary markets. Any stock market lends itself to a whole range of deceptions designed to take advantage of the relative ignorance of others. In the eighteenth century for instance, when most of the dealings were in government funds, the familiar techniques were employed of acting on information not yet in the market; of inventing false information to suit one's book; of going bear of stock; and of operating a bear squeeze. We shall deal later with the issue of 'insider trading' which is still with us. All this has long been known, but it continues to present a problem to those who wish to safeguard the integrity of the market, because different kinds of people trade in it and vastly different assumptions can be made about the level of knowledge to be expected of them. Put bluntly, the professionals should be able to take care of themselves, downright fraud apart. Non-professionals however are, and have always been, at the mercy of the professionals. So the state has felt that they needed some protection. We smile at the folly of the South Sea Bubble, but overlook the Poseidon mine story in our own time. The elements are essentially the same: investors eagerly purchasing shares promising a fortune, but on information which proved fraudulent.

The feeling that it was necessary to protect people against their tendency to be deceived by the unscrupulous extends to the primary market. The promoters of companies in the past had a high old time selling stocks in hopeless enterprises by the most outrageous puffery. It was not only gamblers who 'Took a punt', but solid citizens who were deluded into thinking that there was a quick road to riches. On the way, friends of the promoter could enrich themselves by getting a preferential entitlement to buy the puffed stock at issue and sell it after it had gone to a premium. Not all such companies failed, or the issuer would have been discredited.

The basic stance of the authorities has been to let people rue the results of their own cupidity, but they have over the years become ever more concerned to save them from the consequences of their own folly. This is partly because of a quite proper concern that fair play demanded that the cards should not all be held by one set of players, partly because too many people being hurt financially was politically unsettling, partly because a modern state needs a way of marshalling its resources and people will become reluctant to participate if they cannot trust the system at all, and finally because the system itself may be undermined if the scams get bit enough. The damage caused in the last century by the failure of Overend and Gurney, and in the 1970s by the secondary banking crisis, illustrates that undermining the banking system is like an earthquake—no one knows where the solid ground is.

The UK system has generally not depended on primary or even secondary legislation, but on a mixture of both with rules made by various non-statutory bodies some of which may, like the Stock Exchange, work under the umbrella of some legislation (in that case the Financial Services Act), some, like the Cadbury Committee, with no umbrella at all. The creation of the Financial Services Authority, from the alphabet soup of regulatory agencies (IMRO, FIMBRA, LAUTRO, PIA, etc.), can only be helpful. Merging the bureau of each and finding a tougher approach will be considerably more difficult. The British preference for fudge on regulation has sweetened but also clogged the system.

The work of the takeover panel is a case in point. It is not a creature of statute. It can change its rules without reference to any other authority. It has no means of enforcing its rules beyond what its supporters are willing to do. Yet UK shareholders have good cause to be grateful to it, because it has succeeded in ensuring relatively equal treatment between them. It has prevented management entrenching itself by using devices such as poison pills. It has established rules of conduct about the purchase of shares in the market. It governs the timetable and what must and must not be said. Many Americans seem to regard it as more of a boon than a curse, and some wish they had the same or similar.

The best-known example of the British approach was the Committee on the Financial Aspects of Corporate Governance, chaired by Sir Adrian Cadbury, and consequently given his name. The issues with which it was concerned had been around for at least one decade, and probably two. Nothing would have happened because of government's wish to keep out had it not been for the sudden collapse of some companies shortly after issuing 'clean' accounts. The accountancy profession and the Stock Exchange felt the hot breath of public disapproval—scarcely surprising as so many had lost money as creditors or shareholders. Even the diligent had some excuse as they were entitled to believe that reputable auditors could be trusted. So a committee was assembled with the active help of the Bank of England, which had long taken an interest in this field as it perceived the damage done to the economy by the gratuitous and remediable incompetence of boards of directors. The government in typical style made no attempt to take it over, and merely loaned an able secretary from DTI and an observer.

The terms of reference reflected its origins. The committee was primarily concerned with the integrity of financial information, not with the perfection of the total governance system. It did in fact stretch its terms of reference, because it found that it could not address questions about the integrity of financial information thoroughly without considering how power is controlled. That in turn took it into structure, process, and standards—hence the wide-ranging recommendations which affect all three.

Anyone can propose a code. The remarkable thing about Cadbury is that few companies ignored its recommendations. As an observer to an OECD discussion commented, 'The British view codes as the law, and elsewhere, the law is treated like a code—voluntary compliance only!' True, the Stock Exchange has the power to delist any company that does not disclose its compliance, but that would injure some of the very people Cadbury was trying to protect, the owners. Companies that do not comply must say so and why, and this too has been generally observed. Considering that Cadbury had no legal backing the extent of compliance is remarkable, even with the two veiled threats in the background: from government to legislate if it had to (rather hollow) and from the institutions to exert pressure (a little less hollow, especially if the company turns in poor results). The unofficial message read into Cadbury was 'Conform or perform'; the institutions were not too likely to trouble companies whose figures consistently sparkle. That complacency has been undermined, and institutional shareholders are beginning to consider that corporate governance will help prevent future problems, and there is little point in using the code as a stable door to slam when the horse has bolted. Shareholders therefore have an interest in regulation and their voice is heard too rarely in the debates on ensuring it is effective. Regulation is a friend of the market, and not its foe.

The Development of the Joint Stock Company

ALL over the world people conduct trade through a wide variety of different structures. Numerically the largest number are sole traders whose 'lifestyle' businesses have no formal structure at all. In so far as they become entangled with the law, the most relevant will be the laws of contract. Partnerships too—where two or more people (there may be a maximum number under the law) go into business together—are to be found everywhere, governed by the laws of each particular country. (In the case of the UK, still by the Partnership Act of 1890, a great consolidating Act, but nowadays regarded as unsuited to modern circumstances in many respects.) Some countries like Germany provide a legal framework that is a hybrid of partnership and company, and some significant enterprises use it.

Partnerships continue to be useful and economical in the UK for certain types of enterprise. In general however they suffer from three characteristics which may well be disadvantageous—depending on the type of business to be conducted (quite apart from any taxation issues). The first is that, lacking a separate legal persona, they are affected by changes of partner. Secondly, under UK law, the partners' liability is unlimited (though there are plans to amend this). Thirdly, they are not a convenient way of mobilizing capital from a wide range of sources. Unlike some other countries, the UK has always tended to favour the marshalling of resources from a wide range of savers direct to the organization that wished to use them, rather than rely too heavily on the banking system. This preference went hand in hand with the development of arrangements for buying and selling the interests in the company that savers obtained.

From the Middle Ages it was clear to our forebears that if savings were to be attracted the savers must have some safeguards so that they would not be ruined if they made a small investment, especially as they might know relatively little about the enterprise and had no control over its conduct. The common law provided remedies for creditors but did not provide a suitable framework to protect long-term investors whose aim was to participate in the prosperity of an enterprise that might continue for years. So what we find quite early in British commercial history is that a structure was developed to meet these needs, whose principal characteristics were:

- A separate legal persona in the form of a company or corporation.
- Capital divided into shares, for which a wide range of people might subscribe. The liability of shareholders stopped with this investment; once the shares were paid up, there was no other call on them. The shares were tradeable, and from early days there was an active market in them. It was thriving in the eighteenth century. This is important, as 'exit' was seen from early times as an alternative to the monitoring function, which, given the communications of the time, would have been difficult to exercise.
- Management in the hands of professional managers, who were paid salaries but might not have a proprietorial interest.
- A board of directors, technically appointed by the shareholders with a duty to protect their capital and answerable to them for their stewardship of the company. They were separate from management.

This was the kind of structure the early joint stock trading companies used, but a separate royal charter or Act of Parliament was required to incorporate them. The state's interest was partly economic (it obtained revenue in various ways) and partly political. At its best the framework worked well, and although the East India Company for example certainly had its ups and downs these were not due to the nature of the law under which it was incorporated. In the days of poor communications effective control was always a problem. It became clear quite soon that the joint stock company had great potential, but it also provided the unscrupulous with a wonderful opportunity to take advantage of the gullible.

BACK TO THE BUBBLE

The South Sea Company illustrates the dangers. It was started in 1711 to take over part of the National Debt. The company agreed to pay a dividend of 6 per cent per annum in exchange for a monopoly of the trade in the South Seas, which was mostly slavery. It did not earn enough and the directors pursued a policy of ramping the shares, to such good effect that the price went up to ludicrous levels. On the way up many speculators were handsomely enriched—on paper—and their success encouraged the promotion of many other dubious enterprises, including one 'for carrying on an undertaking of great advantage, but no-one to ask what it is'. Its promoter collected 2,000 guineas in subscriptions in a single day and decamped with the lot in the afternoon.

The South Sea Company did not collapse instantly. The £100 shares touched £1,000, and by the end of August 1720 were still £810. Then the rot set in, and a month later the figure was £190. The directors tried to staunch the collapse by promising a dividend of 30 per cent for that year and 50 per cent for the next year. But the shares became valueless and thousands were ruined.

The result of the Bubble was a sharp reaction by Parliament in the form of the Bubble Act of 1720 which prohibited unincorporated companies from acting or presuming to act as corporations. It also prohibited the use of charters for purposes other than those for which they were originally granted.

The framework of the joint stock company was therefore familiar well before the industrial revolution, but it was only obtainable by specific statute or royal charter and either was a cumbersome and expensive process, best suited to major projects. The Bubble Act and the accompanying loss of public confidence made it almost impossible for companies to raise further capital by public subscription for 100 years. Businessmen devised a new form of association under deeds of settlement in which members took shares and agreed to abide by the regulations.

The Bubble Act was not repealed until 1825—at the dawn of the railway age. The rapid extension of a network to cover the country, promoted by various companies and funded by public subscription, with each company needing its own Act of Parliament, together with precedents in the USA, led in due course to the first general enabling law. Parliament was however wary of making joint stock companies generally available, fearing not so much the accretion of economic power, as fraud. It was felt that the public would be easily robbed by unscrupulous company promoters; besides, the South Sea Company cast a long shadow and the many failures of over-promoted railway companies were a warning. Eventually however the pressures became too great and Parliament moved, though with caution.

FIRST STATUTE ON COMPANIES

The first Act introduced was the Joint Stock Company Regulation and Registration Act 1844 (7 & 8 Vic. c. 110 and 111), which we can find sandwiched in the statute book between 'an Act to indemnify persons connected with Art Unions and others against certain penalties' and an 'Act to amend and consolidate the Laws relating to merchant seamen; and for keeping a Register of Seamen'. Its scope is narrow in that it does *not* confer limited liability on shareholders; Parliament felt that this really would open the floodgates to unscrupulous promoters who would gather in public subscriptions, run off with them, and leave the poor unfortunate creditors to whistle or pursue the shareholders to repay the company's outstanding debts. The way to make shareholders resist such promotions was to leave them with this liability. The shareholders, in other words, would have a direct incentive to monitor the company's solvency and therefore its progress.

In some ways however the new law was broad. It set out in some detail the responsibilities of the parties (arguably better than the current laws in some cases). Paid-up shareholders for instance are entitled to be present at general meetings of the company; 'and also take part in the discussion thereat; and also to vote in the determination of any question thereat; and that either in person or by proxy, unless the deed of settlement shall preclude shareholders from voting by proxy; and also to vote in the choice of directors; and of every auditor to be elected by the shareholders' (s. XXVI). The 'deed of settlement' fulfilled a similar function to the modern memorandum and articles (which were introduced by the 1856 Act). From the very beginning the shareholders were intended to have a real role. The government was sensitive to the possibility of their being cheated and defrauded, so it intended them to have sufficient powers and rights to protect their interests.

The powers of directors were defined: (s. XXVII):

(1) To conduct and manage the Affairs of the Company . . .
(2) To appoint the secretary if any;
(3) To appoint the Clerks and Servants and to appoint others as the occasion shall require;
(4) To remove such Secretary, Clerks and Servants and to appoint others as occasion shall require;
(5) To appoint other persons for special services as the concerns of the Company may from time to time require;
(6) To hold meetings periodically and from time to time as the concerns of the company shall require;
(7) To appoint a Chairman to preside at all such meetings and in his absence appoint a Chairman at each such meeting.

The Act was felt defective in many quarters, in one main way: the principle of limited liability. Its introduction was keenly debated. Mr Muntz, the Member for Birmingham, feared the worse. 'The Directors would manage the Company, not the Company the Directors' (*Hansard*, 139 col. 1393). He found an ally in Archibald Hastie (ibid.):

It was stated that America had prospered under the law, but there capital was extremely scarce and barely sufficed to carry on great schemes; but in England where there was no want of capital they could not anticipate the same results from the application of the principle of limited liability as had been the case in America. The principle of limited liability had produced injurious effects to commercial credit both in America and in France by inducing reckless speculation and systematic frauds upon credits.

The debate showed that it was indeed foreign competition that had spurred Lord Palmerston's government on—even to the point where the need for a company to have capital of £20,000 to qualify was dropped. In the debate in the House of Lords (*Hansard*, 139 col. 2038) the Marquis of

Lansdown put the argument in language that a Thatcher government would have applauded:

The bill was one that rested, and legitimately rested, upon the principle of free trade. By that principle there was established and would be hoped to be maintained in the country the doctrine that any two parties had a right to make a contract in the way most beneficial to themselves; and if one person chose to enter into that contract exposing the whole of his fortune, and if another person chose to enter with the contract exposing only a limited part of his fortune then one had as good a right to do so as the other provided care was taken that the parties with whom they were contracting were made aware of the conditions in which the contract was made.

The Bill was duly passed and is known as the Limited Liability Act 1855, 18 & 19 Vic. c. 133.

The 1855 Act did not touch the main clauses of the 1844 Act, which remained intact. It was this that had established the framework of the company as we know it, including the production of accounts and balance sheet (s. XXXIV), which had to be produced at the general meeting (s. XXXVIII). It gave the shareholders a right 'During the space of Fourteen Days previously to such ordinary Meeting and also during one Month thereafter . . . to inspect the books of account and the Balance Sheet of the Company, and take copies thereof and extracts therefrom' (s. XXXVII). These rights were subject to any contrary provision in the deed of settlement or any by-laws.

The auditors' rights could not be so excluded: 'The Directors shall deliver to the Auditors the half-yearly or other periodical Accounts and the Balance Sheet . . . and they shall examine the same' (s. XXXIX); 'It shall be lawful for the Auditors and they are hereby authorised to inspect the Books of Account and Books of Registry . . . throughout the Year and at any reasonable Times of the Day' (s. XL); 'The Auditors may demand and have the Assistance of such Officers and Servants of the Company and such Documents as they shall require for the full performance of their Duty in auditing the Accounts.' They had fourteen days 'To confirm the Accounts or report specially thereon' (s. XLI). The directors had to send all shareholders the balance sheet and the auditors' report (though this could apparently be excused if the deed of settlement so provided).

The Act even covered directors' conflicts of interest (s. XXIX). Contracts in which a director was interested had to be approved in general meeting. The Joint Stock Companies Act 1856 consolidated and amended the existing company law. Recent statistics from Companies House (21 May 1996) show that of 1,106,648 live companies in England and Wales, eight date back to 1856. There are 1,625 companies registered before 1896 that are still listed. Of the 64,535 listed Scottish companies, 160 were registered before 1896.

The 1856 Act included a schedule A and a table which covered the same ground as table A (confusingly so called) in the 1862 Act which drew heavily upon it. Here we find ourselves on even more familiar territory as the schedules and table A governed with some precision the conduct of general meetings. The voting arrangements are clearly weighted in favour of the small shareholder. Here are some points from table A of the 1862 Act:

Subsequent general meetings shall be held at such time and place as may be prescribed by the company in general meetings; and if no other Time or Place is prescribed a general meeting shall be held on the first Monday in February in every year at such Place as may be determined by the directors. (clause 30)

Clause 37 describes what constitutes a quorum.

The Chairman (if any) of the board of directors shall preside as Chairman at every General Meeting of the Company. (clause 39)

The Chairman may with consent of the meeting adjourn any meeting from time to time and Place to Place. (clause 41)

If a Poll is demanded by 5 or more members . . . (clause 43)

Every member shall have
   One vote for every share up to 10
   One vote for every five shares 10–100
   One vote for every ten shares beyond that. (clause 44)

No person shall be a proxy who is not a member of the company. (clause 49) [The principle of one share, one vote came some time later.]

An amusing contemporary view of the company in society at the time of the early legislation comes from *Punch* (29 (1855): 34), which took a characteristically lighthearted stance on the 'THE NEW LAW OF LIMITED LIABILITY' with a skit on the debate in Parliament:

and we therefore call on Parliament to say whether the following cases will fall under the new Act.

If a person sits in a draught, will the new law limit his liability to take cold? . . . If a man goes into a Chancery suit will the proposed enactment limit his liability to be ruined by lawyers?

A year later, in 1856, Parliament passed a Joint Stock Companies Act that consolidated and amended the existing company law. Banking and insurance companies were expressly excluded from its provisions. The memorandum and articles were introduced in place of the deed of settlement. Companies had to file an annual return, and companies that had registered under the earlier Act had to re-register.

The serious conclusion is this: Parliament was driven by the vastly increased scale of enterprises to facilitate the marshalling of resources. The railways and the great industrial enterprises of the day demanded them. International competitive pressures spurred the government on. It knew that the concentration of power was open to abuse and that the possibilities of fraud were extensive. It also knew that the framework of the common law was inadequate for the task. The thrust of the statutes is to balance power with accountability. That is why there is attention to detail on directors' powers from the beginning and so much said about the rights of shareholders and the conduct of general meetings.

The first leading textbook on companies appeared in 1866—Gore-Brown, now in its forty-fourth edition. The statute books show that there have been no fewer than twenty-three different Companies Acts since 1856. Some have been on particular points like the requirement imposed in 1867 to file with the Registrar contracts to take shares, or the 1980 Act which defined the criteria of a Public Limited Company. Others have been more general or consolidating. Prominent among these were the Acts of:

1908 (a consolidating Act);
1929 (a consolidating Act which also introduced new features especially in relation to Board of Trade inspectors);
1947 and 1948 (the latter consolidated the former together with the 1929 Act and confirmed the new provisions of the 1947 Act);
1985 (a consolidating Act, since changed in some respects by the Companies Act 1989).

Looking back over the last 150 years it is not too fanciful to say that, despite the numerous changes, the Companies Act we have today still resembles its predecessors of the mid-nineteenth century, and in some ways it has aged gracefully, though this is as much due to British pragmatism as anything else. The bone structure of the very first Act is still there but it has lost its original bloom and 'improvements' have made it bloated. It has had too many face lifts. It has long needed a thorough overhaul, and the government's announcement of a thorough review is therefore welcome.

An indication that this is so is the number of occasions when executives cannot simply look to the law, even UK law. Directors must familiarize themselves with European directives; ever changing (and improving) professional accounting standards which have been incorporated in the 1989 Act; the rules of the Stock Exchange; the rules of the Takeover Panel; the codes of Cadbury and Greenbury, and other shareholder guidelines or modifications to the above such as Hampel.

Directors: The Legal Framework

THE legislation which sets out the framework for companies in the UK, the Companies Act 1985, entrusts the conduct of business to the directors, of whom there must be two (s. 282), without distinction as to whether they are executive or non-executive. The concept of the board is not mentioned, nor the chairmanship. The provisions of the Act are mainly concerned with the proprieties. All companies must have a secretary, and in the case of a PLC he or she must be qualified. There is no such requirement for directors.

Nothing is said about the management of the business until part IX of the Act and precious little then though there is a raft of clauses dealing with matters like disqualification (s. 295) and removal (s. 303) and a lone sortie into management in section 309 which requires the directors 'to have regard to the interests of the Company's employees in general as well as the interests of its members'. The clause uses the phrase 'in the performance of their functions', but these are not defined. It is assumed that the directors can decide for themselves what their functions are to be, in the light of the memorandum and articles of association which will invariably provide that the business of the company shall be managed by the directors who may delegate as they think fit. It is left to the directors to decide how much they should do themselves and how much they should delegate. They are answerable to the members, i.e. the shareholders, for their conduct of affairs.

This basic model provides in principle great concentration of power. It means that in practice there are two tiers of accountability for its use. The directors may delegate as much as they like but formally cannot evade responsibility; those they appoint are accountable to them. They themselves are accountable to the shareholders. They must see that certain obligations are honoured, such as the filing of accounts, the holding of general meetings at the appropriate time, and the presentation of the accounts to them. There is little difference of substance from the very early days quoted in the previous chapter.

There are certain well-established principles of the common law which define the standard of behaviour for directors, for instance their duty of loyalty and the requirement to act in the best interests of the company.

The fiduciary duties comprise the following: to act bona fide [i.e. honestly and sincerely] in the company's interests; to act for proper purposes; to avoid a conflict of interests and duty; not to make secret profits; not to fetter his discretion; and general duties of skill, care, and diligence. (Catherine Drew, *Law Society Gazette*, 1 Mar. 1995)

Unless a company fails or is taken over, their conduct of affairs is seldom tested in the courts. The standard the court will expect of them will be conditioned by their professional or other qualifications. A director is expected to use the skills he or she possesses and exhibit the care and diligence of a reasonable person. In Britain, unlike the USA, the legal system makes it difficult to litigate against directors since generally speaking it is only the company that can pursue them, and this seldom happens unless control has changed one way or another. The right to sue directors by way of 'derivative action', that is to say on behalf of the company (even if it exists in principle), is seldom exercised as it would be costly and risky and would generally be unrewarding. If the shareholders dislike the directors' conduct of the business, they can as a last resort remove them, but there are other occasions on which they can register disapproval by voting against specific proposals such as changes to the articles or to the capital structure, including share option schemes.

The system of accountability under UK law had two serious flaws. If all the directors were managing the business the degree to which they could be accountable to each other depended entirely on group dynamics. In some companies run by perhaps a trio or quartet of near equals, it might work quite well. But the more common model was for the board to be dominated by the chief executive since the other executives were subordinate to him (rarely her). In such circumstances there was virtually no accountability: to be accountable to subordinates requires mental gymnastics of Olympic standard.

Secondly, if the shareholding were widely scattered, shareholders were in no position to hold the directors accountable in any practical way. If they did not like what they saw, their principal option was to sell their holding. We discuss this later. They do have other remedies under the law, but seldom use them not least because they tend to be difficult and complex and are always expensive. The Law Commission enquiry into shareholder remedies bears this out.

By providing such a sketchy framework the legislators accommodated in a single statute companies of all shapes and sizes. The same basic law covers the corner grocer's shop and British Telecom. All that a company had to do (as far as directors were concerned) was to have a minimum of two. It was left to companies to make what sense they chose of the Act. They could have 100 directors if they wished. The individuals would nevertheless be stuck with their legal obligations. Once upon a time these did not amount to much more than to behave honourably and use what skills they happened to possess. They did not have to be competent, let alone brilliant. They still don't, but they now have a much wider range of statutory obligations and liabilities—though most are protected to some extent by insurance. They themselves did not however have any stipulated executive functions; they could, and sometimes did, delegate the lot—or none. Nowadays the directors have a liability to third parties as a result of various statutes, e.g. section 150 of the 1986 Financial Services Act (and section 47 (False Market)) (misleading statements in listing particulars), or section 458 of the Companies Act 1985 (Fraudulent Trading), or section 214 of the Insolvency Act 1986 (Wrongful Trading).

Small unquoted businesses that did not need elaborate and costly structures took the Companies Act at face value and operated in fact without a board—a perfectly sensible thing to do as long as the basic disciplines were observed. Larger businesses filled in the gaps for themselves either because they saw advantage in doing so or because they were pushed into it, for instance by the Stock Exchange as one of the conditions of listing. The Act for example only provides for one kind of director, but it has long been the practice for some of the directors of quoted companies to have no executive responsibilities. The 'non-executive directors' (NEDS) were appointed to broaden the board's range of skills and experience, to add lustre, or to provide contacts. They were not representatives of the shareholders any more than the executive directors were, since the law did not provide for any distinction between them.

From the mid-1970s there was a growing perception that the malaise of many companies was attributable directly to the inability of the board to tackle the problem of poorly performing executive management. One of the causes was considered to be the weakness with which the board carried out its monitoring function, and it was felt that this would be remedied by strengthening the NED element. It was a consensus that this diagnosis was correct that led to the establishment of PRO NED (Promotion of NonExecutive Directors) in 1981 by the Bank of England, the Stock Exchange, the CBI, the clearing banks, the Institutional Shareholders' Committee, and others. This policy was endorsed by the Cadbury Report, and in effect implemented by it. This is explicitly to improve the accountability of management internally, i.e. to the board. The Cadbury Report stresses the importance of the supervisory element in the directors' responsibilities. The directors may be the same under the law, but the supervisory task falls most heavily on the NEDS just because it is their job to be objective.

This concentration on the supervisory element of the NEDS' role has caused critics of Cadbury to describe it as divisive, creating a 'them' and 'us' situation between the supervisors and supervised. The effectiveness of a board, like any group, will depend to some extent on its dynamics, that is the way its members interact. There may be cases where the NEDS are too heavy-handed, though probably not to the point where the executives become discouraged from taking risks. And there will be cases where a dominant chief executive pushes the board into accepting risks against their better judgement. No rules can cater for all the possible behavioural permutations.

The NEDS on a unitary board do have, and have always had, a dual role, advisory and supervisory; they are not just members of the team with the referee's whistle in their pocket. In actual conduct of business, it would generally be wrong to draw such a clear contrast. Directors do not join boards to fight the executives—they join because they have sympathy with what they are trying to achieve and want to help them in their task. Their loyalty, like that of the executives, is ultimately to the company. They should see their role as ensuring that success, by the company not making avoidable miscalculations; these roles are complementary. What Cadbury has done, and not before time, is to restore a proper balance between them. The importance attached to monitoring reflects agency theory, to which we now turn as we have some doubts about it.

AGENCY THEORY REVISITED

Agency theory claims that as no one works as hard or effectively for others as they work for themselves and there are costs involved in ensuring they perform well and work in furtherance of the owners' objectives. Margaret Blair sets it out as follows (1996: 97):

Managers are supposed to be the 'agents' of a corporation's 'owners', but managers must be monitored and institutional arrangements must provide some checks and balances to make sure they do not abuse their power. The costs resulting from managers misusing their position, as well as the costs of monitoring and disciplining them to try to prevent abuse, have been called 'agency costs'.

For many participants in the corporate governance debate, controlling management abuses while minimizing agency costs is and has been the central problem to be solved. To put the point crudely, owners need to be constantly on the qui vive to avoid being cheated by the greedy and unscrupulous or injured by the stupid. Their first line of defence is the board, which is why NEDS are so important, as they have no (or at any rate much less) conflict of interest. Agency theory has its limits, not least that it is based on a crude model of human behaviour—namely that the naked pursuit of self-interest is all that can motivate people, and in this situation shareholders need a set of carrots (such as bonus and share schemes) or threats (takeover and thereby job loss) to keep management on its toes.

What makes us suspicious of suspicion is that most of us have had the experience of working with colleagues who were as dedicated to the enterprise as if they had owned it. Human motivation cannot be characterized and oversimplified as a perpetual struggle to obtain the maximum reward for the least effort. Above the level of avoiding starvation it will include elements concerned with social congeniality, with the good opinion of one's peers, with satisfaction from achievement, with the exercise of power, or with the stimulation of challenge.

People often speak of money as the main motivator, because they do not really understand themselves, or are afraid to express their hearts and minds. We feel that agency theory takes insufficient account of all other motivations. How else can we account for the fact that most of our greatest companies are run by professional managers, who, if the theory is to be believed, ought to be cheating everyone, especially the owners, as much as they possibly can and in most cases palpably have no wish to do so?

Agency theory gains in plausibility from the very large rewards some directors take. Of course there are greedy executives: we shall deal with them and the special response we think is needed in a separate chapter below. Meanwhile we should remember that in relation to the number of people employed in a company it is at most a relative handful that attract charges of being over-rewarded; that rightly or wrongly people of the same calibre in the professions get as much or more; that money is not by any means the only or even the main motivator of most of us, as there is always a trade-off with the other factors of satisfaction.

COMPETENCE, NOT MOTIVATION, IS THE ISSUE

Our view is that agency theory directs attention to the wrong weakness. The prime purpose of accountability is to maintain standards of competence. Motivation does not of itself secure competence, and a lack of competence has almost certainly ruined more businesses than a lack of motivation. Shareholders are more likely to lose money because the relevant people in the firm are not up to the mark than merely because they are 'agents' bent on pursuing their own interests at the expense of others.

This means that efforts to ensure accountability should be viewed through the wider prism of performance. Companies are more likely to be ruined by fools than knaves. The failure of so many family businesses year by year tells its own story: whether the cause was lack of competence or some external cataclysm, agency theory cannot be held to blame, as those primarily involved were principals not agents.

DIRECTORS AND CODES

The sketchy nature of UK company law in regard to directors and boards has left many gaps which have been filled by various codes and regulations—a typically British and pragmatic way of covering the defects of others, in this case the government. It was for instance the Stock Exchange not the government that laid down conditions about the composition of the board if a company sought quotation. PRO NED produced its own code, and guidance came forth from various representative bodies like the Institutional Shareholders' Committee, the National Association of Pension Funds, the Institute of Directors, the Association of British Insurers, and more recently PIRC. The most important initiative in the UK was consolidating views on good practice in the form of a code by the Committee on the Financial Aspects of Corporate Governance in 1992.

In practical terms, it is the Committee's recommendations on audit committees that have most affected the directors' role. First, the requirement to have such a committee, composed in the way the Report required, ensured that the boards of quoted companies included non-executive directors, some of whom had to be independent. Secondly, the NEDS on the committee were enabled, and indeed obliged, to gain a deeper insight into the figures. Thirdly, their obligations (which the accounting profession and Hampel have since developed) to delve deeply into risk and systems of control gives them a far better understanding of the business. Fourthly, it improves the lines of communication with internal and external auditors. Finally, the committee can itself develop a coherence which reduces significantly the isolation of individual NEDS. The acceptance of the code (with some grousing) has been well nigh universal. (It has been estimated by PIRC that leading companies followed most points already—certainly about three-quarters of the top hundred companies in the FTSE had audit committees.) Its claim to attempt to make best practice general was not unfair. If all companies had already followed all the practices recommended it would have been otiose. If none had, it would have been too much to swallow.

There are no direct sanctions for failing to comply with the recommendations of the Cadbury Code; there are no fines (much less imprisonment!) for a failure to comply. The Stock Exchange requires that companies report on the extent to which they comply, and explain why they do not, if appropriate. The Stock Exchange only has limited powers to police its own listing rules. The ultimate sanction for failing to make a statement about compliance would be for the Stock Exchange to suspend a quotation, which would injure the very people the code is primarily designed to protect—the shareholders.

The code is obeyed mainly because it represented common practice among leading companies and because shareholders have been prepared to back up the recommendations. The extent to which the institutions have lent their support is looked at in Chapter 16, in the discussion on joint action and guidelines.

The media too have played a part. Companies which have not matched up to the Cadbury recommendations have met sharp criticisms in editorials and news comment. The final report attempts to combine the rigour of Cadbury with new narrative reporting on general principles of corporate governance.

Although the dictionary definitions of 'codes' and 'principles' are remarkably similar, the shareholder preference for the former was made plain in various submissions to Hampel, and even the Institute of Chartered Accountants warned against companies treating corporate governance as a 'do it yourself' manual in which basic standards were not considered generally applicable.

For directors who now sit on formally constituted audit committees, and who have to put their name to statements about such matters as the system of internal financial control, there is a heightened sense of accountability. Whilst the Cadbury Code may be pseudo-legislation, the sense of personal liability has sharpened.

Directors indeed now find themselves in a veritable forest of regulation; there is an expanding range of things for which they are personally liable by law, and we have cited some instances above of liability to third parties. In practice they do not feel besieged in an honest and well-run company. Even so, if there is a merger on the cards they will find themselves inundated by the requirements of the Stock Exchange and Takeover Panel. It would be impossible to operate without a raft of professional advisers—all acting at great expense.

What the UK has done with our legal regulatory and pseudo-legal system is indeed to create, at the shareholders' expense, a world fit for professionals to live in. Perhaps there is no alternative. Governments have come to believe that possible prevention is better than dubious cure. The rough world of the commercial jungle is no longer acceptable.

It is a common feature of law that when it confers upon a citizen or a group of citizens power they could not otherwise achieve there are safeguards as to its use. The framework of the Companies Act of the UK provides directors of companies with such power. They may delegate it to managers but cannot abdicate from responsibility by doing so. This is the bare legal framework. What we have suggested is that if the accountability of management to the boards does not operate effectively, the enforcing mechanism is pseudo-legislation rather than the law itself—and this in a world where great companies control more resources than small nations. There is a clear case for streamlining the various sources of law, regulation, and pseudo-legislation, which at times are in conflict and certainly cause confusion. A further question is where regulatory responsibility does, and should, lie. Currently a range of agencies, some statutory, some not, have a role in relation to boards. These include the Department of Trade and Industry, the Financial Services Authority, the Stock Exchange, and the Takeover Panel, not to mention the Monopolies and Mergers Commission and various European bodies with jurisdiction over UK companies. There is currently no single regulator for companies. Let us hope that the issue will be tackled during the proposed review of company law.

OVERSEAS MODELS

The architecture of the modern corporation or company is so familiar to us that we have ceased to consider the engineering of its structure. It is by no means the only possible kind of structure as a glance at the alternatives attests.

All developed countries faced the broadly similar problem of how to marshal savings for long-term projects and introduced broadly similar company legislation. In the USA it was regarded as a matter for each state, not the federal government, though in recent years the Securities and Exchange Commission (SEC) and the New York Stock Exchange (NYSE) have compelled a degree of uniformity of practice in certain areas such as information flows and board structure. The Germans took the view as early as the end of the nineteenth century that the general meeting was not an adequate forum for the shareholders to hold the directors to account, and that the state could not act as supervisor, so they introduced the concept of a supervisory board to represent their interests, giving it important but limited powers and entrusting management either to a separate board (*Vorstand*) or, in the case of a smaller company, to a general manager (*Geschäftsführer*).

France went in the opposite direction, by concentrating power in the hands of the chairman/chief executive, the *président directeur général* (PDG), with a *conseil d'administration* (the board). In reality the *conseil* had little power or authority. In 1966 the French government introduced a two-tier system as an alternative, which companies could choose; but very few did. French companies invariably had a dominant or significant shareholder; few had widely scattered shareholdings on the UK/US model. The *conseils* are gradually developing a larger role, especially if major shareholders are represented on them. And there is a movement to protect minority shareholders. But 'gouvernement d'entreprise'—corporate governance—as a subject only started to attract attention in 1995/6. The subject is live in Japan too. The Japanese legal framework is based on the US/UK model, but it works differently, when it works at all.

Such a brief comment on some of the features of the various legal frameworks conveys little about how they work in practice (see Charkham 1994). There are however some aspects which are important enough to warrant attention. The first point to notice is a natural reflection of general attitudes, namely whether a country prefers individual to collective responsibility. German law lays the responsibility for management on a board (the *Vorstand*). France gives great power to the PDG. In the USA power centres on the CEO. The Japanese, as is their wont, operate collectively, but through a system of informal committees, not through the board itself, which is a formal and ratifying body, only spurred into real action in the direst emergency.

The second matter is the importance of litigation. Though the UK and US statutes are not very different in principle, legal procedures are. The number of civil lawsuits brought against UK directors is infinitesimal (and then generally after a takeover or company failure). In the USA by contrast the potent cocktail of class actions, derivative suits, and contingency litigation exposes directors far more, despite the Business Judgement Rule (broadly: the courts will not doubleguess management decisions made in good faith). In Japan litigation is seen as a shameful failure of human relations and is very rare.

The third element is the role of the banks (which we shall deal with in a later chapter in regard to the UK). Banks are of course important in all countries and tend to be the main source of external finance in the early stages of company development. With this goes influence, though how much a given bank will wish to exercise depends on the bank's policy, the state of the company, and the skills of the particular bank official. Banks generally want to intervene as little as is consonant with protecting their funds. In many countries the banks may be shareholders as well as lenders—and have a seat on a supervisory board too; this is the case in Germany. In the USA the experience of the great crash led the federal government to limit by law the extent to which banks could take shares in industrial firms (the National Bank Act, the Glass Steagall Act, the Bank Holding Company Act). The cumulative effect of these Acts as interpreted by the courts is to enforce passivity on the part of the banks in respect of their industrial clients. So US banks nowadays have no role in corporate governance, whereas in other systems, however rarely, reluctantly, and tardily, they do. Japanese banks have been known to parachute in rescue teams; and German banks to broker rescuing deals. French banks too tend to get heavily involved (for a discussion of the issue of bank passivity in the USA, see Roe 1994: 51 f.).

It is an oversimplification to attempt to draw too clear a distinction between the systems in which the banks play an important part and those in which the stock market provides a means of changing management through a contested takeover, but there is important difference in the way they work.

The use of the terms 'bank based' and 'market based' is descriptive but inaccurate. The banks do indeed, as we have seen, play a larger part in some countries than others, but the system is *not* based on them. The stock market plays a larger part in governance in the UK and USA than elsewhere, not so much from its role as a source of capital but from its other role as a market for companies. Exposure to the market poses a threat to incumbent management because in those countries, unlike others such as France, Germany, and Japan, very few shareholders are committed in the sense that they would not tender their shares in a bid. Even in the USA, however, the combined effect of protective legislation in some states and the defensive devices known as 'poison pills' in some companies has insulated them effectively from takeover.

The development of the 'hostile' takeover during the last thirty years has added a dimension that the drafters of company legislation cannot have foreseen (and such a takeover cannot occur of course unless the majority of a company's voting shares are quoted). Some have been inspired by success, e.g. Nestlé's takeover of Rowntree—a classic case of a strategic acquisition. In other instances, however, entrepreneurs spotted the opportunities that arose when the underperformance of management had gone unchecked by board and shareholders, although it had been signalled by a weak share price. Even though they are not prohibited by law, 'hostile' takeovers are rare in Germany, Japan, and France, partly because of the more concentrated pattern of shareholding, partly because the big shareholders and banks between them have left less of a power vacuum, and partly because they are counter-cultural. In each country the status quo is under pressure. Even Germany has seen hostile bids in recent years.

It is not for us to try to assess the relative merits of each country's system, not least because they might not apply identical criteria, since their views of the purpose of companies differ in emphasis and the only fair way to form a judgement is in terms of the success with which they satisfy that purpose. This is not to underestimate the powerful currents of reform in both countries. The fear of takeover in the UK may act as a disincentive to take risk, but how is the point to be proved? The conclusion we have reached is that the purpose of comparative studies is not to create a league table of excellence, but rather to illumine differences so as to provide ideas for making each system work better in its own terms. In the case of the UK attention has centred, and in our view correctly, on improving the quality of boards, and France seems to be reaching a similar conclusion. Now the focus is on shareholders, though the legal and cultural framework is profoundly different. The debate on shareholder value may well be contributing to a review of economic efficiency—spurred by the rise of shareholder activists, in the shape of small shareholder organizations in both France and Germany (see the Eurotunnel example in Chapter 19). But the notion peddled by some in the UK that the shareholder is king and queen among stakeholders is not one which the more republican movements of the Continent would accept. There is not therefore a 'universal' shareholder role, but there may be an emerging global shareholder in so far as the capital markets are becoming international. In so far as the 'global' markets are actually driven by US and increasingly UK activists, their agenda has dominated much of the debate. Even in governance, money talks.

Looking at the legal structure tells us about the architecture of the company, but not how it works. This depends on many factors, social, economic, and political, as we can see from the contrasting patterns of behaviour in countries with similar formal frameworks. But in one point they are united. Some such structure was essential to marshal the resources needed for major enterprises in a modern world. This inevitably led to a concentration of power and to government interference when such power was misused.

6

Shareholders: The Legal Framework

THE Companies Acts from the beginning put in place a structure and set of procedures designed to ensure that the power vested in the directors carried with it commensurate accountability to the people whose economic interest gave them an incentive for making accountability real. There was never any suggestion that the shareholders should substitute themselves for the directors or interfere with the minutiae of management. The directors were to be responsible for running the company, but to be accountable to the members for their actions.

The original model exists today, though over the years the shareholders' protection against unscrupulous promoters or incompetent or fraudulent directors has varied.

The main motivation for buying equity in a company was and remains to share the prosperity achieved by competent management and direction. Nowadays matters are more complex. Some investors find themselves with shares in a company because they have 'bought the index' of which that company is a part. Others buy because in their view the current management is underperforming and there is room for improvement. This may result from internally generated changes, or from externally enforced changes—particularly a takeover.

A new development is the emergence of specialist investors who buy shares in particular companies in order to tackle underperformance by using shareholder activism (for example, the Lens fund, the UK Active Value Fund, and the services of consultants such as Sophie L'Helias of Paris-based Franklin Global Advisers who acts for aggrieved shareholders, be they French or overseas holders of stock).

For mainstream investors, though, a choice will have been made on largely positive appraisal of the company and its potential, relative to its perceived risk, price, and other opportunities for investment. Subsequent events may disillusion them, and if they decide the fault lies with the board they may withdraw their support and vote against them or even propose candidates of their own—and in extreme cases an entire slate. If a board is functioning properly the directors will have assessed the competence of management and taken the necessary steps to maintain it; the shareholders, in other words, only come into the picture when they judge the board has failed to do so.

The shareholders' formal rights and powers are established primarily under statute, and, for listed companies, supplemented by the listing rules of the Stock Exchange. In addition, each company under UK law must adopt a memorandum and articles of association which effectively form the contract between shareholders, directors, and the company and establish the rights and powers of each group. The Memorandum and Articles may vary, but cannot ultimately erode any rights or powers provided under statute.

Although the law provides extensive powers to the directors, shareholders in turn have been given rights to allow their interests to be protected. A number of these need modernizing in order to allow their efficient exercise, particularly in relation to resolutions and the AGM. A number of shareholder rights are rarely used in the UK due to cumbersome administrative procedures. What then are the most important rights and powers that shareholders have?

RIGHTS TO INFORMATION

Shareholders have rights to certain information, including notice of meetings which they may attend if they have been entered onto the register of members which the company is obliged by law to keep. This means that a recent shareholder who, due to bureaucratic delays, has not been entered onto the register may not exercise a number of important rights.

The most important information to which shareholders are entitled is a copy of the report and accounts. In addition, a shareholder may request copies of certain documents, including a copy of the memorandum and articles of association. Shareholders also have the right to inspect certain documents, for example, proposed amendments to the articles, the directors' contracts, and minutes of general meetings of the company.

Members (who are registered as such) are entitled to notice of meetings (twenty-one days for the AGM and fourteen days for an EGM). They also have the right to attend meetings or to appoint a proxy to cast their vote for them; a corporate body can appoint a representative with speaking rights at the meeting, although a proxy may not speak. This is an anomaly which requires redress. Individual shareholders should be able to appoint representatives with speaking rights at the meeting if they so wish.

VOTING RIGHTS

Shareholders also have the opportunity under the law to vote on a number of key issues which will affect the company. They do not have the right to vote on the report and accounts (they can only 'receive' them). Most companies have sought a vote, although some leading companies until recently did not (including GEC). This is not as simple as it sounds because the UK has a bizarre two-tier voting system, which many (particularly overseas) are not aware of. Shareholders are provided with a proxy card in advance of the meeting, which lists the resolutions to be passed and provides a box for them to tick in favour or against. If they wish to abstain, they can write this across the form. Some companies record abstentions, but many do not. The National Association of Pension Funds argued in its submission to the Hampel Committee in 1997 that a separate column for abstention should be provided in order to clarify this option; it is however uncertain whether the law recognizes such abstentions. They may simply amount to a spoilt ballot paper.

The proxy card also invites shareholders to nominate the person who will cast their votes for them at the meeting; in other words, it is not simply a 'postal' vote. The shareholders are appointing someone who will attend the meeting and will cast their vote for them. The proxy form usually states that the chairman of the meeting will act as proxy for the shareholder. If shareholders want to appoint someone other than the chairman, then they must write the name of that person on the form. Some companies provide a separate line for the shareholder to fill in. This may appear to be a rather amateurish process, and it is, but the consequences of this system are profound. First, the proxy holder will have discretion to vote on any business raised during the meeting. If the chairman has been appointed proxy for most shareholders voting and not attending the meeting, he or she will effectively be able to wield those votes to control the meeting, without any recourse to the shareholders to whom the votes belong. If there is a move to adjourn the meeting, amend a resolution, appoint a different chairman, for example, then these proxies will be used. This may present the chairman with a conflict of interest and it is one which needs resolving by reform of the AGM (which we discuss later).

The chairman can also be provided with votes by shareholders on a 'discretionary' basis. In this situation, the chairman holds the vote and decides which way to cast it. This is a clear conflict of interest and the practice should be abolished. On occasion the proportion of votes cast in this way can be substantial. In PIRC's 1996 proxy voting survey there were examples where discretionary votes reached over 50 per cent of those cast. In one case over 25 per cent of votes on the introduction of a long-term incentive plan were cast in this way, making rather a nonsense of the requirement for shareholder approval to be sought. If the shareholders in question hand the decision over to the chairman, then there has been no effective oversight. It is not possible to identify from PIRC's survey which shareholders have engaged in this rather lax form of voting; if they are institutions, then it is an issue of particular concern as they are able to report that votes have been cast, without having ensured that the vote was reliably cast in their clients' interest—unless of course they consider that the best protection for share-holders is for the chairman to making the voting decisions for them!

There is another problem. Despite all the effort, time, and expense that shareholders may have incurred in dutifully voting their shares by complet-ing the proxy form, usually these votes are not used. For all the concern over proxy voting which has been expressed in recent years, the fact that most of these votes are never cast makes the concept of shareholder oversight vir-tually farcical. Most companies have a power in their articles which allows the chairman to take a vote on the resolutions either by a poll (which would bring the proxy votes to bear) or simply by a show of hands of those present at the meeting. Normally, it is the latter. Despite all the sound and fury over proxy voting, the handful (or hundreds) who attend the meeting, represent-ing perhaps no more than a few per cent of the voting shares, will determine the outcome.

If shareholders want to ensure that their votes cast by proxy are actually brought to bear on the business of the meeting, they must attend and seek the support of others in calling a 'poll'. This is ironic, of course, as the sole purpose of providing a proxy vote in the first place is to allow shareholders to vote without having to attend in person. The company's articles will specify how many shareholders present must support the call for a poll. Some companies specify a minimum of two, and there is an upper limit of five specified in the Listing Rules. This may not sound onerous, but, on occasion, there are not sufficient shareholders present who support the call for a poll for it to take place. PIRC sent a representative to Northern Electric's AGM in 1996 in order to seek a poll on a resolution put by shareholders which they had advised clients to support. The resolution sought to limit directors' contracts to one year. At the meeting there was no support from other shareholders for this, and therefore the call for a poll failed and there was no way of ascertaining the level of proxy votes cast. Shareholders may be deterred on such occasions from supporting the call for a poll by appeals from the chairman to withdraw the request, on the grounds that it will cause delays, administrative complications, and irritate other shareholders pre-sent. Lunch may even be waiting! It is common for the chairman to ask for the call for a poll to be withdrawn on these grounds, as at both WPP and EMAP, where the chairman added that as the proxy votes showed that the resolution had been passed, there was little point in proceeding. In both cases, this was correct, but the levels of opposition to the resolutions in question was substantial, regardless of the fact that unless a poll was called the proxy votes were effectively not cast. In the report of the Hampel Com-mittee it is suggested that this two-tier voting system be left in place, but that chairmen announce the numbers of proxies they hold for and against the resolution, after the vote on the show of hands. This is a fudge. The show of hands should simply be abolished. Two companies in the UK have done this—SmithKline Beecham, which was wary of its American shareholders being disenfranchised by the British system after the merger, and British

Aerospace, which wanted to avoid the public relations irritation of potential defeat on a show of hands by protesters against the arms trade who bought shares in order to attend the AGM. PIRC supported this move by British Aerospace on the grounds that the only fair system was for there to be one share, one vote.

Among the voting rights which shareholders have, the most important is the right to approve the appointment of directors, although this may be a once and for all opportunity as many companies have exempted some or all of their executive directors from any requirement to stand down in future. The Hampel Report has finally put an end to this by advising that each director should seek re-election every three years. Companies as varied as ASDA and Pizza Express have made use of exemption provisions in their articles in order to pick and choose who stands down each year. The chairman, Archie Norman, was notably absent from the ballot paper at the 1996 AGM of ASDA and the whole board of Pizza Express (bar the lone non-executive) did not stand down in 1997. The situation is further complicated by lack of clarity over the proportion and time scale over which directors may be required to stand down. Apart from the exemption for executives, which is allowable under UK law, there can be a variation on musical chairs which prevents shareholders knowing precisely who will be coming forward at a particular meeting. The company's articles may specify that one-third are to retire. This proportion may include those directors who do not intend to put themselves forward again. The articles will require that newly appointed directors must be approved by shareholders, and these may be included in the one-third. If the board's number is not divisible by three, then rounding up or rounding down may further vary matters. The result is that, under the current provisions under companies' articles, there is no guarantee that all the directors will stand down every three years. Whether they must be included in the 'one-third' (or thereabouts) who retire that year will depend upon various other factors. It is common for companies with controlling shareholders to exempt their appointees from routine re-election. This issue has become important in the United States, where some shareholders have been pressing for all the board to retire for re-election each year, rather than 'staggering' the elections. This means that a vote can be directed specifically at the person with responsibility. For example, if there is a row on remuneration, shareholders may be in the position of not having a member of the remuneration committee standing down on whom they can vote (as was the case at British Gas in 1995). It was a pure coincidence that the person responsible for the decision declaring the derivatives losses at NatWest in 1997 was facing re-election.

The law requires that companies seek shareholder approval for an appointment; it also requires shareholder approval for the removal of a director (unless in certain carefully specified circumstances including insanity and criminal conviction). However, this element of the Companies Act can be overridden by amendment to the company's articles. An example of how contentious these variations can be is provided by the case of EMAP, which embarked upon a hazardous course by introducing new rules at its 1996 AGM to allow the board to sack directors via a 75 per cent vote. This amendment was opposed by two non-executives, who were in due course removed. However, having given an undertaking at the AGM that the new rule would not be used to remove the directors who had opposed its introduction, EMAP was obliged in the event to convene an EGM to seek shareholder approval for the removal. A significant proportion of shareholders opposed the introduction of the rule and, in the event, the removal of the two non-executives. In the ensuing months, the departure of the non-executives was followed by the resignation of other key executives. This change made to the articles therefore appeared to reflect deep-rooted conflicts within the company, and in the course of introducing the new rule, the directors effectively removed from shareholders in future the right to give their consent (or not) to the sacking of a director they had previously elected.

Companies do not always have it their own way in this area. At Eurotherm in the same year, the non-executives (in this case) duly removed a chief executive who they considered was not performing to standard; they were sharply rebuked by a group of influential institutions who considered they had targeted the wrong person and insisted upon his reinstatement.

The Companies Act also makes a gesture at ensuring that directors are not too elderly, particularly if they are executives who have been shielded from the vote for many years by exemption from a requirement to retire by rotation. Although the provision can be overridden by amendment to the articles, directors over the age of 70 at the time of the AGM must give special notice of their age in the notice of meeting and retire for re-election at the meeting. Many companies in recent years have amended their articles to remove this requirement, including BTR, which removed a retirement age of 65 in order to facilitate the appointment of a new chairman taking on the post at age 66.

Shareholders also have the right to approve the final dividend (although, bizarrely, not interims which may be paid during the year). Some companies avoid this vote by declaring a series of interim payments. Examples in recent years include the Royal Bank of Scotland and Hanson, prior to the demerger.

The shareholders are also provided with an annual opportunity to approve the appointment of the auditors, and to authorize the directors to pay their fees. The auditors in turn have certain rights, which are rarely exercised, but also offer protection indirectly to shareholders. For example, if the auditors are not put forward for reappointment by the directors (i.e. are effectively sacked by the board) the auditors are entitled to have a statement circulated and to attend the AGM to explain their position. Auditors also have the right to resign voluntarily of course, and occasionally do so. Coopers & Lybrand resigned as the auditors of Eidos over concerns with the company's corporate governance arrangements.

The directors can exercise the powers of the company in general terms, but must seek shareholder approval for certain specific matters, notably to seek approval for any alterations in the company's share capital. This includes relatively small capital alterations, such as the issuing of shares to finance share option schemes for the executives or other employees, through to major alterations linked to acquisitions or disposals.

Any amendments to the articles of association or the memorandum must also be approved by shareholders. This is not the dull and bureaucratic matter it seems. Shareholders have become increasingly careful about rubber stamping proposals to amend the articles. Although they must scrutinize the proposals at the company's premises (or their solicitors') careful attention has flagged up efforts by some companies to reduce shareholder powers. One example was at Hanson in 1991 where the company proposed to raise the threshold of shares required to propose a director for the board from one shareholder to 10 per cent of the issued equity capital. PIRC coordinated an effective transatlantic proxy campaign to get the proposal voted down, and although it was bundled with a highly popular proposal to introduce a scrip dividend, there were sufficient 'no' votes in the company's postbag in advance of the meeting for the company to cancel the EGM and leave the articles well alone. A new meeting was convened the following month to approve the scrip dividend on its own.

Attached to the rules in the Companies Act is a model set of articles under table A which many companies have adopted. The company may (with shareholder approval) amend or vary these, and the law specifically states 'unless otherwise approved in general meeting'.

SPECIAL AND ORDINARY RESOLUTIONS

Minority shareholders are in part protected by the fact that certain classes of proposal must be passed by special resolutions which require a qualified majority of 75 per cent. Alterations to the share capital and amendments to the mem. and arts. require a 75 per cent majority. Besides these general rights to information and to vote on proposals put forward by the directors, shareholders also have the power to intervene. Chief among these powers is the right to lodge resolutions, subject to stringent conditions. The shareholders may use this power to put a resolution on any issue they consider relevant, subject to the general provisos elsewhere that the resolution does not interfere with the day-to-day business of the company, and does not (as an investment advertisement under the Financial Services Act) contain false or misleading information; the normal laws of libel and defamation also apply. The Companies Act sets various conditions for the introduction of these resolutions, for instance requisitionists must undertake to pay the reasonable costs of circulation unless these are waived and must either represent 5 per cent of the share capital or 100 individual shareholders with equity on average worth £100 each; in addition, a tight timetable for lodging a resolution must be followed. The shareholders are entitled to put forward a 1,000-word supporting statement; there are no rules regarding the directors' 'right to reply' although usually a copious amount of material is provided in the few cases where shareholders have actually requisitioned a resolution.

Some companies have adopted rules which make it easier for shareholders to put forward a resolution. The charter of incorporation for the Bank of Scotland allowed that any individual proprietor (as shareholders are called) can put forward a resolution. Similarly, Great Universal Stores allowed that an individual shareholder could put forward a resolution. Neither had faced a resolution from shareholders in recent years, but, with a policy of safety first, removed the rules. The Bank of Scotland agreed with PIRC that although it would adopt the Companies Act provision of requiring 100 shareholders or 5 per cent, it would not impose costs.

The difficulty of exercising the right of shareholders to introduce a resolution is reflected in the small number of cases in which companies in the UK have faced this. In recent years, the few companies to have faced resolutions from shareholders have generally been privatized utilities, with concern over executive remuneration being the most common reason for shareholders intervening. Here the local private shareholder base largely comprises customers, who through the local press have had an effective means of pursuing their cause, and identifying other possible supporters.

In one case, Northern Electric, the proposal was put forward by a group of the company's pensioners who were attempting to resolve a pension dispute via a shareholder resolution. In this case, the directors put forward a parallel resolution seeking the members' permission for the directors to waive costs. One of the most effective examples of the shareholder resolution being used in recent years by small shareholders is at Yorkshire Water. Here the local shareholders banded together in an organization representing shareholders, but highlighting customer concerns.

The other utilities which have faced a shareholder resolution were rarely under any real threat. The resolutions had largely symbolic value, and received only token levels of support, but they highlighted the impracticalities of the system, although it is intended to provide shareholders with redress. In hearings to the House of Commons Select Committee the UK Shareholders' Association explained the problems they had faced in trying to table their own resolution at British Gas. The group had drawn up a resolution which proposed that the company's articles be amended to put an upper ceiling on the amount that could be paid to the executive directors. This would have extended the scope of an existing article which provided for a ceiling on the directors' fees (paid only to the non-executive directors). The resolution was put forward according to the required timetable, and with sufficient backing to meet the requirements of the Companies Act (100 shareholders with an average of at least £100 each).

Once the resolution was lodged, it could not be withdrawn. In effect the group would have to accept an unknown expense in lodging the resolution. Unable to accept this potential liability, UKSHA reluctantly decided not to proceed.

In the event, British Gas faced two other shareholder resolutions on the same theme at its AGM that year, one sponsored by a Scottish medical academic, Professor Lamb (whose name added to the journalists' menagerie—fat cats, and Cedric the pig at the AGM). Professor Lamb's resolution was publicized by the *Guardian* newspaper, and he was provided with several thousand potential requisitionists for the action. It is doubtful if each of them realized that they were potentially signing up to a resolution for which costs could be recovered. The uncertain nature of the law on this point is a clear deterrent. Could costs include the postage? A proportion of printing? A charge for the time of the company directors, secretary, and advisers in dealing with the resolution? The cost to the company of the heavy public relations campaign and response published by the directors which is mounted in order to defeat such a motion if it looks remotely like attracting support? The law is silent on these points at statute, and there is no case law. The only caveat is the notion of 'reasonableness' in setting the price.

PIRC was equipped with legal advisers and clients who were institutional investors—pension funds willing and able to take the risk of launching such an initiative. The resolution filed by PIRC was drafted to limit the potential liability, and lodged with a covering letter which attempted to define the scope of costs which could reasonably be recouped by the company. Of course, such legal advice itself cost money. At the AGM, attended by over 4,000 shareholders and covered by editorials in newspapers from the *Sun* to the *Financial Times*, the sense of popular revolt was palpable. Despite the ban on journalists at the meeting itself, a smuggled camcorder under the anorak of a BBC journalist who had bought shares at privatization provided some home movie footage for the main television news programmes of the day. The vote marked a watershed in shareholder resolutions in the UK— Professor Lamb's resolution which called upon the company to establish a committee representing consumers and employees to review the company's performance was supported by just over 9 per cent of the vote. PIRC's resolution calling for a review of the company's policy on executive remuneration was supported by nearly 17 per cent of the shareholders. The turnout was nearly double the previous year, and in winning the vote the company chairman had apparently spent the previous months in personal visits and presentations to leading institutions, sent a special letter to all shareholders attempting to rebut the claims made by PIRC in its briefing materials, and changed the venue to accommodate the thousands who wanted to attend.

The vote on British Gas became a defining moment for many pension fund trustees who for the first time asked their investment managers what they intended to do. For others it pointed to the fact that they did not have procedures in place to allow for a reasoned consideration of the issues. Others discovered (too late) that the votes had already been pledged, or cast, and were faced with the argument (wrongly) that there was nothing which could be done to overturn the decision. (All votes can be changed at the AGM itself on a poll.)

The media spotlight was on the institutions: they were under intense scrutiny for the first time on a voting issue. The question was the rationale behind their decision to support the board in a case where it appeared that executive management had abused its power. Some argued that shareholder resolutions in principle were a motion of no confidence in the board; if there were sufficiently serious problems to warrant a resolution, then the board itself should be removed. This is characterizing a shareholder resolution as the equivalent of a nuclear deterrent: they will never be used because of the potential damage to the company and thereby to the shareholder. The result would be mutually assured destruction in which both the target and the proponents of the resolution would lose out as the resolution caused the company to be undermined.

If this line of argument is followed, every shareholder resolution would be so regarded and none would be passed for fear of damaging the very interests they were designed to protect—both the company and the shareholder. It would be tantamount to asserting that the only weapon in the shareholder's armoury was atomic. This is clearly hyperbole. There *may* be resolutions which are aimed at unseating the board, but to interpret all disagreements on matters of policy in such a way is unwarranted. When set against the US situation in which shareholders provide AGMs with shareholder resolutions in their hundreds (some of which are actually passed), perhaps we can conclude that US companies have had their performance gingered up by the presence of shareholder resolutions; rather than being viewed as a nuclear attack on the company, they are seen as a useful protection for investors against gross misjudgements by the board, or failures of policy or strategy, which do not warrant the sacking of the complete board. The notion that directors are either approved (warts and all) or ejected from the board was clearly viewed as too narrow a range of options by the framers of statute. In our view they were right to afford shareholders the opportunity to intervene on issues of policy or strategy, and resolutions should be reformed to allow them to become a more effective tool for accountability to shareholders.

The law does not provide shareholder resolutions as a blunderbuss. There are two forms which can be put forward by shareholders—ordinary or special. An ordinary resolution has advisory status only. If passed by shareholders the resolution simply provides the directors with a statement supported by a simple majority of the members in favour of a particular course of action. The directors are not bound by the resolution. A special resolution can instruct the directors in a particular course of action. This requires a qualified majority before it can be passed—75 per cent. This is a significant distinction, and the fact that the law provides shareholders with the opportunity either to advise or instruct the directors is a powerful reminder in itself that the framers of statute did not envisage passive shareholders content simply to delegate in full to the directors, regardless, or simply to sell their shares if there was a market for them.

The situation in the USA is different in this respect. It is much easier for shareholders to table resolutions, but they only have advisory status, regardless of the majority with which they are passed. There have been a number of instances in which shareholders have gone to court in order to seek enforcement of resolutions passed by a majority, but simply ignored by the directors.

Shareholder resolutions should be viewed as proposals put by members of the company to be considered by other members of the company. The directors will give their view of a proposal and say whether they support it. This will weigh heavily in the considerations of the other members, but if the directors are viewed as wrong, misguided, or simply headstrong on an issue, their advice may not be followed.

At Shell Transport and Trading in 1997 there was the rare instance of an ordinary shareholder resolution at a major transnational—not a utility—addressing the issues of environmental standards and human rights. The company had been embroiled in controversy over its operations in Nigeria, where it was in a joint venture with a government controlled by a military dictatorship. When a number of tribal leaders from the oil-producing south of the country were executed, including an internationally recognised playwright, Ken Saro-Wiwa, outrage at the country's record on human rights was expressed even at the Commonwealth summit, which excluded Nigeria from the meeting. Shell acknowledged that its record on environmental standards was poor, in a region of high tension in which local people viewed the oil industry as working with a repressive government which was denying them the fruits of economic development. The episode exposed Shell's lack of clear policy for dealing with its economic role in countries with human rights abuse. Following in the wake of an effective campaign to prevent the disposal of the Brent Spar oil storage platform in the North Sea, and a consumer boycott in Germany organized by Greenpeace, Shell's traditionally closed approach and lack of transparency left it vulnerable to criticism.

The shareholder resolution was lodged by PIRC working with the Ecumenical Council on Corporate Responsibility following months of discussion with the company at board level and beyond. There was intense scrutiny of the resolution by institutions, with Shell organizing presentations to its top institutional shareholders and PIRC in turn organizing a briefing for investors addressed by environmental and human rights experts. By the AGM Shell had responded in positive terms to many of the points in the resolution: it had revised its statement of business principles to incorporate both environmental and human rights policy, it had produced a revised group-wide environmental health and safety report, it identified a member of the main board as responsible for these issues, and when shareholders arrived at the packed AGM on 4 May 1997 in the Queen Elizabeth Conference Centre with the pomp of the state opening of Parliament filling the streets of Westminster outside, they were provided with a report on operations in Nigeria and a new group-wide health, safety, and environment report. At the meeting, John Jennings, the chairman, admitted that in principle 'external verification was desirable'. In a short space of time Shell had made rapid progress. Despite this dramatic shift in policy, tone, and announcements of future improvements, institutional support for the resolution was significant. Ten and a half per cent in favour, and a further 7.00 per cent formally abstained, rather than follow the board's advice to vote against the proposal. In the months following the AGM, Shell made further changes to its policy, championing a leadership role on environmental and social reporting, which would be subject to independent audit.

Shareholders also have the power to move amendments to resolutions at the AGM. This is limited by the general requirement that any proposal

Table 2. UK shareholder resolutions 1995

Year	Company	Issue	Proposer	Proxy vote where poll called for/ (abstentions)
1995	British Gas	Directors' pay	Professor Lamb	9.8%
1995	British Gas	Review of directors' remuneration policy	PIRC	17%
1995	Northern Electric	Remove shareholder 15% limit	Trafalgar House (bidder)	Defeated
1995	Northern Electric	To allow Trafalgar bid	US arbitrageurs	Defeated
1995	Northern Electric	Pensions benefits	Company pensioners	Defeated
1995	NORWEB	Pensions benefits	Company pensioners	Defeated
1995	NORWEB	Remuneration of chairman/CEO	Company pensioners	Defeated
1995	NORWEB	Directors' service	Company pensioners	Defeated
1995	NORWEB	To waive costs of pensioner resolutions	Directors	Passed
1995	Yorkshire Water	Water leakages	Yorkshire Water Watch (consumer shareholder group)	Passed
1995	Bank of Scotland	Directors' remuneration	Private investor	Defeated

Source: PIRC Ltd.

circulated to shareholders should not be substantively altered. This is to ensure that shareholders voting by proxy (usually the vast majority in quoted companies) are not effectively disenfranchised. Some companies have clarified this by stating in their articles of association that only amendments to correct patent errors or technicalities will be allowed. British Aerospace is a rare example of a company which has expanded this shareholder power by stating that the company will circulate any amendments lodged at least seven days in advance of the meeting to allow a vote by other members.

The law restricts the power of amendment to ordinary resolutions. Special resolutions which require a 75 per cent vote cannot be amended in any way or form. This has caused some difficulty at companies where they have accepted the need to make some adjustment on complex issues in response to shareholder concern expressed after the resolution has been circulated.

The general issue of how companies incorporate shareholder concerns is raised by the limitations on the power of amendment. At WPP in 1995 the company convened an EGM to establish a share scheme for the chief executive, Martin Sorrell. The terms were generous, if the performance targets were achieved. Some shareholders opposed this, on the view that the potential beneficiary of the scheme had presided over a substantial fall in the share price without any penalty, and should not be rewarded once the company recovered its former position. In response the company raised the performance targets and scaled down the size of the potential payout. PIRC questioned the company about the legality of proceeding with the EGM as the terms of the scheme had been altered in private discussions with some shareholders, and other members of the company would not have the opportunity to see the amendments before the votes were cast. The company made an effort to address this question by writing to all shareholders explaining that the terms of the scheme had been altered; the only problem was that the letter was posted on a Friday and the EGM was the following Monday. The substantial numbers of overseas shareholders would certainly not be informed in time for the meeting, and many UK shareholders would not be able to attend and cancel their proxy votes on the basis of the new information. PIRC attended the EGM and sought to move an adjournment of the meeting as the sole item of business was to approve a share plan which no longer existed in the form described in the shareholder circular. The chairman replied that, as the changes were in shareholders' interests, it was not necessary to advise shareholders prior to voting on the issue. An effort to adjourn the meeting would have been fruitless in any case as the chairman was designated as proxy for most shareholders, and as such had power to wield their votes over any business raised in the meeting. PIRC did however call a poll which revealed that over 25 per cent of shareholders had voted against the scheme—a high point of opposition in that year.

Overseas shareholders in Marks & Spencers tried to use the power of amendment in order to highlight the problems the company was facing in the United States. The shareholders in question were the Allied Clothing and Textile Workers' Union which represented employees at Brooks Brothers, which Marks & Spencers had taken over. ACTWU decided to bring its concerns to the attention of shareholders in the UK by planning to move amendments to the report and accounts at the 1991 AGM which would call for management action. The union took on PIRC to coordinate a proxy solicitation campaign, and appointed as legal advisers Stephenson Harwood. In the event the company entered into negotiations with ACTWU and the amendments were not moved.

PROPOSING DIRECTORS

Shareholders also have the right to propose directors, although this is a rarely used power. The share-owning threshold for proposing a director is set in the Companies Act as a member (who in theory could own one share only). Some companies' articles require a higher threshold of share ownership, and specify also whether the resolution proposing the director can be ordinary (which requires no special notice, and will be passed on a simple majority) or special (which requires notice of twenty-one days). It is unusual for companies to vary the Companies Act provisions on the appointment of directors, which make this a matter for the board. One exception was the National Freight Corporation, which when privatized allowed for employee shareholders to elect a member of the board of directors whilst their collective stake in the company was maintained at a particular level. Other companies have given special rights to appoint directors to large shareholders. For example, whilst Waste Management in the USA was a major owner of Wessex Water, it negotiated as the holder of 'B' shares to appoint a director who was not required to retire by rotation. It was not clear how appointment by one shareholder worked with the general duty of directors to the company as a whole. Other examples of directors appointed by particular shareholders include many of the cable and media companies in the UK which are developing via joint venture arrangements. For example, BSkyB names various principal shareholders in its articles who are not only allowed to appoint certain directors, but given the power of veto over appointments to committees. A more informal version of this arrangement is the appointment of representatives by shareholders owning a substantial proportion of the shares; for example, at Sainsburys, which has a substantial proportion of its shares owned by a trust established by the founders, and similarly Stage Coach, which is owned in part by two of its directors.

The use of the power to appoint directors by shareholders has been rare. One example was a proposal to appoint a new director to the board of British Steel in 1989 when the company had announced the closure of its Ravenscraig plant in Scotland. Scottish public sector pension funds, and some employee shareholders, proposed a director. His candidacy was inspired by criticism of the decision-making process at British Steel; it was alleged in a House of Commons Select Committee inquiry into the closure that options for the sale of the plant had not been properly explored. He was to be a non-executive candidate with responsibility not for overturning the decision itself, but for reviewing the options in an objective manner. Despite the controversy surrounding the closure, and concerns expressed in the Select Committee report, there was little support for his appointment. Corporate governance was not a well-established concern among the institutions, despite a number of scandals, such as Guinness and Distillers, there was reluctance to interfere with what was viewed as management prerogative.

In recent years, the main other proposals for candidates to the board have come from individuals, with the ubiquitous Noel Falconer proposing himself to the board at a number of companies, from British Aerospace to British Gas. He has rarely attracted support from institutional groups, and therefore the vote on his appointment has usually been token.

The only other significant shareholder effort to put forward a director was by Yorkshire Water Watch, representing local private investors in the company, which fielded a candidate who in due course was also backed by PIRC. This provided a credible campaign as private investors held a significant proportion of the company's shares and PIRC's clients were pension funds with substantial holdings. Their candidate was Diana Scott, well known in the region as the former Ofwat regulator for the Yorkshire area. She won 20 per cent of the vote. Though she was defeated, her campaign prompted a series of changes at the company, and put the spotlight on attempts to restore customer confidence after a period of drought had left reserves of water at low levels. The board had made a series of failed efforts to win customer support for water-saving measures. Among these was a letter sent to local businesses suggesting that industrial water usage could be cut back if companies extended their holiday periods or even moved out of the area. The local chamber of commerce was not amused. A director made misplaced efforts at leading by example on personal water conservation. He attempted to demonstrate on regional television how male customers could avoid running the tap when shaving, by using only a small glass of water, and claimed not to have had a bath for several weeks, as part of his personal contribution to water conservation. When quizzed by a BBC journalist on whether this meant he had not had a wash over that period, he admitted to taking a bath at his mother-in-law's house, outside the Yorkshire area. Public relations disasters such as these did nothing to win over customer confidence, and the company saw major board changes shortly afterwards.

Diana Scott's campaign focused attention on the board structure and Ofwat in its recommendations acknowledged that corporate governance had a role to play in ensuring the company met its regulatory targets. It stated that the board of the water services company should appoint a new director with experience of customer and regulatory issues. The shareholder resolution had failed, but the regulator had picked the issue up and Yorkshire Water revamped its board.

There has been little evidence of pressure from employees for representation on the board, but at the 1997 and 1995 AGMs the General Secretary of the staff association of the National Westminster Bank was nominated. He was not elected, but such interest in corporate governance may be a straw in the wind.

CONVENING AN EGM

Shareholders are also given the power to convene a general meeting of the company. In order to do this, they must own 10 per cent of the company's equity. The general meeting must be convened by the directors within fourteen days of receiving notice. There are no costs imposed on shareholders who follow this course of action, although the high proportion of shares required to pursue this means it is even more rare than a shareholder resolution, and usually involves a life and death issue for the company's future. In recent examples of shareholders pursuing this course of action, overseas investors have sometimes played a key role.

By the mid-1990s shareholder discontent was brewing at Saatchi and Saatchi. The chairman had presided over a 90 per cent fall in the share price, and a number of US investors were persuaded that it was time to act. The Saatchis had presided over electoral campaigns for the Conservative Party and counted among their clients prestigious companies like British Airways. This glittering reputation appeared to have distracted attention from a tarnished financial record. The Americans were not sentimental, and were more used in their home market to kicking down doors if polite requests for entry to the boardroom were ignored. The British institutions may have taken the view that, since they had supported the restructuring of the board, time should be given for the newly appointed non-executives to work their magic. British patience is renowned. In the Saatchi case US shareholders were not prepared to wait. They decided to force the board's hand by threatening to call an EGM to remove the chairman. In the event he resigned.

Americans were also behind another effort to use the device of an EGM to pursue a change in strategy. Northern Electric had successfully repelled a takeover bid from Trafalgar House which was seeking a source of stable earnings. US investor Guy Whyser Pratt was on the wrong side of the betting on which side would win in the bidding war, and called an EGM which sought to overturn the board's recommendation. The EGM was duly convened and his motion was defeated, although he claimed victory after the event as the board went into negotiations with a preferred bidder.

The EGM route has also been pursued by the UK Active Value Fund, which has taken stakes in underperforming companies in order to change the board and revive the company's performance. American giant CalPERS invested $200m. in the fund shortly afterwards, in a clear sign that international pressure on underperforming companies was stepping up.

Fund manager Hermes raised the stakes in the investment trust world in 1998 by teaming with others to call an EGM at the Brazilian Smaller Companies Investment Trust, and ejected the board. Hermes has also linked up with the US-based Lens Fund to launch a UK fund with similar aims.

In addition to their rights and powers via the formal procedures of the company's meetings, shareholders also have powers to petition the Department of Trade and Industry if they consider that their interests are not being protected, for instance where directors have not appointed an auditor or where they have not complied with a request for an EGM by shareholders. Shareholders may also appeal to the court for redress if they consider there has been wrongdoing in the company. Both of these routes are particularly complex and expensive, which inhibits their satisfactory implementation. The regulatory framework in this respect requires an overhaul and the Law Commission has recommended as much.

COMPANY REGULATION

Besides their legal rights derived from the company's own articles, the common law, and the Companies Acts, shareholders have some protection from other laws and pseudo-legislation. The listing rules of the London Stock Exchange provide protection in various ways, by reinforcing the provisions on the information contained in prospectuses for instance and ensuring some liquidity in the market. The insider trading laws, for example, are designed to prevent the counterparty to a transaction from benefiting by information not generally available; and the Stock Exchange lays down strict rules about transactions by directors. The rules of the Takeover Panel secure equal treatment in a takeover. The rules of the accounting profession are intended to ensure that those who study company accounts receive as fair and accurate a picture as possible—always bearing in mind that accounts are a snapshot only.

There are some categories of company which have a specific regulatory regime, in which the interests not of shareholders, but of others, are to the fore. Prime examples are the utilities, where monopolistic suppliers are regulated in the consumers' interest via a plethora of agencies with the family suffix 'Off'—Oftel, Ofwat, Offer, Ofgas. The regulatory regime specifies targets for pricing, investment, and even (for the water companies) environmental standards. Shareholders in these companies need to appreciate that the simple market mechanisms do not apply and unless the directors achieve the standards set down by the regulator they can be penalized.

This gives shareholders a direct interest in how regulated companies are performing in relation to their regulatory framework. In recognition of this some have incorporated performance in these areas into the targets the directors must achieve before bonuses and share schemes can be awarded. This is wholly appropriate.

The public interest is also directly expressed through the regulatory regimes under which banks and insurance companies operate. Most are now themselves publicly quoted companies with numerous shareholders like any other commercial enterprise of similar size. It is not an exact likeness however because they are supervised by the Bank of England under the Banking Act or by the Department of Trade and Industry. The establishment of the Financial Services Authority in 1997 has brought together the plethora of self-regulatory bodies spawned under the auspices of the Financial Services Act, and the Labour government shortly after election transferred some regulatory responsibility from the Bank, leading to some confusion over the ultimate division of labour. The Authority has embarked upon a round of detailed consultation regarding its remit and representation, and the picture will not be clear for several years.

Banking supervision is undertaken primarily to protect the integrity of the financial system. All banking depends on confidence as no building society or bank in the world could survive the simultaneous decision by their depositors to withdraw their funds. Banks survive because those depositors are confident that they do not and will not need to do so. The effects of a collapse of such confidence would be so catastrophic that no government could walk away from it. The price of cure would be so high that they invest in prevention.

The knowledge that there is a regulatory regime should on no account lull shareholders in a bank or insurance company into any lapses of vigilance. Indeed there is all the more reason to look at the way the boards work. Even at banks shareholders should realize that the Bank of England looks at whether individual bank directors are 'fit and proper' but it does not assess the collective competence of the board. That is up to the shareholders. Their opinion of the top structure is as apposite in banks as elsewhere. If shareholders want even regulated companies in which they invest to prosper, the price is greater, not less, vigilance.

The Role of Banks

IN a book about UK shareholders' rights and duties, it may at first sight seem odd to include a digression about bankers. Yet it would be such an omission that would be odd, considering what a large part banks play in other countries and how great their interest may be even in the UK. Indeed in the modern world there is no enterprise without its bankers to hold its cash, transmit its payments, lend it money, and perform a host of other services.

This was not always so. Without attempting a potted history of the UK banking system and its relationship to commerce and industry we can see that in the Middle Ages such enterprises as there were had to manage without bankers at all. It was not until the partial repeal of the Usury Laws in 1545 that bankers from Lombardy and elsewhere began business in London and the goldsmiths of London were able legally to take deposits, pay interest on them, and recycle them at a profit either to the state or for private economic activity. A century or so later Alderman Backwell, at the sign of the Grasshopper at the Royal Exchange, had a wide-ranging banking business, including money-changing, insurance, and loans. By 1664, King Charles II owed him £286,042. (By 1672, the monarch owed in all £2.25m. and stopped payments from the Exchequer; many were ruined.) Backwell's clients included traders like the Muscovy Company. The Bank of Scotland from its foundation in 1695 was engaged with commerce, by discounting bills of exchange (which produced an income of £1m. in 1800). 'The cash credit was theoretically renewable each year, but this tended to be rolled over year on year and increased in line with a particular business's expansion' (Cameron 1995) *Plus ça change* . . .

Until the industrial revolution, the banks' main customers (other than private individuals) were farmers and landowners and the related industries like brewing and the wool trade. They served too the craft industries of which the livery companies of the City of London and elsewhere are a reminder. To these involvements, the banks added the emerging firms in manufacturing as the industrial revolution got under way. With the exception of the companies chartered or incorporated by statute, the firms and enterprises to which the banks lent were characterized by one crucial feature—the proprietors' entire assets stood behind the loan. That did not stop firms failing and sometimes bringing down the banks that had supported them. The troughs in economic cycles always left a trail of destruction. One graphic figure—from the USA—tells the story. In October 1857 alone, which followed a period of expansion in the early 1850s, no fewer than 1,415 banks failed.

Closer to home there was a banking crisis in Scotland that brought the Western Bank and City of Glasgow Bank to their knees. Deposits were rescued, but the shareholders in the Western Bank lost their capital. Spink (1977) gives lists of failures of both private and joint stock banks. Some had a very short life; Table 3 contains a few examples from a long list. But we are anticipating.

When incorporation became general (in the UK from 1844 onwards; see Chapter 4), it did not, as we have seen, at first carry with it the privilege of limited liability for the shareholders, so those who founded or subsequently took a stake in a company were or should have been aware of how dependent it was on their bankers' support and what part (if any) the bankers played. To have risked one's entire fortune without this knowledge would have been folly. The pressure would have diminished after 1855, when limited liability was introduced, but even then the shareholders stood to lose all their investment—and as the companies were unquoted, there was no easy exit if they did not like the way the company was run. (In many cases shareholders bought partly paid shares and were liable for a further call if this proved necessary.)

We need not be concerned here with the banks as providers of services

Table 3. The rise and fall of local banks

Location	Trading name	Partnership name	Started	Failed
Ashton-under-Lyne	Silverstor Lyne	Sikes & Co.	1797	1800
Exeter, Devon	General Matthew Lee	Yeates	1809	1814
Leeds	Leeds Cantile	John Holmes & Co.	1864	1875
Reading	Reading Bank	Marsh, Deane, Westbrook & Deane	1788	1815
Liverpool	Albion Banking Co.		1836	1842
Birmingham	Borough Bank		1837	1840
Manchester	Commercial Bank of England (Manchester)		1834	1840
	Imperial Bank of England		1836	1839
	Manchester People's Bank		1910	1912
	Royal British Bank		1849	1856
	Yorkshire Agriculture & Commercial Banking Co.		1836	1842

(e.g. as registrars or trustees or even insurers as well as providers of services in the forex and futures markets); in those functions they are similar to others. Their position as providers of funds is unique in so far as they may well have charges over a company's assets (which no other supplier has). The multifaceted relationship of a bank with a company—as provider of various services plus provider of funds—gives it a particular and unique significance, but it is the specific role as lender that matters to most shareholders.

Most young companies depend heavily on their bankers as the primary external source of finance. Some go to venture capital firms or business angels for assorted mixtures of debt equity and mezzanine finance. The instruments have become increasingly varied, imaginative, and complex. Many companies remain heavily dependent on the traditional banks throughout their life, for only about 2,000 of the 900,000 companies in existence have raised capital from the public through the Stock Exchange and its various markets. Even when they have—and these alone are the subject of this book—an important relationship with their bankers tends to persist.

The traditional model is for the quoted company to raise long-term capital on the capital markets, through equity shares, perhaps supplemented by bonds, straight or convertible, or debentures. (The range of instruments is wide.) A company nowadays has many other sources of working capital. It may lease many of the assets it needs rather than purchase them: it may discount its sales invoices with factors. But banks still remain the principal source of short-term trading finance in the well-established way, often on the security of a fixed or floating charge. In the case of short-term trading finance the level of debt or credit oscillates (whether in the form of loans or discounted bills) and for this purpose a short-term lending instrument like the overdraft is ideal—the company only pays for what it borrows and the bank can in principle call in its debt at will.

Companies and banks do not always distinguish between long- and short-term finance: many an overdraft oscillates at levels that suggest that part of what the banks are providing is in essence core capital. This is particularly true of small companies, where the proprietors may well be reluctant to sell any of the equity and raise money that way. The inappropriate use of the overdraft still happens, but far less than it did, as the banks have developed medium- and long-term instruments to meet the companies' longer-term needs, perhaps together with an overdraft for more volatile short-term trading requirements. The Bank of England's fourth report on finance for small firms (1997) states that term lending accounted for 65 per cent of the overall borrowing figure of £34.8bn. in June 1996, up from 49 per cent in 1992. It continues: 'Even so a recent survey suggests that 17 per cent of small firms were still using overdraft finance for long-term business expansion.'

Many major companies now run sophisticated treasury departments well skilled in finding the most appropriate and least expensive form of finance to meet their needs. All this is well understood. Shareholders and analysts may calculate from the accounts what a company appears to owe its bankers, but this does not necessarily give the whole picture. The figures relate to one particular point in time; they may be 'window dressed', i.e. presented in such a way as to suggest a falsely rosy view of the true state of affairs; there is no indication of what facilities are available. A further concern is the use of derivatives which can as one accountant put it turn the balance sheet to jelly, produce profit, or reduce risk—but which of these is likely is not clear to the readers of accounts. Shareholders do not know and cannot make assumptions about their company's relationships with its bankers.

From the shareholders' point of view the transparency is limited, in that they do not know how many banks their company uses and have no rights to obtain such information. There is nothing wrong in principle in using more than one. For those trading in many countries operating convenience may require more; they may simply not wish to have all their eggs in one basket. That however is only the start of it. In the 1980s it became fashionable for companies to establish a treasury department to specialize in the handling of funds and this sometimes was regarded as a profit centre in its own right. Its managers naturally shopped around for the finest rates when the company wished to borrow. Bearing in mind that at certain times in a trade cycle banks have more funds to lend and therefore became more competitive in lending them, there was a veritable explosion in the number of banks a company used, more than 200 in some extreme cases. Sometimes the loans would be on a bilateral basis, sometimes through a syndicate of banks. So anxious were the banks to lend that they themselves did not always know the other sources of the company's finance, the total amount, and the terms on which it had been made available. The banks in syndicates relied too often on the leader to have done its homework and to have a residual interest; neither was necessarily true. None of this was visible to the shareholders: the numbers in the accounts for borrowing do not reveal how many different lenders there are or the details of facilities.

If a company appears to be prosperous, shareholders are most unlikely to be concerned about the fact that it has a multiplicity of bankers. Even if they knew it would not of itself be a warning of impending doom. Only at the first whiff of trouble does its significance come home to them. The eagerness of bankers to lend is nothing compared to the undignified scramble to retrieve their funds if they scent trouble. Given the terms of some lending contracts, it was only too easy for the whole edifice to collapse; given the nature of the syndicated arrangements, it was possible for one lender to precipitate a crisis.

It was this scenario that caused the Bank of England to develop the 'London Approach'. It worked like this: if a group of bankers to troubled Company X wished to prevent banks withdrawing support at a critical stage, they could approach the Bank of England to convene a meeting of its banks. The aim was to produce a standstill—to buy time in other words—so that everyone could obtain the relevant facts and decide in a measured way whether the company could survive and value be thus preserved—or not. Sometimes the conclusion was reached that the company was too far gone to save. More often, however, the standstill produced a solution. Many a company trading successfully today owes its survival to the good offices of the Bank of England at a crucial moment. The Bank's money was never involved: it was, and is, a classic case of the beneficent use of its influence for all the parties involved to remedy a weakness of the market.

In all this the shareholder came nowhere. The fate of the company was entirely in the hands of its bankers. There was usually very little opportunity for the shareholders to regroup and consider whether they would like to subscribe to the company's survival (e.g. by a rights issue to pay off part of the bank debt). The complexity and time scale of such an operation were thought to rule it out, not least because the company had left it very late to seek help. The shareholders could not see how many banks were lending to their company. More importantly they could not see the relationships between the company and its bankers, though had they known they might have made some inferences. They might indeed have asked.

Bankers in the UK do not want (and never have wanted) to get too involved with client companies. They have not bought shares, regarding this as a poor use of capital (on which they could get a better return by skilful lending commensurate with risk); and they have not wished to be committed to the point where a company's failure might even marginally impair their own credit. Having said all that, a bank often finds itself with a developing relationship—especially as the range of its services has extended. Most importantly, the staff at the bank will form a view of the competence of the management of the business and of its prospects: they will be able to distinguish the periodic ups and downs to which all businesses are subject from terminal decline, and offer support accordingly. The effect of the Insolvency Act 1986 has been, it is said, negative in so far as it makes bankers more reticent to advise ailing businesses lest they should be deemed to be shadow directors and therefore exposed to the penalties attached to wrongful trading, were that to be proved.

Relationships of course exist between people, not institutions, though a tradition of relationships between the people in institutions creates a framework for continuity. The process is not at its best if personnel often change—and banks have to grapple with the tension between growing able staff for higher posts by moving them frequently, and keeping them in a location for a longer period where they can build up relationships. There is simply no short cut to the development of confidence through experience. Systems cannot substitute for this.

Once the treasury departments in companies felt it their duty to squeeze the last basis point from every deal, they had sounded the death knell of relationship banking; there was always someone to offer a better price. With the syndicate system companies found themselves indebted to banks they did not choose, who cared nothing for them, and who were quite incapable of distinguishing a setback from a disaster. In recent times new guidelines have been published.

There were always exceptions. Some companies decided as a matter of policy that the maintenance of relationships was worth a few basis points if it came to the crunch. They knew that they did not always borrow funds as cheaply as they might but were conscious of the possible need for support if conditions grew harsher—as they sometimes did. Their foresight was generally rewarded. Banks do not like to get a reputation for turning their backs at the first whiff of trouble on companies that have reposed trust in them.

All this is of material importance to shareholders. If a company fails, they come last in the queue—after bankers, other preferential creditors, et al., and there is seldom anything left. It is therefore very much in their interest that a company should pick its bankers wisely and nurture the relationship with them, so that a temporary downturn is not transmuted into catastrophe. Paul Spencer, the treasurer of Hanson Trust PLC, writing in the *Banker's Digest* (27 Mar. 1992) of Beazer, noted that 'It had recently consolidated all its borrowing facilities, derivative exposures, etc. into a multi finance agreement with approximately 90 banks. The difficulties of working with this group were immense. There were too many banks, with a range of disparate objectives, compounded by the different facilities, exposures, and risk profiles that each bank had.' His solution was, 'either deal with as small a group of close relationship banks as possible, or as is the growing fashion, have bilateral loans where possible'. From the bankers' point of view the relationship is immensely valuable, not only as a source of revenue from various services, but also because with relationships goes information, and with information goes influence. To this aspect we now turn.

One of the distinguishing features, it is said, of 'bank-based' systems such as those in Germany and Japan is the influence the banks wield over their client companies. The relationship in both cases may be buttressed by shareholdings, and in Germany by a seat on the supervisory board as well. In fact, many companies in both countries are cash rich and do not depend on the banks for funds at all, so matters are not as simple as they may sound. Besides, bankers are not naturally interventionists anywhere—it is not their style because it is risky. Bankers generally want safety and they want it at the lowest price. Taking responsibility for advice, let alone applying pressure, is a higher price than many will willingly pay. It may be forthcoming in a limited way if a relationship is good enough; or it may be provided if a situation is serious enough, perhaps as a condition for renewing a facility. But bankers realize their limitations in running other people's companies, and no one anywhere can expect too much of them. The current mood of the bankers in Germany is to get less involved in companies, partly for commercial and partly for political reasons—there are fears about the banks gaining too much power. Even bank-based systems are under intense pressure to meet the twin tests of enterprise and accountability.

Having said that, there are extreme positions in the UK (and elsewhere) where a bank has formed the view that a company could trade out of a situation given a better lead, so management changes have sometimes been 'inspired'. A Japanese bank has been known to parachute in a rescue team to save a business and in the course of doing so to get new management in place: it does it as banker not shareholder (though it may hold shares) to show the world it accepts responsibility and honours its obligations to a client which flowed from being the lead bank. From this account, and from what was written above about the London Approach, we can detect a structural/procedural defect in the UK's arrangements—what we might dub 'the missing link'.

Standing back for a moment and looking at a highly geared company at work, we see that it draws its funds from a range of sources. It has equity capital, possibly loan capital like debentures, and it has bank loans, term and overdraft—as well as a range of other facilities like leases and swaps. Each of the groups supplying these various facilities has its own contractual terms. The only time the groups get together is on the coat-tails of a disaster—and then not all of them. Shareholders in particular have little chance, though very often they have the most to lose. The bankers are high up in the queue, and can generally salvage something from the wreck. Sometimes the shareholders might well have concluded there was no point in throwing good money after bad, as the facts, when fully revealed, made it clear that survival was impossible (Polly Peck would have been a case in point). In others, a restructuring with shareholder participation might have saved the day. The missing link is precisely that opportunity to participate in reconstruction: at least they might have the chance to decline!

To state the outlines of a problem on which so much ink has been spilt is not to solve it because the obstacles to any arrangement for involving any shareholders are high. If a company is sorely pressed it needs the continued support not only of its bankers but also of its suppliers; delay can be fatal. We recognize all that—and yet still believe that there are cases where shareholders have the opportunity—and perhaps the right—to play their part in refinancing, though the time scale for making decisions must necessarily be short.

There is one other difficult and contentious area between shareholders and bankers which the Cork Committee faced many years ago (1984), but did not resolve. Banks have a preferential position as creditors on the back of their fixed and floating charges over the company's assets. This has two effects. First, it enables them to continue their support for a company at the point when the claims of others (like creditors and shareholders) are impaired or even valueless. Secondly, if the support in the end proves inadequate, others will bear a greater pain than if they had withdrawn their support sooner. 'Scared of living and feared of dying', the banks hang on and hope. Would a restructuring early on with shareholders' support help? Should the banks retain the preferential position that a general charge provides? Realistically, there are few cases, one suspects, in which share-holders would want to increase their risk: but it would seem to us a reason-able function of the capital markets that they should have the opportunity of doing so if it can be timed right. Existing shareholders faced with a rights issue to save a company may take that option rather than just cut and run (in a market in which the shares, unsupported, have little value). Much depends on the view that is taken of the company's real potential; at the moment they are right out of the game.

To the extent that a quoted company usually constitutes part of a market index, it seems to us that some such provision is especially necessary, because shareholders who 'buy an index' cannot cherry-pick. As they are locked in, they ought at least to have a chance of helping a rescue when the circumstances suggest this might be advantageous.

The company is increasingly seen as a community of complementary interests (the stakeholder concept). Each of these interests is best served by cooperation. Shareholders and bankers should not be viewed as compe-titors. Bankers for their part will benefit from the commitment that comes with a deeper relationship (where a better flow of information will result in better-informed economic decisions). One of their rights which is of poten-tial benefit to themselves, to bankers, and to all other interests is to put more money in when it is needed. They may not use their right, just as a banker may not lend more, or an employee may depart for another job, or a creditor may stop supplies. There are formidable obstacles to effective participation because in a 'workout' time always presses, facts are often unclear, there are a multiplicity of differing interests as well as bankers, and so forth. Besides, when a company goes down it may be the case that the institutions have taken to the lifeboats long before and it is only the private shareholders who are swimming about in the water. This means that mobilizing shareholders to express a view let alone put their hands in their pockets is not easy. But we live in a technological age and it is not impossible. They might, if invited, be prepared to play their part and subscribe further funds if thereby a company can be saved—provided that the new money they put in is not subordinated to the banks and other debts. This is not an easy area—especially for multi-nationals—but it ought to be tackled. The Bank of England has long been keenly aware of the problem and internationally discussions have taken place under the auspices of INSOL, which in 1997 convened a conference in New Orleans of those interested in insolvency problems. Unfortunately this did not lead to a clear solution.

Action will need to take into account the development of debt trading. In the latter half of the 1990s the practice developed of banks selling some of the debts owed them by troubled companies. The purchasers would buy these at a discount (say 75p in the £1) in the hope that if the company traded its way out of trouble, they would be repaid in full and thus show a handsome return. None of this affects shareholders directly, but it means that the company itself has no control over who buys its debt and the faces around the table in any bid to sort out a troubled company's affairs will be different (and perhaps unfamiliar if the new purchasers of debt have no history of relationships with the business). The very fact that debt is being so discounted conveys to shareholders in graphic terms the plight of the business in which they have the misfortune to be invested. A place at the table needs to be found for shareholders.

The Ownership of Companies

OWNERSHIP and control are concepts axiomatic to corporate governance. It is important to understand what they signify. Before plunging in, we ought to look briefly at what we mean by 'ownership' and its relationship to 'control'. They are complex notions in relation to companies. There is no need to start a semantic debate, but we ought at the very least to see what they entail in practical terms.

The concept of individual ownership (as distinct from communal or public ownership) is so much part of our heritage and everyday lives that we take it for granted; we take for granted the rights that go with ownership in regard to exclusive use and disposal so long as these do not infringe the rights and interests of others. To have laws and for these to provide a remedy against those who deprive people of what they 'own' is the mark of a civilized society as is its capacity to enforce these remedies. Legitimate ownership, in other words, gives us title to enjoy our property, and by implication denies it to others, and it allows us to deal with it as we will. Such an attitude towards private ownership was common across the developed world by the nineteenth century. The definition of what is and is not a public asset has often been a vexed issue—witness the public disquiet over the enclosures centuries ago and debates on privatization more recently. The doctrine of communism redrew the boundaries between public and private property to such a degree that the very structure of the latter was undermined. As the ex-communist world gradually recovers from that nightmare, investors trying to develop joint ventures or acquire assets there sometimes find themselves bereft of what they had always regarded as the natural landscape—laws governing contract and ownership. They have found once again that a healthy market economy depends upon a legal system that acknowledges and defends property.

Notions of property are not 'natural' but socio-political, given force by the law and social mores ('Thou shall not steal'). The assumptions we make here in the UK are the result of long development, and some of the basic concepts which our law reflects can trace their origins to Roman law. The penalties we exact for breaking the law have changed. We no longer deem it necessary to protect property by a law *ad terrorem*—and hang people for stealing a sheep or a lamb.

Private ownership means many things, according to the circumstances. Take a simple example. If you buy a taxi, you may be said to 'own' it. Within the law you may do what you please with it, and if you please give it away or consign it to the scrap heap. The law does impose obligations on you if it is used, such as maintaining it in good condition whilst it is on the road, and paying its road tax and insurance. Mandatory insurance, and the requirement to hold a driving licence and obey the Highway Code, illustrate that the law may impose duties on an owner to safeguard the rights of others. Furthermore you may also be said to control it. If however you ask a driver to drive it for you (having ascertained that he is qualified), you have to a large extent lost control; you may lay down rules but whoever is in the driving seat is in control. As owner you may change the person in immediate control when it is physically possible to do so (but may be liable to damages if the way you do it is a breach of contract).

What if three of you buy the taxi jointly? You may be said to own it jointly, but what does that mean? You do not each own a third of each part like the wheels or cylinder block. For the concept to make sense there must either be general law that covers such a situation or a specific agreement or both, so that the parties know where responsibility rests and the profits flow.

Even in the simple case of car ownership we see that in most circumstances ownership implies an obligation. This is usual, and the obligation may be extensive. The same is true with other possessions, be they animals or bricks and mortar. Animals are protected under the law from cruelty or neglect, and if we own a house we very soon find that we may not be able to do with it as we wish and must have an eye on noise and nuisance generally. If it happens to be listed, we have some responsibility to maintain it. That responsibility is owed to the state and it is the state that will enforce it for the benefit of future generations. The state has armed itself with a panoply of remedies from fines to compulsory purchase orders.

If we are a trustee of property, we are acting on behalf of others, and we may have special duties in regard to our stewardship which we shall revisit in a later chapter when we come to examine fiduciary obligations generally. In short, the law in the UK has long recognized that ownership confers certain rights, that obligations go with them, and that there are various ways in which such responsibility may be enforced. Our society is not all 'take'.

If we consider the concept of ownership more deeply we soon see that it is not absolute as the object of our ownership is not fixed. Anyone with a deteriorating house in the country, or for that matter a rusting car in a garage, will confirm that is so. πάντα ῥεῖ as the Greek philosopher put it—everything is always in a state of flux. For practical purposes we may behave as if this was not so, though repair and maintenance bills remind us otherwise.

If the object we own is animate—perhaps we farm—we know our property will need very careful attention if we are to maintain its value, but we do not ask the permission of the animals which belong to the farm when we want to transfer its ownership. We do not ask the employees on the farm or for that matter in any other kind of enterprise either. It is regarded by all the parties (as matters now stand in the UK—in some European countries there are rights of consultation enshrined in the law) that part of their implicit contract with the company when they enter employment is that the ownership of the company may change without their permission, and more often without any kind of consultation because formally the change of ownership of the company does not affect their individual contracts with it. A similar position arises in the law of real property; the agreement of tenants does not have to be sought if the landlord wishes to sell his or her interest.

A sole proprietor working alone in an unincorporated business will of course have to obey the law, but within its constraints he or she will have extensive rights as to how to conduct its affairs; the owner will also be personally responsible for its obligations. His or her rights of ownership may extend beyond its tangible property and include the goodwill that has been built up. Many a dental practice for example has changed hands on the basis that goodwill was of value as well as the dental chair and the other tools of the profession. (Goodwill is a term of art in accounting, but otherwise it may be defined as the propensity of the customer to return to where satisfaction has been received.) The practical task facing the purchaser will be to ensure that the goodwill he or she has bought does not evaporate.

If the business has employees, ownership is less absolute. They cannot be traded. They have contracts with the business, actual, implied, or both, and do not need to stay with a new owner—as many a purchaser has discovered when the main assets being antipathetic to the new regime walked out through the front door. The value of ownership is contingent on the continuity of goodwill of the employees as well as the customers. In other words, the notion of ownership of a business is not the same as the ownership of an inanimate tangible asset or group of them. Nowadays a purchaser of a business will find that he or she cannot easily vary the employees' contracts, because of the protection afforded them by the Transfer of Undertakings Provisions.

What was true about the joint owners of a taxi is also true of joint owners of businesses, however constituted. The rights and obligations of each part owner must be defined either by specific agreement or by law—and that includes the rights to exercise control, whether tactical or strategic. In all cases of joint ownership, the ownership of a part is naturally a far more limited concept than the ownership of the whole. So, when we come to talk about shareholders 'owning' a company, we need to look carefully to see what that actually means. In the case of our three joint owners of the taxi we would need to examine or determine what agreement they had made about sharing rights and responsibilities. In the case of limited liability companies we start with the statute, since that is where the general rights of share-holders are laid down. We need also to know the common law rights. We must examine the company's articles of association, as these may restrict certain rights, confer others, or impose certain obligations (they might for instance restrict transfer of the shares—uncommon in quoted companies, but frequent in private companies).

Here we must return to the point that the incorporated company has a persona, in law, that is separate from its proprietor(s), be they a multitude or a single person. What anyone gets when they buy shares in UK companies is a series of clearly defined rights, as described in the earlier chapter.

Even if an individual shareholder's rights are added together they currently fall so far short of what we normally associate with 'ownership' that it is misleading to think of each minority shareholder being an owner of the company. Only when a group of shareholders act together in sufficient weight can they exercise collectively what we might call the control rights of ownership. Each shareholder owns a bundle of rights, most of which have been described above; but even these may be limited by some particular condition attaching to the shares, as used to be the case with 'A' shares which had no voting rights (J. Lyons and Co. Ltd. was a case in point, and so was the Great Universal Stores PLC until they voluntarily enfranchised the 'A' shares in 1994). At the time of writing holders of shares in the Savoy Group will find they have enhanced or reduced voting rights, depending on the class of share they hold. In recent years, the trend has been for companies to have only one class of ordinary share, though they may well have preference shares as well, and these generally carry no votes. There are still supporters of 'A' shares especially among the smaller family-dominated companies, and the CBI appeared to be relaxed about them, unlike the Association of British Insurers which is bitterly opposed (*Investors' Chronicle*, 22 Nov. 1996: 19).

Under the present UK laws, fully paid-up shareholders who are beneficial owners have no obligations though they may have certain limited duties, like declaring a stake after it reaches a certain size. Indeed the original purpose of the limited liability company was to give individual savers a chance to venture their funds without further liability of any kind (once the shares were fully paid) even if the company failed.

CONTROL

Control is far from a simple concept. It is inherent in the basic structure of the company that it is open to the directors to decide what control over its affairs should be delegated and under what conditions; in a large company they will delegate all the day-to-day decisions that fall to be made in the conduct of business. In no company however can the directors absolve themselves of the ultimate responsibility by delegating. When we talk about 'changes of control' it generally means total control—the right to take the important decisions that guide the company's destiny, and this includes the key appointments. The context is usually a change of ownership, but it need not be so. Roe (1994), quoting Chandler, refers to the same phenomenon in different language—the separation of ownership and management. The reason why we are differentiating between ownership and control is to drive home the point that from a practical standpoint we do not have to ask the question 'Who owns the company?' A determined group of shareholders none of whom can be said to own or control the company alone may by acting in concert bring the company under effective control as surely as if the ownership of a majority of shares had found its way into one person's hands. Having exercised this control, perhaps by changing the top management, they can dissolve their temporary alliance. The ownership of shares need not have been transferred.

Thus we can distinguish between 'shareholder control' and 'management control'. The latter is normally vested in the board of directors—and they delegate it as they think appropriate. Shareholder control on the other hand is limited to certain important specific issues; if in a minority position (as most are) they must act together, in sufficient strength to have a voting majority or in practice a strong coherent minority. The issues include approving dividends and distributions, capital reconstructions, winding up the company, etc., but the most relevant to our discussion is the power to appoint and remove directors and auditors. Shareholder control, without itself changing, can be used to change the board, that is to change management control. Of course the concepts are not always distinguished. A takeover will often change both shareholder and management control at one fell swoop. And often when a company is or becomes a wholly owned subsidiary, management control by the parent or shareholder control by the parent become indistinguishable.

If enough shareholders decide to change the board, they will in effect bring about a change in management control; this can be accomplished without the ownership of a single share changing hands. What the board itself can actually do depends on what is being controlled. Controlling a capital-intensive business like a power plant is a very different matter from controlling an advertising agency. Irrespective of the nature of the business the concept of controlling it can also only be defined in terms of the rights afforded to the various parties. Take for instance the right of the owners to shut a plant. As many companies in Europe have found to their cost that right means quite different things depending on where the plant happens to be. In some countries the obligations to consult the employees and the costs imposed make the process of closure far slower and costlier than in the UK. A more deliberate process may however be less wasteful for the economy in the long run; downsizing at the double tears the social fabric and imposes its own costs.

Even with all the restrictions, the right to control a business in the sense of controlling its major decisions is seen as having value, because it is the route to improved managerial control and hence to enhanced value. That is why there is a bid premium whenever a takeover is mounted. *Acquisitions Monthly* and AMDATA calculated that the bid premia (comparing the offer price with the price a month earlier) were 46 per cent in 1986, 38 per cent in 1988, and 32 per cent in 1990.

As noted above, the ownership of the company in the sense of controlling management resides theoretically in the body of shareholders as a whole. Unless it is special business or an extraordinary resolution, this means a majority of those voting—far short of 51 per cent of the outstanding equity. The law is silent upon the point, but the Takeover Panel decided that the effective point at which control passed was 29.9 per cent, so if anyone exceeds this level, they must bid for the remaining shares. This not only safeguards shareholders in the sense that it secures equal treatment for them, but it also to a large extent stops management being hamstrung by a large shareholder who obstructs without controlling.

If however we examine the structure of many Continental companies we find that a much smaller percentage confers control, thanks to the particular voting structure. In Italian groups (Barca 1995) we see that ownership of a majority of the shares as such may mean precious little if voting control is vested in a handful of family shareholders. In their paper on 'Ownership and Control' (based on a lecture by Meyer in 1993) Franks and Meyer (1994) set out the main strands in the literature. The principal reasons, in logic, for transferring ownership are either to appropriate all the increased rents which follow the acquisition or to combine these with those that flow from economies of scale or synergies as a result of the merger.

If shareholders wish to put control of the management into other hands (in economic terms 'change their agents', as the management are directly or indirectly the agents of the shareholders) without transferring ownership they can do this by changing the composition of the board, but the benefits that flow from the changes will be realized by a whole raft of shareholders among whom the promoters of change are likely to be a minority. This gives rise to the 'free rider' problem which many have wrestled with. Another reason to change ownership is seen in break-ups aimed at realizing undervalued assets. Such purchasers are not interested in the survival of the company but are content to keep what they want (if anything) and get the best price they can for the rest.

If the analysis suggests that fundamental changes in management control are needed and that at the same time further investment is required, a change of ownership may be considered as essential both to ensure the necessary powers and to distribute the fruits of investment appropriately. As in all cases of takeovers success will depend on the skill and sensitivity with which they are conducted. There are too many cases of value being impaired.

Integration may be desired for strategic reasons as well as to change management control in order to save costs or reach new markets or just to market more effectively; size is not without its benefits. Typical examples of this were Glaxo's purchase of Wellcome or Nestlé's of Rowntree. In such cases it was by no means clear that the purchaser wanted to fire existing managers. Such deals may be inspired by their competence rather than the reverse, and the top people in some cases have made their way in the bigger group, as for example Sir Derek Birkin did in RTZ or Richard Giordano did in BOC. The use to which control is thus put is a very different matter from the case where the purchaser thinks little of the incumbent management. Whatever the rhetoric, some takeovers seem to be made for reasons that belong to the psychiatrist's couch rather than to cool economic analysis.

There is a class of cases where changing ownership is clearly not essential, and indeed may be detrimental. The market system predicts that if management under-utilizes its assets, the share price will ultimately fall and management will be displaced by those who can do better, whether with a change of ownership or not. In 'improving' the underperforming company the use of shareholder control is not primarily restructuring or integration, but to force out the existing directors and replace them by people calculated to perform better. If the main problem is a handful of underperforming executives, this can be remedied by using shareholders' powers. Why go to the costs (huge) and bother (enormous) of a change of ownership? 'Releasing trapped value' is the way that the price rise in the target's shares is sometimes described. It looks as if no one pays. They do of course—the shareholders who remain in the new enterprise; where are the enormous costs of the transaction coming from, not to mention the restructuring costs? Over the years there have been many cases where management has had a less than sparkling record, which could have been remedied by changing management control and putting it into new hands.

It makes no sense at all to create larger and more complex structures unless there is a sound operational reason for doing so. Many of the modern conglomerates are a clumsy way of securing operational efficiency in the divisional companies. The subsequent demerger of so many is proof of this. It has been a marvellous game—for the investment bankers and other financial wizards who have collected their dues in agglomeration and again on break-up. It used to be said that what had been joined together by investment bankers in holy conglomeration shall by no firm be put asunder. We can now add a rider—except by another investment bank. Who pays? Why, the shareholders of course, who apparently could not see where their interests lay in the first place, namely in distinguishing between ownership and control. Had they done so judicious cooperation would have been enough to set in train the chain of events to bring about the change of operational control at minimum cost without seeking a change of total control and taking the risk of throwing the company into a new composite structure that had less logic than the old.

Shares as a Home for Savings

IN the Great Britain of the late twentieth century almost every adult is aware of shares. The Report of the Committee on Private Share Ownership (1996) states that 20 per cent of the adult population have direct investments in the stock market; if collective investments are added, the report estimates that 12.5 million people hold shares. Millions more have a claim on funds, whether a life insurance policy or a pension scheme, whose main assets are shares. It is important to remember that this is not so even now in most parts of the world and was not so in these islands until quite recently, for two simple reasons, resources and opportunity. We now consider both.

SOME HISTORY

In the British Isles for most people in the first part of this millennium life was a bare battle for survival—to produce enough to satisfy the landlord or to live on from one's smallholding, or to produce a surplus of a particular crop to sell for cash to buy necessities, or to produce goods or supply services with the same object in mind. Many failed. Illness and hunger took their toll; the expectation of life was short. A tolerable old age was only possible by virtue of physical strength, a supportive family, or the rights of a tenant or of a smallholding, or of proprietorship of a trading business (perhaps as part of a trade guild). For the vast majority the amount of surplus wealth available as savings for investment outside the land or business was limited. As time went on the exceptions to this grew. For centuries the ownership of land was the main source of wealth, and it continues to be important. Even today, 90 per cent of it is owned by 5 per cent of the population. As trade developed there were successful merchants up and down the country, based in large towns. By the late Middle Ages London had a whole range of trade organizations (the livery companies) whose wealth was manifest and some of whose leaders like Sir Richard Whittington became famous. Land-related industries like brewing flourished. 'We are not here to sell a parcel of boilers and vats, but the potentiality of growing rich beyond the dreams of avarice.' Thus spake Dr Johnson, acting as an executor to Thrale, a brewer, as related by Lord Lucan to James Boswell (1823). Wool fell into this category too and many prospered from either producing the cloth or acting as entrepreneurs between the growers and weavers.

Even for those with surplus funds there were relatively few outlets other than the acquisition of more estates. Many went in for conspicuous consumption: if one could not invest, one might as well enjoy—after all the tax man was never far away. One might impress. As Cobbett noted (1832), rich men in the wool trade vied to outdo each other by building great parish churches that the local residents could never have filled—even before rural depopulation. Many, to improve the quality of their existence in the next world, left huge funds for charitable ecclesiastical or educational purchases. The roll call of the benefactors of Jesus College, Cambridge (founded 1496), like many others, bears witness to this stream of generosity (and perhaps egotism); as does the foundation of many great schools, such as Dean Colet's St Paul's (1509). The great livery companies of the City of London to this day dispense charity of some £20m. each year as a result of benefactions to them over the centuries.

To those who are used to having a wide range of relatively secure institutions like banks or building societies in which to lodge our surplus funds (and from which to draw interest on deposits), it is easy to forget that, until relatively recently, most people did not have any surplus funds and those that did had relatively few places to put them. Savings for the wealthy would be in the form of gold and silver and there were few places where these could be lodged profitably. Many households kept their valuables in great iron chests, which are to be seen to this day: in ages even more lawless than ours keeping them thus was both dangerous and unproductive. We have already touched briefly on the development of banking, but might just note in passing the difference between that (where the bankers took deposits from savers) and moneylending, where the principals' own money was lent. This distinction accounts for the persecution of the latter; it was easier than repayment. Gradually, however, under foreign influence (emanating in Florence and Venice), banking became more respectable, and the good goldsmiths of London certainly had a part in it in the early days. The magnificence of their London hall still bears witness to their success.

As times became more settled under the Tudors and trade developed, many more small businesses had sleeping partners, people who would invest their surplus worth and expect in return a share of the profits. As overseas trade developed two forms of enterprise emerged. The distinction is thus described by Trevelyan (1942: ii. 59–60):

This movement of merchant capitalism athwart the old municipal and guild system had been apparent in the wool trade as early as the age of Chaucer. In Elizabeth's reign it took another great step forward in the rise of the Overseas Trading Companies of a new type. They were of two kinds. First the 'Regulated Company', in which each member traded on his own capital, subject to the common rules of the Corporation; such were the Merchant adventurers who had a great past as well as a great future as exporters of cloth; the Eastland or Baltic, the Russia, and the Levant Companies. The other class was joint-stock—the East India Company; the African; and two generations later the Hudson's Bay. In this second class, trade was conducted by the Corporation as a whole, and the profits and losses were divided among the shareholders.

To each of these companies, whether regulated or joint stock, a geographical sphere of operations was assigned by royal charter, and no 'interloper' from England might trade therein. . . . These Elizabethan companies were in many respects similar in their privileges and functions to the 'chartered company' that helped to develop and disturb the interior of Africa in Victoria's reign.

The companies themselves were created by Act of Parliament or by royal charter. The aim was to stimulate commerce, produce revenue for the government, and, later, to extend British political as well as commercial influence. The instrument was monopoly, and of course monopolies excite jealousy, so they were (if profitable) constantly under attack. Two extracts from an earlier book make very clear the differences between regulated and joint stock companies (Cawston and Keane 1896).

Here is a regulated company—the Turkey Company, in 1681—attacking: 'They breed up any person under the notion of an East India merchant because anyone who is master of money may purchase a share of their trade and joint stock.' And the East India Company's telling reply: 'It cannot be denied by a reasonable man that a joint stock is capable of a far greater extension as to the number of trades and largeness of stock than any regulated company can be. Because, in joint stock, noblemen, gentlemen, shopkeepers, widows and orphans and all the other subjects may be traders and employ their stock therein; whereas in a regulated company such as the Turkey Company is, none can be traders but such as they call legitimate or bred merchants.'

As a home for savings, the regulated companies (and all the other guilds composed primarily of working 'partners') were not significant. The joint stock companies were, and some like the East India Company prospered mightily. Some figures illustrate the point. To defend their monopoly the Company offered in 1698 to lend the Treasury £700,000 at 4 per cent. And when a new Act was introduced the same year the old company subscribed £315,000 to it; the entire £2,000,000 was subscribed in two days. By the time we reach the amalgamation of the old and new East India companies in 1702, the total contribution to public funds was £3,200,000. The company's history makes fascinating reading but that is beside the point here: it was a home for savings for a wide range of people.

The famous episode of the South Sea Bubble was described earlier. The result was the Bubble Act of 1720 (not repealed until 1825), which prohibited unincorporated trading companies from acting as corporations and limited the use of charters to the purposes originally intended. Trevelyan puts its effect into perspective (1942: iii. 99):

Joint-stock methods had suffered a setback with the bursting of the South Sea Bubble in 1720, but they lived down that discredit and men learnt to be a little wiser in the future. The joint-stock company was admirably suited to the social structure of that aristocratic but commercially minded century, for the landed magnate could, without becoming that abhorred thing 'a tradesman', meet on the board the City man and act with him, and to the political influence of the one could be joined the business brains of the other.

The number of people with surplus wealth to invest steadily increased through the eighteenth and nineteenth centuries and one outlet was to lend it to the government, where debt was managed by the Bank of England. Trevelyan (1942: iv. 27) was on a different issue but his vivid description confirms our point—the investing public had grown apace.

At the beginning of George III's reign the 'fund holders' had been reckoned at 17,000 persons, and about one seventh of the total debt was at that time held abroad, largely by Dutch investors. But after Waterloo only a twenty fifth part of Britain's now colossal debt was held by foreigners. In 1829 official statistics showed that the fund holders numbered 275,939 persons, of whom more than 250,000 were small investors, each receiving an annual interest of £200 or less. This meant a wide diffusion of safe and easily realizable wealth among a very great number of families.

It appears therefore that as early as the eighteenth century British investors with surplus savings had a relatively wide choice—beyond land, one's own business, or more consumption; they could put their money into the funds or more adventurously buy shares in the limited but growing numbers of joint stock companies created under Act of Parliament.

Some joint stock companies were bona fide and produced a varying stream of profits from which the shareholders received dividends. Thomas Mortimer (1798; this was the 12th edn. of a book first published in 1761) quotes the example of Parliament intervening in 1767 to force the directors of the East India Company, which had declared a six-month dividend of 6.5 per cent in May, to rescind it; and imposed a limit of 10 per cent per annum. The shares moreover fluctuated but could, if the timing was right, produce handsome capital profits. Mortimer published tables of the prices of East India stock for the years 1791–7 showing fluctuations as follows in each of the years mentioned: 1791–35.75 per cent; 1792–41 per cent. Others however were scams, that is to say the operations were not wholly genuine and the market was manipulated. In financial markets at all times and in all places gullibility and greed can be exploited by the unscrupulous.

The willingness to take risks in investment has been reflected for 300 years in the readiness to turn aside from the safe (the funds) to the risky (shares)— perfectly logical the more risk can be measured and the premium for taking it assessed.

There is a delightful passage in *The Forsyte Saga* which makes the point: 'They had all done so well for themselves, these Forsytes, that they were all what is called "of a certain position". They had shares in all sorts of things, not as yet—with the exception of Timothy—in consols, for they had no dread of life like that of 3 per cent for their money.' (Galsworthy 1923: i. 25)

Class was an important ingredient in the economic cuisine. The industrial revolution was essentially a middle-class phenomenon, though when it got under way a few (but only a few) landowners committed substantial resources to it—not always successfully. What it did do was widen substantially the range of people who had surplus funds to invest, and who—a new development—did not see the land as the natural place to put them. Some did, to be sure and shook the factory dust from their shoes as fast as they could, before turning themselves into country gentlemen. Others did better, retaining their—more or less—active commercial interests even after buying their country estates. (The Chamberlain and Baldwin families were not atypical: screws and steel were the foundations of their enhanced gentility.)

A whole new range of opportunities arose with the railway age. Even at this distance one can sense the excitement—for the first time mankind was not limited to the speed of the horse. It was a major revolution and like all revolutions claimed its victims. Here is Kynaston (1994: i. 102–3):

Railways were a great case in point of City involvement that was crucial but not always beneficial. In the 1820s the pioneer Stockton and Darlington Railway borrowed heavily from Richardson, Overend & Co; in 1833 the first London meeting of the Great Western Railway took place at the fine old Jacobean house in Lime Street then occupied by the firm of Anthony Gibbs, with the firm's head, George Henry Gibbs, becoming a director and a loyal supporter of Brunel; in the same year George Carr Glyn joined the London board of the projected London to Birmingham railway (eventually the London and North Western), becoming chairman four years later. Then in 1835 came the City's first railway boom, as the number of officially listed companies (twenty-one in July 1835) almost trebled in the next twelve months. 'The whole active interest of the Stock Exchange have lately directed their almost exclusive attention to Shares in Railways', noted the *Circular to Bankers* by February 1836, adding that 'the operations and purchases in them have been greatly accentuated by orders from the country, but especially from Lancashire'. What is significant, though, is the extent of misgivings felt by those most closely concerned with the new railways, or at least the respectable, non-speculative ones. 'I have done everything to stop the gambling in our shares not to the satisfaction of the Stock Exchange here or of the share brokers elsewhere', Glyn himself wrote in October 1835. But even though the line was not yet built, he was unable to restrain extreme bullishness in the Birmingham shares, a phenomenon analysed the following February by George Gibbs, the cousin of George Henry, senior partner of the merchants Gibbs Son & Bright of Bristol and Liverpool, and himself until recently on the GWR board:
  'The advance in these shares has been at least £55 in the last twelve months and yet for my life I cannot discover one fact bearing upon their value on which any rise can

reasonably be built, that was not as well known before it commenced as it is now, with one single, and that to my mind alarming, exception—the patronage of the Stock Exchange.'

Bates of course condemned the boom out of hand—'there is at present great madness abroad in regard to rail roads . . . it is going too fast & will inevitably lead to disastrous results'—but for the Stock Exchange itself there was a greater good, even after the boom collapsed in 1837. This was the creation of a major and permanent market in non-government securities, sustained over the years by the high volume of shares issued by the railway companies, thereby ensuring ready marketability. 'Home Rails', in short, was set to become a feature of City life.

Disaster followed. Railway speculation peaked in 1845. The ensuing collapse engulfed members of Stock Exchange who were hammered and halted the projection of new lines.

Long before the railways, 'the funds' had become an important outlet for savings. The British government found it an effective way to tap the public's wealth. The sum of all the public funds on 5 July 1798 according to Mortimer (1798) was £443,709,979 18s. $4^1/_2$ d. on which the annual interest was £17,334,388 18s. 11d. Here indeed was a way for the public to invest savings so as to produce a safe though modest income stream. There was some hope of capital gain through good timing, though this was limited; the downside was limited too. The genuine saver could provide for his old age; the gambler could move in or out of the stock trying to take advantage of the price changes which took place as a result of or in expectation of changes in interest rates (themselves responding to changes in external circumstances).

With a ready market go frauds. Anyone who believes that these are a product of our more venal age should read Thomas Mortimer (1798). The reader will encounter bulls and bears (see a reference to 7 George II 'An act the better to prevent the infamous practice of stock jobbing'); and a chapter on state lotteries: 'A lottery is a kind of public game at hazard, which had its origins in Italy, as far back as the time of the ancient Romans, and continue in practice in that country, in France, Holland and England as a mode of raising money on easy terms for the service of the State.'

In its pages the observant reader will recognize many of the tricks still played behind regulators' backs—false market rumours to help a cheap purchase or dear selling; front running by those anxious to exploit those who would follow the false scent. Even so, the crucial fact is that with all its faults, its inadequacy of information, a real market had been established and was working in which government stocks, and shares in non-governmental enterprises, would be traded. Surplus savings could be invested in parcels of convenient size and relatively low transactional costs; even more important, the liquidity of the market made selling relatively easy. Thus when the effects of the industrial revolution and the development of the railways burgeoned in Britain in the mid-nineteenth century, the model for mobilizing capital widely was already familiar, and the market was at hand to provide liquidity.

The government had put in place by 1855 the machinery for creating what is in essence the modern limited liability company. This facilitated the growth of family businesses, which would take in outside capital without losing family control (and no longer suffered the disadvantages of being partnerships), and also the creation of quoted companies, which could tap the capital markets and provide liquidity for shareholders. Those who risked their savings by buying shares in unquoted companies were from the outset and still are at the mercy of those who control them since exit is difficult and power negligible.

By the seventeenth century there was an active market in shares in trading ventures. It was conducted in the coffee shops around the Royal Exchange. By 1673 the government felt it necessary to restrict the number of brokers to 100. But by 1698 there was a daily price list on sale recording the fluctuating future of companies. Issuing shares to finance a venture was accepted prac-tice. The name 'Stock Exchange' dates from 1773 when a new Jonathan's Coffee House in Threadneedle Street was built as a venue for conducting business. It moved to Capel Court in 1802. By 1850 the Stock Exchange had 864 members dealing in fewer than 300 securities.

By the end of the nineteenth century the stock market was extremely active—but not in a wide range of domestic UK industrials. The forerunner of the *Financial Times*, the *London Financial Guide*, showed on its list, on 20 January 1888, 22 railway stocks and nearly 100 mines amongst many other foreign stocks and bonds. At the peak of the railway boom the South England official list quoted 280 different railways shares. By 1849 failures had reduced the list to 160. Here is the entire list of domestic equities (categorized as miscellaneous):

Allsopp Breweries
Bryant & May
EC Powder
Guinness
Hotchkiss Ordnance
Hudson Bay
Kynoch
R. Bell
Spratts Patent
Metropolitan Music Hall
Aerated Bread
Barretts Brewery
Telephone
Construction
American Brush & Light
Maxim Weston

Swan
International Financial
Bryant Powis & Bryant
Welford & Sons
Wickens Pease & Co.
Forders
Harrison Barber
Simson & Mason
London Pavilion
Royal Music Hall
Metropolitan Music Hall
New Explosives
Morris Tube
Nordenfelt Gun
Railway Investment Trust Board

By 1 January 1914 the picture had changed; shares were listed under specialized headings. The number of UK companies listed under the main ones are as follows:

gas, electric: 11;
hotels and catering: 12;
iron, steel, coal, engineering: 33;
motors and cycles: 9;
newspapers, printing: 9;
shipping: 9;
telegraph, telephone: 16;
textiles: 28;
theatres, music halls: 9;
trains: 4.

But this contrasts with more than 150 companies listed under the heading 'Eastern plantations and other companies'.

Equality of treatment came nowhere—Kynaston again (1995 4: i):

Life in Capel Court could not have gone on without the existence of a substantial class of people willing to invest or speculate in stocks and shares. When in March 1898 there occurred the spectacularly successful flotation of Liptons the grocery chain, with Panmure Gordon and Helbert Wagg as co-brokers, Sir Thomas Lipton took personal charge of the invidious matter of who got what. 'Dukes and Marquises were allotted in full', according to the story passed down to Alfred Wagg; 'Earls, Viscounts and Barons received 50 per cent, Baronets and Honourables 25 per cent, and the general members of the public nil. I believe a certain number of Society beauties were considered as ranking equally with Dukes and Marquises for the purposes of allotment'. Three years later, when a National Telephone issue brought out by Morgans fared poorly, Dawkins commented to Jack Morgan that 'our underwriters have all behaved very well and are not dissatisfied, with the exception of one Peer, to whom we gave a share at the personal request of Mr Everard Hambro'.

As Kynaston makes clear, the main finance houses much preferred foreign bonds (and to some extent stocks). There has been a school of thought which for many years has attributed the failure of British industry to keep pace with its competitors after 1870 to the preference by those with funds to invest to send them overseas: the undoubted skills of the City in operating internationally made London probably the most favoured centre for foreign government loans. It is less certain however that this actually crowded out British industry, though it may have been a factor given the parallel attitude of the banks which continued then, as before, and as now, to see themselves as the suppliers of short-term money and not as providers in effect of long-term debt or equity.

SAVERS' CHOICES

By the end of the nineteenth century savers seeking income had a wide range of choice.

- banks;
- government bonds;
- industrial and commercial quoted shares (both individually and collectively in investment trusts);
- foreign government bonds;
- land and property;
- private enterprises.

Then as now there were collective and managed savings such as insurance policies. The Prudential was founded in 1848 and was then known as 'The Prudential Mutual Assurance and Loan Association'. It started writing life insurance policies in 1860.

Much depended on circumstances. As time progressed savers acquired greater confidence in certain types of deposit such as those with building societies, knowing them to be supervised. (Mistakenly they believe the same of banks, although in fact they are only safeguarded up to £20,000, and the collapse of Barings in 1995 brought home to many their vulnerability.)

From the savers' viewpoint what matters is risk, security, income, and capital growth; the balance between these factors depends on circumstances and taste. We have traced in outline the development of the range of available outlets to illustrate from the savers' point of view (barring sentiment and principle) their indifference to the use to which savings are put so long as they are productive in the way they want. (War Loan was sold on sentiment; some investors avoid tobacco or drink shares on principle—both are becoming more significant in markets, as ethics is seen to underpin investment returns.) What a bank does with its deposits is only of interest if it jeopardizes their safety; if Nick Leeson's judgement had been better the

Barings' depositors would not have trembled. How a government spends its funds may be immaterial to the holder of gilts, provided that the yields to redemption take account of inflation (or the bonds are index linked). There have been enough defaults on government securities this past century to make such a sense of security seem rather optimistic; in the catastrophic German hyperinflation between the wars holders of government bonds lost all.

The so-called 'cult of the equity' which marked the years since the Second World War is not just a reflection of the wish to get a better return than government bonds provide. It is a direct reflection that business has to adjust to inflation in order to survive and that shareholders' returns reflect this adjustment whether held directly or in some form of collective savings. The holders of German equities did *not* lose all their investment in the period of hyperinflation.

There are two types of such investment in an industrial or commercial company—direct, and through the market. By direct investment we mean the purchase of shares in an unquoted business in whose operations the investor is not engaged. 'Business angels' is the modern name for private external backers of small businesses and they have always been about; more common is the family enterprise in which several subscribe but only one or two are active. This type of investment falls outside the scope of this book, but it should by no means be assumed that the relationship between the executive and the shareholders in such a company is an easy one; readers will have examples within their own range of knowledge about the tensions, not least when the executive appropriates more of the profits by way of remuneration than the other shareholders consider reasonable. It ought to be possible to assume that people who risk their savings in such enterprises ensure that they can stay close enough to the action to tell whether the directors' stewardship is satisfactory; indolence and optimism too often negate such an assumption.

During the time when so many of the institutions described above were being developed, there was no support for the needy or indigent, other than the Poor Laws which were harsh and patchy in their application. If they had employment, people worked till they dropped, or in old age depended upon family support or savings. Against such a background there developed various institutions designed to encourage savings in a form accessible to those with lower incomes such as friendly and provident societies: insurance companies like the Pearl and the Prudential catered for the same needs. The money that people put into these various funds was so to speak 'free' savings: it was what was left after a decision not to consume all the money earned or acquired. This itself was a major decision, often taken with some pain.

The welfare state has created a different climate. The old imperatives have gone. The state, raising money by taxation or borrowing, through National Assistance and unemployment benefits provides a wide range of support for the sick, old, and unemployed. Eleven million employees are members of an occupational pension scheme. A further 5 million are contributing to personal pensions. These are all 'fixed' savings. It is not surprising that the UK has a rather low savings ratio. The Central Statistical Office gives an average personal savings ratio of about 10 per cent for the five years before 1995—far better than it had been in the 1950s but still below Japan which averaged 12 per cent in the years 1981–7 and Italy at about 13 per cent in 1996 and 1997. Lester Thurow (1996: 296) takes the three years 1990–2: USA 3 per cent, Europe 8.3 per cent, Japan 18.5 per cent; and contrasts this with 1960–9: USA 11 per cent, Europe 17.3 per cent, Japan 22 per cent.

The state aims at assisting survival, not ensuring a high level of comfort—and is finding the financial burden of doing even that barely tolerable. If people aspire to a better standard of living in old age they must make further provisions through collective instruments like insurance policies or pension funds. For millions more there is the slow acquisition of property by means of a mortgage. By the time these kinds of savings have been made, the 'free' money available for further investment is not normally substantial for the ordinary family unless some windfall occurs—be it the pools or an inheritance, in the form of a family house.

For a family to have a surplus for investment in shares means that its existing financial commitments must be covered as well as 'normal' expenditure to whatever level has been determined. The government-backed range of savings instruments now contains many that are a hedge against inflation as they are index linked; this looks safe enough if people believe the government will continue to be able to honour its obligation. 'Sid's' purchase of denationalized stocks fell into a special category, being regarded not like other shares but as in a group of their own in terms of risk and security.

There is a wide range of people with some 'voluntary' savings to make—and a wide choice of what to do with them. Many run accounts with building societies or have national savings (which caters for those who want to gamble with income whilst preserving nominal capital through premium bonds). Millions bought denationalization shares. For those who can afford it looms the opportunity of investing in a huge range of industrial and commercial companies whose shares can be bought on the Stock Exchange. 'Huge' is used advisedly; the UK has a far larger number of domestic quoted companies relative to other countries, given the size of their economies.

The discussion here concerns only that part of 'voluntary' savings people have decided to put into shares, in other words after their basic asset allocation decisions have been made. In fact the Inland Revenue reported that the liquid assets held by the UK population in 1993 were divided into 63 per cent cash, 29 per cent listed UK securities including unit trusts, and 8 per cent government or foreign securities (Committee on Private Share Ownership 1996).

In a perfectly ordered world any savers would have made such a decision after attempting to define their objectives and assess the best ways of attaining them. Given the performance of equity shares over time against other forms of asset they would by no means be illogical to wish to acquire some. Should they choose a collective scheme (unit and investment trusts) or buy shares in individual companies, and if so which and how many? For the time being we shall defer looking at collective schemes and return to them when we examine institutional investors.

The reasons for buying shares in general may be to gain a real return over a relatively long time period. Yet the decision-making process is not always clear, for which product, or what company. How did the choice come to be made? Was it by close observation; through a tip; by advice from a broker, banker, or accountant; on the encouragement of the press? Or was it some combination of some or all these? Had they considered alternatives in the same sector, or other sectors, or foreign shares of the same ilk? Have they read the report and accounts? What confidence do they have in the company's leadership and why? If it is their money they can stand on the seashore and throw it in without answering for their conduct. It is often said that gamblers secretly want to lose. So let us assume that our investors do not fall into that category. Is their choice considered and logical?

All purchases of equity shares are purchases of risk capital, though the fact is often forgotten. Even institutions, which know this perfectly well, are inclined to treat equities as if they were bonds when they put pressure on companies to maintain dividends in the face of poor results which do not justify them. No one would argue that the risks are equal: some companies are clearly much more speculative than others.

The buyer or seller in the market for popular shares is in a maelstrom of activity in which 'investors' and 'gamblers' jostle anonymously. There are two clusters, which overlap at the edges. Stags fall clearly into the latter category; they have no intention of holding. An insurance company's considered purchases, made for the medium or long term, fall into the former. A 'shorting' fund—where the sole activity is to sell shares short in the expectation they will fall—must be speculative in nature. Certain types of activity in the derivatives market are similar: there is no intention of buying and holding the underlying stock. Other activities in derivatives are more in the nature of insurance. Some purchasers bring to investment activity the language of the racecourse, but they may in fact be making an each-way bet; if the price rises quickly they may hold, but if it wavers they may cut their losses. Long-term investors may nevertheless play the market. Company chairmen who watch holdings in their company's shares with care will note with interest the transactions of some pension funds which move in and out of their stock during the year to take advantage of its volatility—they have a standing order to buy at n and sell at $n + x$.

Returning to where it all began, we must not lose sight of the basic fact that the invention of shares in limited liability companies was not to enrich stockbrokers or investment banks or any other intermediaries whatsoever, but to harness savings drawn from a multitude of people for a multiplicity of enterprises producing the goods and services they need.

The Private Shareholder

WHEN the 1844 Companies Act made incorporation generally available without a specific Act of Parliament, the shareholders had an enormously strong incentive to monitor a company's progress—they were liable for its debts were it to fail to the full extent of their personal assets. Although the 1855 Act relieved them of this threat, they still had a strong incentive to monitor as there was no open market in its shares. There might indeed be limitations in the articles of association on how they were to dispose of them, for instance requiring them to be offered first to the directors or existing shareholders.

To this day, therefore, if savers invest in an unquoted company they have a special incentive to follow the company's progress carefully. Having followed it, the courses open to them if they are disappointed or dissatisfied are limited. If 'exit' is restricted, savers have to turn to the other means at their disposal of safeguarding their investment. There is in fact only one—to replace the directors, either by voting them out if they come up for re-election or by convening a meeting to do so. Often, however, the articles relieve the directors of the need periodically to seek re-election (entrenchment), so even this possibility may be foreclosed. Besides the distribution of shareholdings in many private companies often protects the board.

The criminal processes of the law are cold comfort to those who have lost their investment as cases like Maxwell show only too clearly. Mounting a challenge to incompetent but honest management in the civil courts is an enterprise of high cost and great legal uncertainty. The rule in *Foss and Harbottle* (1843) effectively protects managers from being sued for acts which could be formally validated (because of the board's control of voting power). Anyone taking a minority stake in an unquoted company must be presumed to know all this.

Shareholders with the controlling interests in the company do not of course always see eye to eye and splits especially in family business can often be nasty in the way divorces are nasty, because of the cocktail of warring financial interests and emotional recrimination. In such cases the 'outside' shareholders may find themselves in a pivotal position. The formal position of minority shareholders in an unquoted company is therefore weak. Even so, good relationships may exist between them and the directors. They may meet informally from time to time, there may be exchanges of views between them. It is to be feared, however, that the nature of power is such that most executive managements brook as little interference as they can; and that the nature of human cupidity is such that as long as a company appears to prosper most of its shareholders will not wish to concern themselves with the finer points of its policy and performance. A juicy dividend cheque is an effective tranquillizer—at least until the truth can be concealed no longer.

For the minority of such shareholders who seek to peer more deeply, there has from the very outset been the right to examine the report and accounts and to question the directors on them at an annual general meeting. There never has been however an obligation on the directors to answer such questions. The potentiality of mustering enough votes to force change can only seldom be realized. The private shareholder in an unquoted company has very little protective clothing against a harsh wind. Put another way, the board is not effectively accountable.

The value of private shareholdings has advanced, but we are concerned with accountability and what counts for that purpose is the percentage of shares held, for with them go votes and therefore power. Overall, the private shareholder has dwindled in importance and, thereby, influence from about two-thirds in 1957 to less than 20 per cent in 1997. The report of the Committee on Private Share Ownership (1996), chaired by Sir Mark Weinberg, compares the 'Direct individuals' with pension funds (27.8 per cent), insurance companies (21.9 per cent), and overseas holders (16.3 per cent). Unit and investment trusts held 8.8 per cent (1996: fig. 2). In the 1996 Share Ownership Survey done by 'Direct and Collective Investment in the UK' it was stated (1996: fig. 3) that 26 per cent of the population held shares directly or collectively.

The decline in the proportion of shares held directly had for some time been a matter of concern to the Conservative Party, which as a matter of doctrine believed in a 'property-owning democracy' in which many members of the public held a direct stake in British companies. This, it was felt, would engage their sympathies for British industry in general, and their particular interest in the particular companies selected. It would reinforce their belief in a free market system and help to lay the ghost of socialism. As it happened, a convenient opportunity arose of implementing the policy.

When the Conservative government returned to power in 1979 it embarked on a process of returning the nationalized industries to private ownership. The main motive, it appears, was to remove government from direct involvement in major industries, for both parties had found it difficult to handle them on many fronts—unions, prices, investments, and salaries to name a few. In addition, the sale of some or all of the shares would raise substantial sums of money. If the business passed out of government hands it would no longer have to finance borrowing outside the definition of government expenditure, thus affecting the Public Sector Borrowing Requirement (PSBR). Finally it provided a practical way of introducing a wide public to the joys of the stock market for the first time. Great efforts were therefore made to market the shares widely—the 'Sid' concept—and in order to entice 'Sid' to buy, the sales were made on favourable terms. The government had a genuine dilemma, as it stood to look stupid if a privatization issue flopped or wicked if millions of people bought shares which soon depreciated in value. If Sid made a profit—realized on paper—who knows but that he might feel the capitalist mantle on his shoulder and vote Conservative. In terms of the number of direct shareholders the increase was dramatic—from an estimated 3 million in 1979 to a peak of 11 million. This had shrunk to about 9.5 million by 1995. Taken with the aggregates mentioned earlier, the figures suggest that the proportion of shares held directly in nondenationalized companies continues to fall.

Private investors in quoted companies are much better placed than their counterparts in unquoted companies. They will have additional sources of information (from the newspapers, brokers, as well as from the company itself). The Stock Exchange moreover regulates the flow of information in the interests of openness and equality of treatment (and the rules of the Take-over Panel protect them too). They will be able to escape by selling in the market if they do not like what they see before them—whether or not they are showing a profit on their original purchase. UK capital gains tax somewhat restricts this freedom of investment for big holders of successful shares, since a percentage of the capital gains (over a certain limit, and adjusted for inflation) goes to the government. Shareholders find no difficulty in selling shares in major companies and the efficiency of the London stock market means that the difference between the buying and selling price is small. The spread is much larger, as a percentage, for shares less frequently traded. Of course they sometimes lose money on an investment, but they are after all susbscribing to risk capital.

As late as 1963 a majority of shares were owned by private shareholders. Given that they hold less than 20 per cent in aggregate, and the number of shareholders is large (as a look at any report and accounts will confirm), it follows private shareholdings will be fragmented. Such fragmentation may be useful to the efficient working of the stock market, but in terms of the power of management, it means there is virtually no accountability since individually the number of votes a small shareholder commands is like a pimple on St. Paul's. Directors are however usually not wholly insensitive to criticism especially if it is well directed. So individuals might—and still do—exert influence to some extent, but they have no power. Real accountability implies power. If they band together as shareholders' associations sometimes attempt, the situation can change. In the words of the old motto, 'L'Union fait la force'.

The fragmentation of shareholdings in public companies and the attendant lack of accountability of management were famously noted by Berle and Means in their seminal work '*The Modern Corporation and Private Property*' (1932). Their analysis in relation to private investors still holds good as cited for instance by Roe (1994). The broad thrust of the argument is that fragmentation of shareholding makes the mobilization of power economically unviable. Individual shareholders would have to pay too much; the bulk of the benefits would accrue to others. This has been dubbed the 'free rider' problem. Roe puts it thus:

Most public companies are held by many shareholders owning only small stakes. In the Berle–Means era, shareholders were mostly individuals; even today, individuals directly own half of all stock in US companies, and even though intermediaries own the other half, rarely does a single intermediary own more than one percent of any individual stock of the nation's very large firms. Because of atomization, an active shareholder cannot capture all of the gain from becoming involved, studying the enterprise, or sitting on the board of directors, thereby taking the risks of enhanced liability. Such a shareholder would incur the costs but split the gains, causing most fragmented shareholders to rationally forgo involvement. In the language of modern economies, we have a collective action problem among shareholders—despite the potential gains to shareholders as a group, it's rational for each stockholder when acting alone to do nothing, because each would get only a fraction of the gain, which accrues to the firm and to all of the stockholders. This shareholder collective action problem is then layered on top of a principal–agent problem—agents, in this case the managers, sometimes don't do the principal's, in this case the stockholder's, bidding perfectly.

Note however that the UK differs from the USA in that intermediaries often hold more than 1 per cent. It is this which provides the potential for action. We return to this point later.

There have been examples on either side of the Atlantic of attempts to mobilize the voting power of individual shareholders through membership of some form of umbrella organization and there is little doubt that by means of well-argued campaigns, perhaps accompanied by a shareholder resolution, they have succeeded in exerting some influence. Matters are different elsewhere. In Germany, shares are in bearer form and have to be put in the hands of an authorized depositary, usually a bank. There power is indeed mobilized (though there are legal safeguards to ensure that the banks do not vote contrary to the owners' expressed wishes; if the owner has expressed no wish the bank may use its discretion). To some extent this mobilization of individual shareholders' votes in Germany is a fortuitous by-product of the form of the instrument in which shares are held.

LEGAL REDRESS

Any standard US work on this subject would have at its core a stream of legal precedents of all kinds. Shareholder lawsuits do not figure in this book because there are so few of them in the UK. The reason for this is that the process in the UK civil courts is not as helpful to litigants, who may have to face heavy costs if they lose, and cannot get lawyers to act on a contingency basis (no win, no fee). Class actions are difficult to mount and derivative suits virtually unknown (where a plaintiff sues the directors on behalf of the company). Many UK directors are nowadays covered by directors' and officers' insurance, but it would be difficult to find many instances of where these policies have paid out on a *civil* claim. Many consider that the litigious environment of the USA frustrates as much as it protects.

TAKEOVERS

Private shareholders now take for granted the possibility that the company in which they had invested might be merged, restructured, or taken over, and regard this as part of the normal operations of the market. The bid for British Aluminium in 1958 marked the beginning of a new era; it was financed in the City of London, and successful even though the company's management opposed it. It was a takeover, not a merger in the old sense. The private direct holder might well find this new world agreeable. It usually meant that there was a premium at which he could exit. It was however a rough world in which a small shareholder could be left stranded with a minority interest which commanded a lesser price than the control stake. The City's response was the creation of the Takeover Panel in the 1960s which ever since has set out rules to produce a process which secures evenhanded treatment for all shareholders, and ensures that the companies are not damaged by extended wrangling and litigation. There may be cases when a shareholder regrets that a takeover has succeeded, because he or she felt that there was nothing much wrong with the old company—and indeed there may not have been. At least they have serious options if a bid succeeds; they are not oppressed.

INFLUENCE

The private shareholder, in practice, is virtually powerless. Even to exert marginal influence requires:

- information;
- acuity;
- time;
- opportunity;
- organization (banding with others).

Information means as a minimum receiving the report and accounts and studying them and commentaries on them. This is the first fence and many shareholders fall at it because the report and accounts do not reach them. This occurs in cases where the shares are held in nominee accounts, generally by a stockbroker. There need be nothing sinister in this—it makes administration cheaper. But it means that the shareholder has no voice and no votes unless determined (at a price) to secure them. The votes are not generally exercised by the stockbroker either; they just disappear into a 'black hole'. Generally speaking, the shareholder has to pay to get what he or she needs. Few bother. In these circumstances the very basis of the Companies Act is undermined.

The introduction of Crest made matters worse. In a document published by PRO SHARE in May 1996, there is a description of investors' three choices under Crest—the least costly of which is to use a nominee. Charges are to be expected too if those who elected to become ordinary nominee members want information about the company and so forth. Crest itself charges sponsors £20 per annum for each sponsored member. How much sponsors charge for their various services is another matter. Table 4 sets out the different features of each of the options listed above and is designed to help investors choose the route which suits them best.

Even if a shareholder is able to cross the first hurdle he or she has to understand the material. The modern tendency is to require companies to produce more and more information. The trouble is to understand what it all means, and this often calls for a high degree of sophistication. It is to be

Table 4. PRO SHARE'S advice to private investors

	Hold share certificates yourself	Use a nominee	Become a sponsored member
Ease of settlement	Less certain	Guaranteed	Guaranteed
Availability of company information	Yes	Subject to arrangement	Yes
Access to information on special events, e.g. scrip dividends, rights issues	Yes	Subject to arrangement	Yes
Availability of shareholder perks	Yes	Subject to arrangement	Yes
Record keeping	Do it yourself	Service provided	Service provided
Legal title to share	Yes	No	Yes

Source: PRO SHARE (1996).

hoped that most companies are scrupulously honest about interpreting performance and prospects as part of them—but even they naturally do not offer an assessment of themselves compared with others in their field. One good set of accounts taken in isolation may if thoroughly analysed reveal a great deal about the company's progress over recent years and about its view of the future—but they may reveal little about the context, especially world economic, political, and trading conditions and competitors' performance—without which they cannot be fully understood.

Of course, shareholders can do all these things for themselves, but they need not only the information and basic acuity but also time. There are in the world doubtless many such people, some of whom do this as a business, others who bring to bear the experience of a lifetime in business or the professions. But there are far more who do not and could not. Some will be gamblers who buy and sell shares like commodities, caring little what the company does, and concentrating instead on what the market will do. The rest, if they buy individual shares at all, do so for miscellaneous reasons like a tip; admiration for a particular product or service; advice or hunch; or loyalty to a local firm. Such holders care little for report and accounts; some will hold till Doomsday. Some major UK companies now offer a simplified short report to all shareholders and a full set of accounts, free, to those who request them. One told us that, out of their 180,000 shareholders, less than 1 per cent did so.

The number of individual shareholders interested in the question of the board's accountability may be small. What is more they cannot as a general rule pursue such an interest indirectly by buying a unit trust (in US parlance a mutual fund). Roe puts it like this:

Mutual funds, despite huge financial resources of $1.2 trillion—half in stock—rarely participate in corporate governance. They channel funds from distant individuals to industry, gather information about industrial investments that their owners cannot easily get and evaluate, and do the paperwork that individuals begrudge. They are not intermediaries that get funds from disparate investors, combine them into concentrated holdings, and then enter the corporate boardroom to represent their shareholder beneficiaries and, if need be, check management. (Roe 1994)

In fact, there are some exceptions to this rule—notably M & G in the UK and Fidelity in the USA. The fact remains that investors in such pooled vehicles have no right to participate or even be consulted on the corporate governance policy of such funds.

In the UK nowadays the sum of individuals' interest in equity shares is as great as or greater than it has ever been—but indirectly through collective savings rather than directly and individually. Many people are interested both ways. They have rights under some occupational pension fund and possibly through an insurance policy, and also hold some shares direct. As direct holders their influence is, at best, marginal and their power vestigial.

Those who act on their behalf as guardians potentially have power especially if they make common cause with others like themselves. Certainly, as we shall see, the most powerful have real influence; collectively they have great power. Ought the individual shareholder to be concerned about this?

Any idea that all shareholders are treated alike is now untrue. Some companies assert that any direct shareholder will be granted an audience by a director if he or she requests it, but this would obviously be impractical if too many attempted it. Even the institutions do not command equal attention. In general the bigger and more powerful an institution the better their access to a company's management. Even if they do not hear a single fact or shadow of a fact that is not generally available, the mere meeting is itself hugely valuable as it helps them assess the confidence they can have in a company's pronouncements. Moreover, a company's meetings with analysts and other intermediaries do not just rehearse what all shareholders already know. If all these meetings were so restricted would the protagonists waste time and money on them? Such meetings are supposed to steer clear of market-sensitive information; perhaps they do, but the market sometimes moves after they have taken place.

Should the private shareholders care about this? Should they assemble in platoons and march down Threadneedle and Throgmorton Streets in protest? We think not. We feel that the greater interest now being taken by institutions (of which more below) is a step forward; that the difference in access for individuals is to be expected; that individual shareholders should be reassured if those in charge of their collective savings are concerned with the accountability of management—it means that at long last the Berle and Means analysis is less valid than it was. The direct shareholders in the UK are now the 'free riders'—they stand to benefit without cost to themselves from the exertions of the institutional shareholders.

If direct shareholders want to exert more influence, there are three courses open to them:

(1) (For the very rich)—buy enough shares to be significant.
(2) (For everyone)—do their homework and write to the company; and attend general meetings, being prepared to speak if necessary. Write to the media where it is warranted. Even in the best-run companies mistakes are made, accidents happen, injustices and unfairness ensue, managements get over-defensive.
(3) Get together with like-minded shareholders and form some kind of association or consortium that can mobilize the proxy votes, and in effect turn itself into an institutional shareholder with corresponding influence. Some organizations like PRO SHARE do exist, but they do not aim to garner proxies. The UK Shareholders' Association is a small but growing band of informed investors. Make no mistake—that will cost money: but unless and until it happens the private direct shareholder is

doomed to be a hanger-on to institutional coat-tails. But that is far better than in the Berle and Means days when there were no coat-tails about!

THE EMPLOYEE AS SHAREHOLDER

The Conservative government 1979–97, in pursuit of their general policy of encouraging more people to have a stake in British capitalism, encouraged employees by tax breaks to take shares in their own company by one means or another. Many companies have indeed introduced Employee Share Ownership Plans (ESOPs). Some employees take up such shares because they are proud of the company and believe it will prosper, though there are bound to be some who do not because they do not identify with it and do not wish to have a further commitment to it: or simply have no spare cash. Virtually no employees in the UK buy shares with aggressive intent, in order to harass or embarrass the board at general meetings. If that were their aim ESOPs would be no use to them as the shares are voted (if at all) by the Plan's trustees. So the activist would have to buy in the market, and few do. In other countries matters may be different. There is an anecdote of a public company in India whose employees bought so many separate small parcels of shares that the board had to hire a stadium to accommodate the numbers. The general meeting lasted two days and the questioning was penetrating because knowledgeable. Employees in the UK are only just beginning even to consider their special position as shareholders. The potential role in corporate governance deserves to be explored.

Some companies distribute shares by way of bonus, through option schemes, which nowadays tend to reach beyond executive directors to other levels of management and even ordinary employees. It is scarcely to be expected that a senior employee will make a public (or even a private) nuisance. Their ownership of shares will be confined to receipt of private benefit. Those who have thus acquired shares and have left the company stand in the same relationship as other shareholders, but are probably better informed.

THE CONSUMER AS SHAREHOLDER

Large companies touch our lives at many points, mainly as consumers. We may decide to buy shares in them too—and some of the denationalized issues, for instance British Gas and British Telecom, made shares available to customers on a special basis. When the fracas over the chief executive's pay arose in 1995, British Gas found itself playing host at the AGM to 4,000 shareholders who were evidently mainly customers. Customers do not have the inhibitions of employees in speaking out—and may well have a good insight into how a company is performing. Any chairman of a company supplying consumer goods or services must be prepared to face irate questions about some wrong, real or imagined—and occasionally be astonished by praise from the satisfied. The customer as shareholder is an issue of real concern for utilities, and some have exerted effective pressure, via groups like Yorkshire Water Watch, or provide management with another form of contact with their consumer base which is an opportunity to learn and thereby improve services and competitive position.

DIRECT AND INDIRECT HOLDINGS

The financial interest of the British public in the stock market has never been greater, but most of it is through collective savings; trustees and managers stand between them and the companies whose shares are held. They are beneficiaries and have a claim against the fund or company. They do not have a direct interest in any particular asset the fund holds at a particular moment, whether it be a work of art, property or shares. It has been suggested in some quarters that by electronic means the beneficiaries' views could be sought on matters appertaining to a particular company which is currently in the fund's portfolio—whether a takeover bid should be accepted for instance. Technology will facilitate democracy. The Pensions Act provision allowing some trustees to be elected by members is a step towards direct involvement. We still have a long way to go in ensuring the private shareholder plays an effective role in corporate governance in the UK.

Narrower Share Ownership

THE proportion of equity shares held directly by individuals has shrunk dramatically in recent years from two-thirds in the 1960s to less than 20 per cent today. This is not because equities have proved unattractive. Although there have been short periods in which equities have been a poor investment compared with gilts (and indeed with property), any long-term graph shows their superiority. BZW's annual Equity–Gilt Study shows that the annual real return from equities between 1918 and 1996 was 7.8 per cent per annum compared with just under 2 per cent for gilts. A Californian economist, Bryan Taylor, has produced figures for 1700–1995 which show that, if income were reinvested and no tax deducted, £1 in gilts would have grown to £630,000 over the period and £1 in equities would have produced £51,554,000!

Of course, the general picture includes many exceptions—companies which have not kept pace or which have failed altogether. An index is not a convoy; the companies which comprise it do not all move at the same pace. In general however the stock market has proved its worth as a means of maintaining the real value of savings in the face of inflation. On those grounds alone, there is a sound basis for investing in equity shares.

As we noted earlier, individuals' total interests in equity shares have never been greater, but they are now generally indirect, through pension funds, insurance policies, or some kind of collective investment such as unit trusts. Indirect investment in these ways has supplanted and extended direct individual holdings. The performance of equities is therefore of greater importance than ever before.

CHOICE

For the individual direct investor, as for others, the selection is of course the key. The choice is bewilderingly large. The financial world teems with advisers (all of whom, quite naturally, charge for their services). Picking stocks, and indeed picking advisers, is far from easy. There is no problem as long as people really understand what they are doing, but that is a far cry from advocating that everyone should become a direct investor. We have doubts about the policy of advocating 'wider share ownership' unless the investor falls within one of the following categories:

(1) a holder of a *significant* stake in a quoted company by inheritance, purchase, or perhaps options;
(2) knowledgeable about markets and companies;
(3) a gambler;
(4) a small buyer of stocks in a limited number of companies, for example, in denationalized utilities.

For those anxious or interested to receive it, an avalanche of advice is available on investing in shares. Much of it is contained in newspapers and journals; some will come from professionals—lawyers, accountants, bankers, stockbrokers. With so many sources to hand we do not need to add our measure on how to set about it. Our theme is after all the shareholders' role, not the choice of particular stocks or even particular forms of collective savings. Naturally people who invest in shares must in their own interest monitor the result of their purchase, or ensure that someone competent does it for them just as they would any other kind of asset.

All share transactions cost money, so the person who constantly massages the portfolio will keep the broker happy. To avoid such expense many 'lock up their shares and put them away'. Some of these have died rich, if their choice in the first place turned out to be felicitous. There comes a time when it is right to sell. There is no company in the world today whose record and performance do not require periodic consideration by those who invest in them—and there never will be. What about our four groups?

The first group are mainly concerned with their own companies, which they may be presumed to understand. The second group, the experts, can readily do this for themselves. The third group, the gamblers (using different and shorter-term criteria), can look after themselves. The fourth group, who have generally been the buyers of the great utilities, may hope that in the long run they have a small portfolio of unexciting but reliable investments, unlikely to affect the blood pressure.

In terms of their governance role, we can expect each group to be different. The first will be active and involved. The second group, the experts, will be on the qui vive to support initiatives that they think will benefit them. They may however have made an a priori decision to deal with all problems via the Wall Street Walk—i.e. 'Why vote?; if we like what we see, we stay with the shares; if we don't like it; we sell.' They vote with their feet. The third group— the gamblers—also fit this category. Backers do not give horses a sermon in the paddock.

The fourth group might have thought at one point they were in for a quiet time—no ripple of disquiet could trouble the serene countenances of the boards of denationalized utilities. Governance was not expected to be an issue. This has not proved the case. Issues have arisen which the small shareholders can perfectly well understand and evaluate (much more difficult on technical issues) and they have had an opportunity to take sides.

That leaves the possibility of a fifth category, which by definition is not proprietorial (or they would be in group 1), not knowledgeable (or they would be in group 2), not just gamblers (or they would be in group 3), and interested in more than denationalization issues (group 4). They are potentially a large number as the generations change and the funds released by the sale of property need to be invested. Their best interest demands *ex ante*, interim, and *ex post* advice—with selection, monitoring, and disposal. They can construct their own portfolio or opt for a collective savings scheme like a unit trust (mutual fund) or an investment trust or some variation. In all forms of collective savings the investors are paying a price (for none of these services come free) for someone else to do their worrying for them. But they are not out of the wood because:

- Selecting the appropriate vehicle is far from easy as the choice is vast. The private investor needs not only disinterested but also expert advice even in this.
- As services do not come free the investor must know what they will cost.
- An institution, whatever it is and however long it has been established, is actually run by people of various ages and varying ability. Naturally it wants to do well to keep the business, but any look at comparative tables will demonstrate that performance is not constant. Investors know that moves are costly, but they cannot avoid making a judgement from time to time about the relative decline in a fund's performance. Such a judgement is by no means easy to make, and itself may require expert advice.
- Investors are protected nowadays by all the rules of the multiplicity of supervisory organizations operating under the Financial Services Act. Even so they might just keep an eye on the amount of trading, if the organization has discretion (as is customary). 'Churning', as it is called, is not unknown, even now.
- Savers know, though they sometimes forget, that equity capital is risk capital so that any investment they make, direct or collective, is by definition risky to some extent. If they do use a form of collective savings they will want to know that risk is not being compounded by the managing organization being itself unsafe.

When it comes to handling other people's money there have been the lazy, the incompetent, the careless, and the downright wicked. There are always those who lie in wait for the greedy or gullible by offering extraordinary returns. Such returns go with extraordinary risks, always, inexorably. At worst, as in the Barlow Clowes case, sharks await. There is a bewildering choice of well-established unit trusts and investment trusts—they are doubtless scrupulously honest but they do not always do well since human judgement is not infallible. Sometimes their performance must be monitored (and it is always wise to keep an eye on their costs of management). If he or she elects to use their services the private investor leaves the monitoring of the individual companies in the portfolio to the body managing the funds but still has to solve the riddle of how to get expert advice about the choice of collective instrument. It does not matter how many layers there are between the investor and the company. The investor cannot escape the role of being the ultimate guardian of his or her own interest, and the price of this is vigilance.

INDIVIDUALS' MANAGED PORTFOLIOS

Some private investors in our fifth category do not wish to invest through a collective savings scheme: they feel they can do better, given the right advice. They often put themselves in the hands of stockbrokers or bankers who are given full discretion to run their portfolios for them. In doing so they too have invariably surrendered any minuscule governance role they might possibly have. They ought to be aware that conflicts of interest, with the best will in the world, beset stockbrokers. If a stockbroker is serving a company and needs to place its stock, does its loyalty lie to that company or to the clients whose accounts it manages on a discretionary basis? Do those who tip shares always disclose their own positions? Firms try to face up to these conflicts, but conflicts they remain.

Here is an extract from a stockbroker's letter to its clients (February 1997) that speaks for itself:

Conflicts of interest: Your attention is drawn to the fact that when we give you investment advice, we, or some other person connected with either or both organisations, may have an interest, relationship or arrangement that is material in relation to the transaction or investment concerned. However, our employees are required to disregard any such interest when making recommendations to you.

Your attention is also drawn to the fact that when we recommend a transaction to you, we:

(a) could be dealing as principal for our account by selling the investment concerned to you or buying it from you; in such a case, the fact will be disclosed on your contract note; or

(b) could be matching your transaction with that of another customer by acting on his behalf as well as yours;

(c) or we could be buying investments in which we are involved in a new issue, rights issue, takeover or similar transaction concerning the investment.

THE MISSING SIXTH

By way of a coda to this part of our analysis we add a sixth class of investor, now no longer with us and seldom mentioned in the literature. The references in the earlier chapter to the stock market a century ago and the newspapers reporting it drew attention to the shortness of the commercial/industrial list and the length of the foreign list. There are three factors easily forgotten. First, that in many of the countries in which their companies operated there was no capital market. To raise money on the capital markets entrepreneurs had to come to London or another international centre, and London was good at supplying their needs. With the effluxion of time, local capital markets developed in many countries, so London was not so necessary even though it continued to be useful. Secondly, many of the enterprises were small and dealings in the shares few. Presence on a list does not imply great liquidity.

It is however the third reason which is most relevant: the existence in the UK of thriving local stock exchanges in centres other than London, e.g. Glasgow, Birmingham, Nottingham, Bristol, Manchester, Liverpool—this list is not exhaustive. What this meant was that there was a class of local investors who knew a great deal about the local companies. They were knowledgeable about their performance and prospects. Doubtless there were many disappointments and losses and many must have rued over-prolonged loyalty. But they did at least know what they were about and the people who dealt for them were probably known to them too. There is a greater care in maintaining relationships in smaller communities as no one can easily escape the consequences of fouling them up. With the disappearance of most of these exchanges, that particular class of investor has shrunk, though some still survive for essentially local companies quoted in London. Incidentally, the London list of a century ago included not only the larger national and international companies, but also local London businesses—such as the theatres and music halls.

The doctrine of 'wider share ownership' is at best likely to prove unnecessarily risky except for the knowledgeable, if that programme means direct holdings of individual, non-utility shares. The right haven for such investors is a form of collective savings and even then they must keep an eye on the continued effectiveness of the managers, and their costs.

A much better slogan would be 'Deeper share ownership' as coined by the Social Market Foundation in their pamphlet of the same name. The purpose of this would be to persuade would-be investors that using their savings to buy shares is a rational step only if they really understand what they—and what the company—are doing. And subscribing to a collective savings scheme like a unit or investment trust only makes sense if they understand what the relevant managers are doing, how they are performing, and what their services cost.

Even then investors have to remember at all times (and it is only too easy to forget after a long bull market) that the market can be a switchback. The long upward trend line referred to at the beginning of this chapter covers numerous breaks in the market and the small investor is notorious for getting timing wrong. In the Great Crash of 1929 Groucho Marx recalled getting a curt message from his stockbroker, 'Marx—the jig is up'. Like others he had been buying on margin and was financially wiped out. Professor Louis Lowenstein makes the point well (1988: 102–3). Private investors might well enquire how much those who actively manage their money have consistently outperformed the index, taking expenses into account. Research in the USA suggested that few do so, and therefore that 'buying the index' is the logical route for the passive investor on grounds of cost and effectiveness.

CRASHES

At least until recently, we had largely forgotten about the crash of 1929. There had been stock failures before, and of course banking panics and failures. But this one time the process seemed interminable. When the worst appeared to be over, the worst had yet to happen. Of $50bn. of securities sold to the American public from 1920 to 1933, approximately one-half had become absolutely worthless by 1933. By 1934 almost half of the foreign securities sold to American investors in the seven years 1923–30 were in default. Nor was it just a matter of new issues. The aggregate value of the stocks listed on the New York Stock Exchange on 1 September 1929 was $89bn. Less than three years later, in 1932, their total value was only $15bn. And these were the best of companies, the blue chips.

Volatility has since unsettled many markets, and their investors. Just in case readers should imagine all this is simply history, consider the 'Weekend Money' section of the *Financial Times* of 3/4 August 1996. This included articles by Barry Riley entitled 'Mutual Funds Ride a Roller Coaster—In the US they're all Go. In Japan they've Nearly all Gone'; by R. Taylor on an investment trust called 'Tottering Kepit Heads for an Early Grave'; and by K. Goldstein-Jackson called 'Time for a Shareholders' Charter'. All of this was long before the 1997 and 1998 switchback rides in the Far East which made volatility a new part of every investor's lexicon.

Entrusting savings to the equity market is over time a rational decision. Even so, with the exception of the groups we identified we have reservations about urging others to enter the market unless they know enough either to evaluate what is going on themselves or to evaluate how an intermediary or collective scheme is performing. We have had cases drawn to our attention where problems have meant the sackings of several: a broker who 'stuffed' a trustee account; a PEP manager who 'churned' a discretionary account; and an honest but misguided fund manager who became so besotted with 'chart-ism' that he forgot about fundamentals. There are the totally honest but bewildered; and the assured but mistaken. The quality of the work by the best analysts is first rate but even they have to build their prognoses on the shifting sands of human personalities. Investment in the stock market is a great game, but the only consistent winners are the experts or intermediaries who take a cut going up or going down, or the professionals who scored when conglomerates were assembled and scored again when they were dismembered. The individual direct shareholder with a small holding is at the end of the game for information, at the bottom of the poll for influence, at the top of the list for a possible rip-off, and the target for the greatest costs, pro rata. Investing is not a game for the reckless, but a serious enterprise for the knowledgeable or for those who are good judges of whom to trust. Others keep out.

The public appears sceptical about investment in any case. The Weinberg Committee found that most of the populace with 'free' funds keep over 60 per cent of them in cash and that they are extremely risk averse, distrustful of the stock market (its accessibility and reliability), and bemused by the complexity of company reports and accounts. There is a telling passage: 'Moreover existing discussions about the enduring of pre-emption rights further reinforces the message received by private investors that the market is run for "those in the know" rather than the private shareholder' (Committee on Private Share Ownership 1996).

This may tell us that people are shrewd, but that does not mean they are knowledgeable. What is more many companies are not enthusiastic about direct private shareholders. In the Weinberg Report, 32 companies were questioned. Ten were neutral and 4 against—compared with the 17 which professed to welcome them. In British Gas, Chairman R. Giordano has let it be known he would like 'to ease Aunt Maud out without any pain' (quoted in the *Financial Times*, 11 Feb. 1996: 5). Commenting on both Weinberg and Giordano a few days later Gillian O'Connor in the same paper concluded, 'To stand a good chance of benefiting from direct share ownership, private investors need to be knowledgeable although not necessarily rich. What Aunt Maud needs is a good tracker fund.'

The Weinberg Report did not appear to arouse much enthusiasm, because the picture it painted is not a rosy one. It shows a cautious, risk-averse, suspicious public, conscious of its own lack of information and wary of attempts to supply that deficiency made by those with a personal interest in the business that ensues. And why should companies welcome small shareholders who cost more to service—if the job is done properly—other than for their inertia and powerlessness? And why should stockbrokers welcome them unless they can charge proper rates for their efforts (which are likely to be much higher pro rata than for big deals)? The Confederation of British Industry posed the question in its evidence to the Committee on Corporate Governance under Sir Ronnie Hampel.

Could the increasing remoteness of private individual shareholders from companies, resulting from CREST and rolling settlement, be counteracted, and their contribution to corporate governance enhanced? If so how? It is unlikely that CREST will materially change the behaviour of the overwhelming majority of private shareholders. Private shareholding continues to be discouraged by the tax and other advantages enjoyed through investing through funds. The Weinberg Report revealed that almost 40 percent of private investors held shares in just one company and made a number of suggestions for widening the ownership of shares in the UK. However, it is impractical to believe that the majority of individual shareholders can have a great impact on corporate governance given their current limited role in share ownership.

In the face of the evidence, the goal of wider share ownership needs redefinition.

CHAPTER

12

Power: The Greasy Pole

THE legal framework of the company was always intended to facilitate the accumulation of power and resources necessary for the size and duration of modern commercial and industrial enterprises. Note that the directors are not exercising power in a personal capacity—they are exercising the powers of the company—as set out in the memorandum and articles—this gives freedom of action, tempered by the shareholders' powers (and the law) to restrain, overturn, or intervene.

People come to power as they come to greatness—by odd routes. As Malvolio read, 'Some are born great, some achieve greatness, some have greatness thrust upon them.' In regard to industrial power some know from the outset that they want it; from day one they have a place in their knapsack for the equivalent of the field marshal's baton—the CEO's credit cards. Others start with more limited horizons but raise their sights every time they register success. Ambition feeds upon itself. Some have a vision of what they want to use power for if they should ever acquire it. Such people seldom do, for the imaginative qualities that are needed to determine the purposes of power do not sit comfortably with the pragmatism (and ruthlessness) necessary to acquire it. When Disraeli after a lifetime's political infighting became Prime Minister in 1874, it was not on the back of a pack of dynamic policies (elections were not often so fought in those days). 'I have', he said, 'climbed to the top of the greasy pole.'

We do not have to search far for the reasons why some struggle so hard for power and defend it so jealously. Being CEO means recognition: not being answerable to other executives: getting more money and perks: having inconveniences reduced. The well-organized CEO in a major company may enjoy some luxury; and is attended by staff from whom even the admirable Jeeves might have taken lessons. The pleasures of power are such that many would accept promotion to the CEO's job for very little more than they are already earning. In days gone by they used to: it is the modern trend to pile Pelion upon Ossa and pay them huge sums. Much of the fabric of British society is built on the premiss that high responsibility does not necessarily require commensurate pay. Throughout public life the top jobs are not marked by huge jumps in pay. This is true of the Prime Minister, the judiciary, the armed forces, and the civil and diplomatic services. There is an argument that their 'rewards come in the form of public recognition, namely honours'. Honours go also to top industrialists. When did a chairman of ICI *not* get a knighthood?

Directors recognize the need to protect their position by organizing to express a common view. In the USA CEOs of major companies have an organization called 'The Round Table'. The Institute of Directors and the Confederation of British Industry do not quite represent the interests of CEOs in the same way, though finance directors have banded together in the 100 Group which has generally pursued an interest in the subject of corporate governance.

PATRONAGE AND NOMINATION

What shareholder activists and the non-executive directors who are prepared to challenge a chief executive may encounter is a sharpness in the response to criticism which suggests a tender point has been touched. And as far as shareholders are concerned, what is a typical tender point? It is the exercise of the power of patronage, which manifests itself in the composition of the board (and of its committees). The exercise of patronage confers pleasure on all the parties concerned. Shareholders in looking at the constitution of company boards will be well advised to bear this thought in mind. 'To whom', they may wish to ask themselves, 'do the directors feel they owe allegiance?' And 'Is the exercise of power by the CEO or chairman so complete that no one however nominally independent will be chosen who is likely to give trouble?' Some chairmen may want the compliant, especially if their search for additions to the board is undertaken at the prompting of the institutions. For similar reasons CEOs often want other CEOs. This is partly for their experience, but it also reflects the fact that another person in the same position as themselves should start with a sympathetic bias. Of course all directors should have sympathy. No one joins a board to quarrel. The borderline is ill-defined, but power and patronage define it in a way that defends the CEO's personal interests, sometimes at the expense of the company's. The Cadbury Code is specific (2.4): 'Non-executive directors should be selected through a formal process and both this process and their appointment should be a matter for the board as a whole.' Paragraph 4.30 of the report falls short of recommending the use of nomination committees though it points out their usefulness. The overwhelming majority of companies have stated that they have such committees, although there is considerable variation in their remit, purpose, and structure (PIRC 1997d). The Hampel Committee emphasized the value of such committees, but stopped short of elaborating any practical advice on the matter in the report published in January 1998.

Significantly, the percentage of companies with such committees is far lower than that of those with remuneration committees. Overpayment is a limited ill; having a sub-optimal board has potentially unlimited consequences. The better the 'recruiting' process, the more effective a board is likely to be; the more effective it is, the less shareholders have cause to intervene.

DONATIONS

One of the aspects of power and patronage is to decide how much of the shareholders' money shall be given away, to whom, and for what: a recent contribution to endow a university of over £1m. by BAT Industries in the name of its recently retired chairman, Sir Patrick Sheehy, comes to mind. Shareholders will wish to disregard sums of money that are *de minimis*— companies have many occasions locally to smooth the wheels of commerce by such gestures. They will also support subventions made to a local community in one form or another that are vital to the conduct of operations there—RTZ in Namibia for example. They will note with interest the number of opera seats a company chairman has at his disposal through the firm's deep concern with the arts. They may view with interest a company's political donations especially if such donations are followed by an honour. And when they see some other munificence perhaps to the educational world they will not wish to cavil at the excellence of the cause or worthiness of its recipients, but might just wonder whether, as it is their money that is being given away, and as the objects are not at all closely related to the benefit of the business (if at all), their authority should have been sought. Directors are empowered to do whatever they think fit for the benefit of the business, but sometimes the line between that and the sheer exploitation of power seems rather blurred. It is a much more satisfactory arrangement if shareholders' authority is sought to distribute *n* per cent of profits. Some years ago, the 'percent' club was formed with just such an object in mind; we do not want to play Scrooge, but feel that all material sums should carry shareholder approval. They are entitled to be consulted about the use for funds which are not for the continuation of normal business activity; such a discipline would also ensure that directors considered carefully how such beneficence was a proper extension of corporate responsibility, and not simply a public relations exercise or patronage of the directors on private causes. Where the director sits on the board of a body which receives money from the company then there may be concerns also about a conflict of interest. Ultimately, the day-to-day conduct of a company is more important than charitable donations, and, arguably, more challenging to the directors. When a company is prominent among charitable givers, and there are grave social consequences to its decision to 'downsize' or replace permanent staff with casual employees in the name of cost-cutting, then critics are right to be cynical about the motives.

Another aspect of power to which we wish to draw attention is the most significant, for it concerns the direction, and perhaps the very existence, of the business. Everyone connected with a business (all the stakeholders, to use modern parlance) wants to see *real* growth however defined; they want to see businesses built up. This is the source of prosperity. It is however a long hard road and a CEO's time in office may be quite short—at least short enough for the rewards of his or her labours to fall to successors. As this is so, many use their power to attain growth, but of a different kind, by acquisition. Sheer size confers status, rewards, and greater immunity from takeover. But does it add value, viewed from the point of view of the company (and of society)? It may, if 2+2 can be made to be worth 6 because of economies of scale, deeper market penetration, better research. But the history of the last decade demonstrates that too many of such expansions lacked commercial logic and in the result produced no more than 5—and sometimes only 4 or less. Shareholders need to watch this manifestation of the exercise of power especially keenly, and it often comes with a complaisant board. Shareholders have not been helped by accounting conventions which have favoured acquisitions against organic growth (though less than they did).

Why do we put such an emphasis on power within the company, which is not a concept that can be translated into numbers for the economists and analysts? Because the history of Western democracy teaches us that we neglect it at our peril. The suspicion of excessive concentrations of central power produced the checks and balances of the US Constitution. It is also reflected in the adversarial procedures of the UK Parliament whereby the executive is challenged. The increased role of the judges through the procedure of judicial review this last thirty years represents a reaction against the abuse of power by the executive. Nor can it be argued that the economic and political spheres are totally different. US laws for generations have been based on a fear of excessive concentration of economic power—everything from the relationship of banks and insurance companies with industry to anti-trust provisions. The UK has its Office of Fair Trading and Monopolies Commission.

The framers of the first Companies Act a century and a half ago intended there to be a concentration of power, and they were unquestionably right. Dynamic leadership was and is essential; and such leadership needs power, not to be choked by a miasma of Kafka-esque regulation. The power does not have to be vested in one person, but perhaps in a duo or triumvirate or small group. The genius of the UK legal system was to invest the company with a persona, with powers, which the directors can exercise. German specification of a single *Geschäftsführer* for small businesses and of a group (*Vorstand*) for bigger ones is instructive. To put the formulation correctly:

it is essential for executive management to have power. That is what the first principle of corporate governance requires.

However—the public is rightly suspicious of power without accountability because those who exercise power, especially if they do so successfully, may get carried away by their own brilliance to the point where they become convinced they are infallible and that opposition is misguided. They tend at this stage to discard those who hold contrary views and eventually make poor decisions which undo totally or in part much of the success they have had. Many companies which fall into this category—those with strong leaders and weak boards—have known success. But the crucial element was the adulation of the media which had so intoxicated those concerned that their judgement was impaired. We could produce examples, but in W. S. Gilbert's words, 'The task of filling up the blanks I'd rather leave to you.' It is not difficult. In our society we expect people to accept responsibility for the effects their actions have on others; the point of accountability is to ensure this.

We do not wish to give the impression that British and American commerce and industry is run by a regiment of egomaniacs (see our earlier discussion of agency theory). We understand very well that many boards successfully achieve the balance between drive and accountability at a high level of competence—precisely what companies need. We also know that many boards spend much time assessing the competence of the CEO and team and doing their very best to ensure that it is up to the mark. The National Association of Corporate Directors of Washington, DC, published the research of S. D. Truskie in July 1996 on the subject.

My findings indicate nearly four out of 10 companies (38 percent) have in place a formal oral and written performance evaluation of their CEOs. This is considerably higher than the rough estimate of 20 percent that we see in the press . . . This trend is not unwanted or unwelcomed by CEOs. Their written comments suggest that many more CEOs view a performance review positively than negatively. Many CEOs reported that a performance evaluation provides clarity in what their boards expect of them, and establishes a mechanism for receiving valuable feedback on their performance.

Even so, there are boards whose standards and judgements are not high enough; and there are boards that are so dominated by the CEO that they are in practice powerless to control him. In the post-Cadbury world such boards should be fewer because of the gowing cohesiveness of audit committees. Power and patronage being what they are, some of these committees will not comprise firm enough members: the chairman/CEO will see to that. So we see occasions, hopefully few, when action is needed and is (to the discerning) seen to be needed. And then, as a last resort, if influence fails, it is a power struggle. This is inevitable. It is not new. It is how the Acts were designed to work from the very beginning.

13

The Rise of the Institutions

SHAREHOLDERS are a diverse bunch. We have looked at the differences between private investors in an earlier chapter. However, there is a broad distinction which can be made between private investors who are buying shares for their own direct benefit, and professionals who are investing on behalf of others. The term 'institutions' is used to describe all kinds of collective shareholdings, save perhaps share clubs. Included in the term 'institution' therefore are both UK- and overseas-based investors in the following categories: insurance companies and pension funds, investment trusts and unit trusts, and the fund managers (either internal or external) employed to invest on their behalf. In addition, there are stockbrokers and the trustee departments of banks, which, although relatively small, do hold shares on behalf of their clients. What distinguishes the institutions from other shareholders is that they are investing money on behalf of others: this puts them in a fiduciary role, which imposes various duties under the principles of trust law. We look at these in the next chapter.

Just as individual direct holders vary from Sid with £100 (in denationalized stocks) to Cyrus T. Sid III (with an international portfolio of $100m.) so institutions vary in size. A small occupational pension fund may have less than £1m. invested, a large one several billion pounds. There is also the chain of command to consider. The phrase 'institutions' is used for both the intermediaries who have the day-to-day task of investing money (such as fund managers) and the body with ultimate ownership of the shares (such as pension funds). In some cases there is overlap, for example with investments and unit trusts, which may invest for institutions or private shareholders. They may be quoted in their own right as companies, and then, in turn, invest their client's money in other shares. Insurance companies are also no longer simple organizations. An insurer may be a quoted company, or not. It may offer fund management services to pension funds, as well as investing its own fund on behalf of policy holders. This means that institutional relationships are complex, and may give rise to conflicts of interest.

Take as an example the Prudential, the UK's largest institutional investor, with over 3 per cent of the UK equity market in its portfolio. The Pru itself is a listed company with a place in the leading index of shares, the FTSE 100. It is a major insurer, selling both life and mortgage endowment policies. It is heavily involved in selling personal pensions to the public and investing as manager the occupational schemes of a growing number of both public and private pension funds. In its equity portfolios are substantial numbers of UK companies, many from the same index in which the Pru itself is quoted. Not only is the Pru a shareholder in these companies, it is also offering commercial services, from fund management of these companies' pension funds, to sales of commercial insurance. The Prudential's situation is not unusual; among the leading fund managers in the UK, a number are quoted companies in their own right. For example, consider Gartmore, now part of National Westminster Bank, which is selling services as banker and other forms of corporate finance to companies in which Gartmore invests not only for NatWest's own pension fund, but for external pension fund clients as well. Mercury Asset Management is a quoted company, but manages money for institutional and private clients.

All institutions must make custodial arrangements to ensure the safe keeping of assets. They also have to manage the money entrusted to them to provide a return on it. Some funds are under the formal charge of trustees whose responsibility it is to arrange both. When it comes to management the institutions can elect to employ people to do it 'in-house' or can farm it out in whole or part to a management firm which may be a specialist fund management firm or a life office or another entity. If they use external managers they may employ more than one firm. Smaller institutions tend to farm out the management of their funds altogether. There is a problem of classification, since some of the funds managed by external fund managers can properly be classified as 'pension funds'. Fund managers are in a critical position when we come to assess where power lies. Whether a fund is under trustees or not depends on what type of institution it is, how the fund has been set up, and what the law requires. Pension funds and bank trust departments have trustees but the other categories do not.

The pattern of ownership and control of equity shares is a complex web. For that reason there is a need for clarity in lines of reporting, accountability, and disclosure of interest.

WHO OWNS WHAT

The pattern of equity ownership in the UK is markedly different from many other developed economies. Share ownership in the UK according to figures provided by PRO SHARE, based on CSO statistics, shows the percentage in various category of owner. The most important point to note is which group in each market is the single largest among the shareholders. In the USA it is

Table 5. Ownership of shares (%)

	Japan	Germany	France	USA	UK
Individuals	20	17	34	48	18
Banks	21	14	6	3	1
Institutions	21	15	18	34	60
Corporate	28	39	21	0	2
Govt. and other	2	3	2	9	3
Foreign	8	12	19	6	16

Source: International Markets Group, a cooperative venture of the International Federation of Accountants, the International Bar Association, and Fédération Internationale des Bourses de Valeurs.

individuals who have nearly half of the shares; in Germany it is corporate holdings; in the UK, institutions (defined here in relatively narrow terms as pension funds and insurance companies). In Japan it is more evenly balanced between corporate, institutional, and private holdings. In France, individuals still hold sway although corporate and foreign ownership is clearly important. The dominance of institutions in the UK is relatively recent. Personal direct investment was responsible for over 60 per cent of shares in the late 1950s with institutions controlling less than 20 per cent in total. Within thirty years, that balance had been all but reversed.

These data are important because they show unmistakably the trend over recent years. The decline in percentage terms of the direct private investor is most marked—though in cash terms their holdings have advanced substantially with the market. The rise in importance of pension funds, insurance companies, and unit trusts is even more marked, as is the growth in overseas holdings.

Institutional dominance of investment is reflected in other ways, in the value of asset investment by members of the Institutional Fund Managers'

Table 6. Trends in % UK share ownership

	1957	1963	1975	1981	1990	1994
Personal direct	65.8	54.0	37.5	28.2	20.3	20.3
Pension funds	3.4	6.4	16.8	26.7	31.6	27.8
Insurance cos.	8.8	10.0	15.9	20.5	20.4	21.9
Investment trusts	5.2	11.3	10.5	5.4	1.6	2.0
Unit trusts	0.5	1.3	4.1	3.6	6.1	6.8
Overseas	7.0	5.6	3.6	11.8	16.3	—
Other[a]	10.9	9.6	10.6	7.4	3.6	—

[a] Banks, charities, public sector, industrial, and commercial.

Association (IFMA). The list of their members in Appendix 4 shows that it covers most of the leading intermediaries in every category except perhaps investment trusts (which have their own association, the Association of Investment Trust Companies, but these nowadays account for only a small percentage of the market). The members of IFMA do much business for overseas clients, institutional and private.

The final point to consider is where these funds have been invested. Overwhelmingly, the institutions have liabilities which require returns which outstrip wage inflation over the long term—for occupational pension funds whose liabilities are denominated in terms of final salary, this is a key requirement. This has led to equities becoming the single largest asset class for the institutions.

This pattern of holdings has led to an immense concentration not just overall by institutions as a group, but within them even tighter control among the relatively small number of investment managers which invest the funds for them. Disclosure on this is a moot point. Although the law requires that holdings over 3 per cent should be disclosed, it is not clear how this applies to intermediaries who hold shares in a company for a range of clients. In aggregate the holding may greatly exceed 3 per cent, although no individual client has as much as that. It is increasingly common for fund managers to declare their holdings on behalf of clients as a disclosable stake.

The disclosed levels of control by investment managers are startlingly high. Here are some examples taken from recent published accounts. At Wassall the 45 largest shareholders held 59.7 per cent; of these Robert Fleming held 12.9 per cent, Gartmore 9.8 per cent, Schroder 4.3 per cent, Abu Dhabi 4 per cent. At British Vita the 90 largest shareholders held 71 per cent; of these Sun Life of Canada held 5.63 per cent, Norwich Union 4.29 per cent, and the Prudential 3.21 per cent. Recent Pearsons accounts showed that 43 shareholders had 54.4 per cent of the equity, and that included in that figure was the 8.69 per cent held by Lazard Frères and associates. Some companies had no disclosed holder with more than 3 per cent, for instance Redland and Coats Viyella, but the concentration was still marked. In the former case the top 100 held 54.4 per cent and in the latter 206 held 73 per cent.

Let us now return to the aggregate figures—pension funds, insurance companies, and the others. These convey an impression of where power might lie, but do not of themselves tell us where it does lie. This will depend in some cases on the arrangements made between the holders of title and the managers of the portfolio or the owners. Considering the simple issue of casting votes at company meetings, the situation can vary enormously between the institutions.

Insurance companies hold shares in their own name or nominee names and vote them (or not). Pension funds' arrangements vary. PIRC research on corporate governance policies indicates that the larger funds are more likely to have policies which require the investment managers to cast votes, report on their decisions, and work within a general policy agreed with the trustees (PIRC 1997*b*). Within the Statement of Investment Principles which is now required under the Pensions Act, trustees are increasingly incorporating reference to corporate governance, and making sure this is set down in the contract with the investment manager. PIRC has advised its clients to ensure they have detailed procedures agreed for voting according to agreed guidelines and special arrangements to accommodate exceptions. The National Association of Pension Funds has also written to all of its members stating that it is good practice to have a policy on the exercise of voting rights and that fund managers should have agreed procedures for handling this part of their brief. Both initiatives follow on from the Cadbury Committee which recommended that institutions exercise their voting rights and declare their policy to 'those with a legitimate interest'.

The growing tendency for pension fund trustees to assume responsibility for the exercise of shareholder power has caused some tension, with the traditional delegation preferred by the investment professionals. MAM wrote to its 440 pension fund clients in 1997 seeking formal delegation of authority over voting shares, and set out, in general terms, the basis upon which the votes would be cast. This was not approved by a number of clients, who in both general and specific cases insisted on retaining responsibility for the decision. This has meant that investment managers are having to establish separate nominee accounts for clients to allow for splitting their vote: for clients which have different views on the same resolution, and then for those funds where they have discretion. At the Shell 1997 AGM, the company provided shareholders with special proxy forms to allow fund managers to split their vote.

Investment managers, particularly those with USA parents (which have practical experience of both the policy and administrative aspects of corporate governance) have used as a marketing feature their ability to provide a comprehensive service for executing their clients' voting policy. Linked to this, particularly in the USA market, has been the growth of specialist consultancy services providing the research, advice, and interpretation of resolutions to assist both institutional fund managers and private investors in the exercise of their voting rights. A younger and less developed market in the UK for the same services is now developing with the two main trade associations, the Association of British Insurers and the National Association of Pension Funds, offering their members guidance over voting issues, new organizations such as the Local Authority Pension Funds Forum and consultants such as PIRC.

Unit trusts, although they employ fund managers and investment trusts, have generally been reticent on corporate governance issues, although there have been signs in recent years that some are prepared to play an active part—and to be quite public about it. M & G for example has a long history of maintaining an interest in the good governance of the companies in which it invests and it tends to take significant stakes and thus concentrate its attention. M & G decided recently to appoint a specialist manager to consider corporate governance issues, as has Hermes, the pension fund manager for the Post Office and BT pension funds, which appointed a corporate focus executive, following a bruising experience over the Granada bid for Forte. Other unit trust managers have also been active; notable among them is Fidelity which has shown an active interest and been prepared to be an advocate for change.

Stockbrokers are the usual resting place for the voting papers for private investors. The stockbroker has the technical right to vote as holder of record, but rarely does so. The beneficial owners seldom interfere (and might well be charged for their pains). There may be exceptions to the general stand-off, e.g. where a beneficial owner holds a large parcel of shares and there is a takeover bid. A more esoteric example of a 'black hole' is stock lending. Here it appears that the borrower has the right to vote, although he will ultimately have to return the borrowed stock, and despite the fact that the lender retains the rights to dividends. This can have consequences in the case of a takeover bid of which people outside the market may not be aware, either because the borrower may vote the stock, or because, if he does not, it will be voteless. The problems for private investors here have been exacerbated by Crest, and some companies have been trying to find ways of allowing private investors to retain their voting rights through in-house dealing services.

As proxy voting research confirms (PIRC 1997*a*), until recently there were too many instances where votes are not cast and relatively few occasions on which clients will go to the trouble of giving a specific instruction to the fund manager. Power hovers uncertainly between the two. It is all too easy to overlook the potent effects that arrangements made for purely administrative convenience may actually have on the real exercise of power. We earlier cited the example of Germany where shares are held in bearer form and must be deposited with an authorized body (usually a bank); the reasons for this are administrative efficiency and security. The result is de facto to confer great authority on the depositaries who have the voting rights to the shares subject to clients' express instructions. Client apathy or ignorance being what it is, the power is effectively transferred to the German banks. The issue of where responsibility lies for the exercise of voting rights is fundamental to the exercise of power. In the UK some of the major fund managers run the portfolio of hundreds of pension funds.

A major change is occurring quietly. At one time fund managers were inclined to argue that their concern for their clients was all-consuming and that they had no direct interest in the companies in which they invested other than to understand when it was in their clients' best interests to buy and sell. As their positions grew, they began to feel that it was in the interests of good portfolio management to have a thorough and comprehensive programme of contacts with companies. Such meetings inevitably provided an opportunity in the course of discussion for them to register their own views about the company's progress and policy, and for them to exert their influence when in their view a company was doing or not doing something they regarded as inimical to shareholders' interests. Of course the company listened but it might well in the end ignore what they said; it is after all the directors' responsibility to decide. The changing situation was clearly set out by MAM, who were quoted as saying, 'Historically we managed investment portfolios on a discretionary basis whilst most of our clients retained their voting rights attaching to shares.' It is still private meetings with companies which play the central role: voting to oppose is a last resort. 'Where we believe that shareholder value is threatened we will request that the board takes appropriate action. In most cases a robust and private dialogue is our preferred way to protect shareholder interests. If we meet intransigence we will either sell the shares to protect our clients' capital investment or we will publicly oppose management who refuse to act on our concerns,' says MAM. This general view was confirmed by a survey of corporate governance guidelines among the top 150 institutions in the UK (PIRC 1997*b*). Few stated that they would attend an AGM (and then only *in extremis*) and it was not clear how any stated view, for example, to support the Cadbury Code, would translate into voting activity (if at all).

However, if the institutions consider their main role is to pursue corporate governance through private dialogue, the difficulty here is that research indicates companies do not consider that their meetings with institutions are productive. Extel surveys carried out each year provide an insight into the meetings between companies and shareholders. All too often, according to the companies, the institutions are poorly briefed, have not agreed an agenda, do not field senior staff, and the meeting appears to have little purpose. Despite this, PIRC's research indicates that institutions place greater weight upon these meetings than they do upon attendance at the AGM or even on the exercise of voting rights on behalf of clients.

One of the clearest examples of the confusion about the role of voting in the PIRC study was in answer to the question: in what circumstances do you abstain? For some institutions this was the most serious indication of concern; for others it represented a state of equanimity, they were not voting because they were happy with the company's performance; others viewed it as a mild rebuke; and for others it was the first stage in a carefully considered programme of exerting pressure upon the company to effect change. In blunt practical terms of course, all an abstention does is to tilt the outcome towards the dominant vote in favour of any given course of action. The subtlety of the situation outlined in the survey must be lost on the companies, particularly in the many cases where the institutions have not even communicated their policies on this issue to the company concerned, and due to the uncertain legal status of an abstention, many companies do not even keep records of votes cast on this basis.

This detour into the complexity of a vote to abstain is simply to illustrate how tentative and uncertain the moves are in the direction of voting as a means of ensuring corporate accountability. The intermediaries to whom responsibility has been delegated for the exercise of power over the UK corporate boards are at best feeling their way between the traditional role of trading shares and the new demands from pension fund trustees (and the public) that votes be exercised. In the midst of this, some firms are developing impressive voting programmes. To bring in the majority the process needs to be addressed by reforms which clarify responsibilities and reporting to clients.

TO VOTE OR NOT?

The intermediaries have had a range of responses to the call for shareholder voting. The pressures for not voting, or when voting to offer automatic support for the board, are palpable. Any kind of voting means that someone has to fill in the voting form. If it is to be done by people who understand what they are doing, they must have considered the report and accounts in good time. To do this against the clock, with the care and attention it always deserves, is more than the present timetables permit and more than fund managers actually want. The institutions might indeed go further and contend that as voting has a cost, it should not be incurred unless there is a benefit. Some would argue anyway that as they have 'life and death' authority over a share without recourse, i.e. they can buy or sell as they choose, they should be left with the discretion over lesser matters, like votes on the chairman's pay or share options or the membership of the board. Failure to vote may have other explanations:

- Administrative error. There are instances where there was an intention to vote but failure to deliver by sheer administrative 'mishap'. One company secretary at a FTSE 100 company complained in private to the authors about the large number of votes which were posted too late to be cast by proxy at the meeting.
- Policy. There may be in place a de facto 'Sell rather than interfere' policy, and this is not uncommon in smaller funds. There may also be a covert policy about not voting on contentious issues, if there is a danger that there might be repercussions. Companies often dislike their own pension funds voting in ways that oppose or censure the management of other companies—it may be their turn tomorrow!
- Conflicts of interest. The conflicts of interest in financial conglomerates that have both a fund management and a corporate finance business can be severe. It is not unknown for instance for a company to complain bitterly to the corporate finance side if the fund managers sell some of its stock. To whom do such fund managers owe allegiance?

This goes some way to explaining why the overall levels of voting in the UK have moved only slowly since the Cadbury Report was published in 1992.

However, there is clearly a boom in the time and effort going into voting by those institutions which are taking it seriously, and even some high 'oppose' and 'abstain' votes. Much of this activity is client driven as pension funds have become more concerned about voting. Speaking at the NAPF conference in 1995, Graham Allen of ICI investment management said,

In essence . . . the policy [of ICI pension funds] covers two main areas: voting policy in respect of normal resolutions and share option schemes; and guidelines outlining the circumstances in which ICI investment management contacts the chairman of a company seeking an explanation of why his company does not meet 'best practice', thereby encouraging change. During 1994, we contacted over 30 company chairmen on such issues as the separation of the chairman/chief executive roles, the retirement of directors by rotation, directors over 70 years, insufficient non-executive directors, and the absence of formal board committees. Whilst one or two of the responses were disappointing, companies have in general reacted in a constructive manner.

There is still a long way to go. Surveys of registrars' returns show that only a small minority of companies have had a majority of their shares voted in recent years (PIRC 1997a). Votes in favour (including discretionaries) averaged over 98 per cent, with scores in the upper 80s and 90s for resolutions on most major issues including the election or re-election of directors, increases in share capital, the report and accounts, and the appointment of auditors. The least popular resolutions of those proposed by the board were those seeking authority to establish long-term incentive plans or share options, or to issue shares without pre-emption rights. Next in unpopularity was the approval of a donation to the Conservative Party. There were several special cases of high negative votes—where the resolution had been proposed by shareholders against the wishes of the board. There is some evidence of shareholder disquiet on directors having three-year rolling contracts (on three occasions the negative vote was more than 12 per cent). And an 82-year-old director had 8 per cent of the vote against him. These negative figures may sound small, but given the forces of inertia and acquiescence, they are not without significance.

Without reforms to clarify responsibilities and to require disclosure, the situation will only improve by fits and starts, when some steady progress is actually required.

14

The Legal Obligations of Institutional Shareholders

IN earlier chapters we have set out shareholders' rights and powers and discussed their general role. We now look at the duties of fiduciary investors. We have seen the dramatic shifts in the ownership of companies' shares in recent years, showing that the institutions now have a role in the equity markets which is dominant. Not only do they control nearly two-thirds of voting rights, in listed UK companies, but via the concentration of fund management business in the UK, as few as thirty or forty individual firms can control the voting decision on behalf of their clients at leading companies. This represents a profound concentration of control. In concluding that institutional shareholders have substantial power, this raises a number of questions centring on accountability and obligation. How might accountability be ensured? Are there are implicit or explicit obligations upon institutional shareholders which ought to determine their role?

Under statute shareholders owning fully paid shares have no obligations. The only requirement under the law is to disclose their identity to the company if they own more than 3 per cent of the shares. Even then, the nominee holder of the account will suffice. If the company wishes to establish their identity it may exercise its rights under sections 212 and 216 of the Companies Act 1985. Failure to disclose may eventually result in a penalty such as losing rights to transfer the shares or vote them or collect dividends.

Apart from this modest requirement to identify themselves, shareholders have no further obligation to the company. The exception is to comply with any Takeover Panel rules that apply. The law is designed to protect the position of the shareholder who has provided equity; not to consider that the substantial powers this confers on the shareholder confer any responsibility. The shareholders can even close down a company by winding it up, subject only to its making the necessary debt and redundancy payments and so forth. There is nothing in UK law, as there is in German law, of a duty to consider 'the company in society' other than a tepid reference in section 309 of the Companies Act to the directors' duties 'taking into account employees' interests'. Perhaps if the companies concerned were not significant in the economy, and shareholders were relatively small and private, this is a situation which would not particularly matter. As listed companies are vitally important to the common weal, and the largest group of shareholders represent the main part of the nation's savings, this situation is not acceptable.

FIDUCIARY RESPONSIBILITIES

As we have seen, most shares are now held by institutions on behalf of others. This puts them in a position of fiduciary responsibility—in other words, they owe obligations to those on whose behalf they invest. There may be a 'constructive trusteeship' in cases where trusts in a formal sense do not exist. There may be more than one class of beneficiary. This raises the question: do the general duties of fiduciaries include a responsibility to the companies in which they invest, which would imply the exercise of voting rights or other shareholders' powers to protect the investment?

Fiduciary obligations rest upon any investor in a position of trusteeship, be it formal via the legal establishment of a trust (such as a pension fund) or simply by holding assets on behalf of others (as with a bank holding someone's deposits). The principal duties of fiduciaries arise under trust law, and are regulated for some categories of trustee under specific legislation, such as the Pensions Act 1995. The general fiduciary obligations of a trustee (or someone in a position of trust) were set out by the Occupational Pension Board in a guide to the duties of trustees (OPB 1997). Beyond following the rules of the particular pension scheme in question and obeying the law, the general duties of trustees are 'To act prudently, conscientiously and honestly and with the utmost good faith; to act in the best interests of the beneficiaries and strike a fair balance between the interests of different classes of beneficiary.' In principle these duties apply to all analogous situations such as life funds, investment trusts (where the 'beneficiaries' are shareholders), and unit trusts (where the beneficiaries are the unit holders).

It must therefore follow that in regard to their position as shareholders, trustees and quasi-trustees must not do anything in regard to the companies in which they invest which would be to the detriment of their beneficiaries and —this next point is important—must take decisions with a reasonable time scale in mind. They are not obliged to take a short-term view, but must bear in mind the interests of different classes of beneficiaries. This means that future beneficiaries are part of their responsibility. For a pension fund trustee, this means considering the position of the oldest pensioner drawing an income from the fund and also the youngest new contributor who may not retire for forty years or more.

Trustees are not relieved of this obligation by delegating to professionals. Although they are bound to take expert advice, ultimate responsibility rests with them. The trustees must, however, retain responsibility to the greatest extent that is lawful, and in practice this normally means that they retain control over broad strategic decisions. They may take advice on asset allocation, such as the proportion of the total funds to be invested from time to time in UK ordinary shares, but they are responsible for the outcome. This does not mean that they must always be right, simply that they have demonstrated the utmost good faith, prudence, and care in their decision-making.

Trustees also have some specific obligations under statutes other than the Pensions Act. For example, the Financial Services Act requires there to be a formal agreement between the trustees and the investment manager, 'which will cover the division of responsibilities between the two parties.'

How far does the duty of care and prudence by fiduciaries extend? Could the beneficiaries take the view that in order to protect their investments, the trustees should ensure their fund managers monitor companies, vote their shareholders, and even have to take positive action if problems are looming? Or is it enough simply to buy and sell the shares in the traditional manner? Does the duty fiduciaries (and quasi-trustees) owe to the beneficiaries impose upon them an obligation to take action in regard to any company in which they are invested? If so, what and when? There is an emerging legal view that the answer to these questions is yes. If the fiduciary has the power and the opportunity to intervene either to protect the investment or to enhance it, then this should happen under their general duty of care and prudence.

In considering what this means in the specific case of corporate governance, it is worth reviewing how the role of trustees has developed over the years. Trustees were never assumed to have special knowledge or experience but to bring general duties of prudence and care to the task of investment, and seek advice from professionals when necessary. In some ways, the trustee system was not unlike the jury system where lay people have ultimate responsibility but are advised and petitioned by experts. There are professional trustees, of course, and if trustees have any relevant expertise they are expected to use it. In the very early days trustees would be set in charge of property, like land and buildings and livestock, assets of a kind with which they were familiar. Their choices of 'investment' were quite limited and they were circumscribed in what they could do.

It was assumed for many years that institutional shareholders, who stand in the position of trustees or quasi-trustees, could discharge their obligations to their clients by making sure the monies entrusted to them were kept safe and by investing them within the parameters the law permitted. In the course of the decisions they made on the choice of investments they were obliged by the law to exhibit the standards of prudence expected in people in their position. Subject to the limits imposed by statute or trust deed and rules, they had the power to choose between different categories of investment such as property, bonds, and (certain classes of) shares. If their personal knowledge was inadequate they were expected to get advice, for to act in ignorance would be deemed imprudent. They were expected to keep money or bond and share certificates safe and not let real property fall to bits.

The general assumption has been that although trustees were expected to see that buildings for which they were responsible did not fall down through sheer neglect, there was no corresponding duty in regard to companies in which they owned shares. There was no explicit obligation to monitor the performance of companies in which they were invested. If they became dissatisfied their remedy was to sell; they might argue that they had an obligation to do so. The assumption behind such a proposition was that all stock market decisions are matters of judgement and their dissatisfaction might be reasonable but in the end misplaced. It was therefore immaterial that with over 70 per cent of shares in institutional hands, a transaction generally shifted shares from one trust to another, i.e. from one set of beneficiaries to another. The transfer would change nothing in respect to the operation of the company itself: to be owned by the hopeful but inert is no more bracing than to be owned by the despairing. A better-informed institution could properly sell the shares in an ailing company. It threw into the market what rugby players call a 'hospital pass'. In the old days there was a fair chance it would go to private buyers.

Until quite recently the general view in the UK would have been that the trustees' duty to appoint professional managers to worry about such matters was quite enough; certainly the very slow and uncertain increase in voting shows that the institutions have not generally felt under any specific obligation to use their votes. The mood in the UK has gradually shifted in recent years. As the debate on corporate governance developed it became accepted in many quarters that the least that institutions should do was to use their votes. In its report, the Cadbury Committee (1992) reflected this tide of opinion when it endorsed the policy statement of the Institutional Shareholders Committee in favour of voting. Cadbury was positive: 'Voting rights may be viewed as an asset, the use of which is of legitimate interest to those on whose behalf the institutions invest.' The Hampel Committee endorsed this view.

There is a growing body of legal opinion which considers that institutional investors in the UK do have a responsibility under trust law to vote their shares. On this view exercising voting rights is considered a necessary part of exercising care and prudence in relation to investment in companies. Courts have begun to consider that the voting rights attached to a share can be considered an asset. Patrick Howell, a QC commenting on the impact of trust law on the voting responsibilities of shareholders, considers that their responsibility is wide-ranging:

Whether the often discussed problem of a low level of UK corporate investment in plant and in research and development is more related to the way financial markets operate or to the attitudes of corporate managers . . . whatever the reasons, if the effect is that certain investment areas in the UK are going to dwindle or cease to exist in the long run (think of major computer manufacturers, or motor manufacturing), then this is a topic of legitimate concern for UK pension fund trustees because as long term investors, their investment choices will become more restricted and they may have to take foreign exchange risks to invest in all the sectors they want. (1991)

He argues that the general duties of care, prudence, and equity (acting solely in the interests of the beneficiaries) apply here as with any other function. This view is that if shareholders have powers through which they may protect the beneficiaries' interests, then they should be used not ignored. Are the trustees relieved of their duties if they are in a minority position, as is the normal case? Howell considers that the duty to act collectively may arise in order to protect the beneficiaries:

Traditionally UK institutional shareholders have been reluctant to exert influence (either individually or collectively) on the management of companies in which they invest, but this may not remain so. Any ideal of stimulating corporate investment is likely to involve some long term commitment on the part of institutional shareholders to the companies involved; and the ability to intervene to prevent some action which is disadvantageous to the shareholders (say an excessive pay off to management) is bound to raise questions of when the responsibility to do so arises . . . trustees have a general duty to consider this exercise (of influence) from time to time. Where shares are held by nominees, this will include giving directions to the nominees on how the voting rights are to be exercised. (1991)

On this view, shareholders in exercising their voting rights must ensure that they are fulfilling their trust law duties. In practice, this means that those in a capacity of trustee must be able to demonstrate that their voting activity is prudent, carried out with care, and for the sole interests of the beneficiaries. This provides a clear benchmark against which to judge their policy on issues where there may be a conflict of interest between the directors of the company and the beneficiaries of the fund.

This view has been tested in court in a situation where the beneficiaries of a trust fund sued the trustees for allowing a company in which the trust fund held shares to go bankrupt. The action was successful, and Justice Brightman stated that:

the trustee was bound to act in relation to the shares and to the controlling position which they conferred, in the same manner as a prudent man of business. The prudent man of business will act in such a manner as is necessary to safeguard his investment.

He will do this in two ways. If facts come to his knowledge which tell him that the company's affairs are not being conducted as they should be, or which put him on enquiry, he will take appropriate action. Appropriate action will no doubt consist in the first instance of enquiry of and consultation with the directors, and in the last, but not unlikely resort, the convening of a general meeting to replace one or more directors.

What the prudent man of business will NOT do is content himself with the receipt of such information on the affairs of the company as a shareholder originally receives at annual general meetings. Since he has the power to do so, he will go further and see that he has sufficient information to enable him to make a responsible decision from time to time, either to let matters proceed as they are proceeding, or to intervene if he is dissatisfied. (*Bartlett* v. *Barclays Bank Trust Company Ltd.*, 1980, CD)

This case related to a situation where the trustee in question was a major shareholder in a private company, hence the absence of an option to 'exit' the situation by trading the shares in the market. To the extent that institutions have stakes which cannot be easily unloaded even in listed companies, the parallel with this situation is clear: the duty of care extends to maintaining the health of the company.

There are some institutional investors even today who would argue strenuously that they have neither the expertise nor means to ensure that companies are well run. For that reason, voting is a waste of time; it is costly; and they are ill equipped to do it. The last point is of great concern if it is true, for it is tantamount to admitting that they do not understand the businesses in which they are invested. The cost argument seems to us to be greatly exaggerated. Research, advice, and administration services are available from a growing range of providers. Costs no longer excuse, though it may mean getting streamlined procedures in place. The position is therefore changing, but some investors will still emphasize the cost of voting, whilst accepting the costs of seeing companies fail through lack of attention. Most of the time voting will be uncontroversial as shareholders will happily accede to the proposals put to them by effective and successful boards. We do not have a picture in our minds of hundreds of companies needing violent proxy battles at frequent intervals, but of a very few that do require attention to a degree, and very occasionally situations where mere voting on the management's proposals will not suffice. There is also a need for standards overall to rise through the diligent oversight of companies and voting plays a vital part in this. Before we leave voting we should add that mere 'wooden' voting is not enough. Trustees ought to have to demonstrate that votes are always cast; if they delegate this duty to managers, the latter ought to have clear instructions on when to refer back, be required to record what they have done, and be prepared to give reasons.

It is the fund managers not the trustees who are, and indeed should be, more aware of the position of any particular company. The trustees should empower the managers and indeed require them to take the appropriate action, referring back in the cases where the company's policy is out of step with the trustees' established guidelines. Faced with this, the trustees may instruct the manager to sell, but if they do it will probably only 'pass the parcel' to another institution, who will have to unwrap it.

Looking at a parallel from the political sphere, we can see that in a democratic state no voter can correctly argue *ex ante* that his or her vote will not count, whatever may be observed *ex post*. No trustees have the right to assume, just because the holding is small, that they are therefore without influence or power. That one may be the crucial vote that precipitates change. Besides, as noted above, selling invariably means a purchase by another trustee, so a problem is transferred, not extinguished.

If it could be shown that votes *in aggregate* were worthless or useless there would be no case in law for suggesting that there should be a duty in law to any person to exercise them. To do so would simply be a waste of money. As things stand, it is certain that the shareholders' powers are highly significant, and in relatively small combination they can be highly effective.

A DUTY TO VOTE?

With the establishment of a statutory framework for the administration of pensions, the possibility of regulation on voting for the largest group of institutional shareholders in the UK has become a reality. During its passage through the House of Lords, Lord Haskell for the Labour Party tabled a number of amendments to the Pensions Bill which would have introduced a duty for trustees to have regard to their voting rights and other shareholder powers in parallel with their other duties; they would also have been required to disclose their policy and ensure that their fund managers kept records which could be inspected by beneficiaries upon request. Lord Haskell argued in debate that this was an issue of central importance for competitiveness and public accountability and was wholly consistent with the principles of trust law which imposed a duty of care upon fiduciaries. He also pointed to the fact that US private sector pension funds holding shares in British companies had a duty to vote their shares, which was putting leverage onto the voting outcome; the apathy of UK investors meant that American pension funds could more readily determine the outcome.

The then Conservative government agreed with the basic arguments. Lord Mackay responded in debate that 'the government strongly believe that institutions should develop constructive, long-term relationships with the companies in which they invest. Regularly voting their shares can be an important part of that relationship.' He added that he accepted voting was 'consistent with the trustees' duties to act in the interests of the beneficiaries' and that such activity was 'crucial to our economic prosperity'.

However, government demurred at the prospect of legislating on the issue. 'There is a significant difference between encouraging best practice, which the government can encourage, and imposing specific or detailed obliga-tions on pension funds which risk being regulatory and burdensome.' Lord Haskell withdrew his amendments, in order to allow them to resurface in the debate on the Pensions Bill in the House of Commons, tabled in summary form by Donald Dewar for the opposition. The focus this time was on disclosure of policy and keeping records. A commitment to review this issue was made in the Labour Party's pre-election document on industrial policy. The role of shareholders has been included for review in the government's fresh look at company law, with President of the Board of Trade Margaret Beckett arguing in a speech to PIRC's 1998 annual conference that she wanted to see a 'step change' in voting and did not rule out mandatory action.

FOREIGN HOLDINGS

It is not just UK shareholders who are considering these issues. The statistics demonstrate the rapidly growing importance of shareholders based abroad. They now hold nearly as many shares as private UK shareholders. Many shares are held in the USA where proxy voting is a well-developed art form: there are competent and active 'proxy solicitors'. They are used to marshalling votes on contentious issues, and have even been prepared to go on the offensive in markets unaccustomed to shareholder activism, such as Japan. They have sought to tackle companies on the Continent of Europe where shareholder returns appeared to them to be inadequate for the sums invested, or shareholder rights are disregarded.

POWER AND INFLUENCE

There are few occasions when shareholders exercise power to change management, or to cause management against its will to alter course or drop proposals. They are given an opportunity to do both if a company seeks to raise more capital, but this is relatively infrequent. There are more occasions when shareholders exert influence and cause management to modify its plans or alter the composition of the board.

The capacity to exercise influence depends in the last resort on the potential to use power. A 0.5 per cent shareholder will obviously not carry the clout of a 10 per cent shareholder, irrespective of the relative merits of their positions. This is the reason why many institutions see their roles almost entirely in terms of influence, which can be exercised privately and informally. Influence is not power in a velvet glove; power remains power whatever the fabric of the gauntlet. Influence is a product of limited or perhaps potential power; and of ultimate timidity and a reticence to use power (which is why it often fails). If shareholders care about an issue enough to use influence, they ought in logic be prepared to exercise power.

We do not in all this envisage an apocalyptic scenario. Most of the time shareholders will wish to use their influence and power to support management. But sometimes—rarely—they will not. Should those who hold shares for others routinely seek to use what influence they possess?

The answer is, yes. Those who are not prepared to do so voluntarily should be required to do so by law.

THE US EXAMPLE

The debate on fiduciary responsibilities and voting has been informed by developments in the United States. The legal and regulatory framework made formal activity in some ways easier than in the UK, disclosure of information was greater, and shareholders could readily submit proposals for the agenda of a company meeting, without fear of costs or onerous hurdles.

Shareholder activism in the USA has its origins with the public sector, industry schemes, trade union pension fund activists, and charitable bodies. Initially many of the early shareholder resolutions addressed social or ethical questions, such as the role of companies in the Vietnam war, their activities in South Africa, and their employment policies at home.

A second wave of shareholder activism was triggered by the flood of take-overs and mergers in the early 1980s. Among other things this prompted the formation of the United Shareholders' Association which aimed to protect the interests of small shareholders. It targeted management proposals such as 'greenmail' or anti-takeover devices (the so-called poison pills) and over-generous remuneration packages.

The Council of Institutional Investors was formed by public sector and Taft Hartley funds in 1984 to represent the interests of institutional shareholders. It actively lobbied the Securities and Exchange Commission (SEC) to liberalize the rules on shareholder action, and also developed policies on shareholder voting for its members. Activist groups demonstrated the potential of voting on a wide range of issues, and as a consequence there has been an explosion in the number of shareholder proposals.

The Investor Responsibility Research Center reported that the number of shareholder proposals on corporate governance issues had increased from under 50 in 1985 to over 250 in 1994; and the number of proposals on social issues had increased from a handful to 100 in the same period. The US rules permit an individual investor to put forward a resolution, and to have it circulated by the company at the company's expense. Many of the resolutions were rigorously opposed by the management of the company concerned. There were allegations that some executives unduly influenced the voting behaviour of their own company's pension funds in order to squash shareholder resolutions which they regarded as threatening management's interests in other companies. This led to a regulatory initiative which has required private sector schemes to have a policy on voting which demonstrates that the exercise of rights is in the interests of the beneficiaries.

The DOL, which regulates private sector pension funds, took a close interest in the debate on shareholder activism and the role of trustees. In a speech to the United Shareholders' Association, the then assistant Secretary of Labor, David Walker, set out the Department's views:

With regard to proxy voting, there has been a major shift in the type of proposals being introduced for shareholder votes, many of which clearly may have an effect on the economic value of the stock. Proxy voting on issues which can affect the economic value of the stock represents the primary tool for shareholders in their efforts to assure corporate accountability (management and otherwise), and to maximise the value of their holdings. This is especially important for pension plans since plan fiduciaries are obligated, among other things, to seek to maximise the ultimate economic value of the plan's holdings consistent with a given level of risk and ERISA's other provisions. As a result of and in view of the increasing importance and changing nature of proxy votes and the rapid growth of private pension plan holdings in corporate equities, it is absolutely essential that plan fiduciaries understand and exercise their fiduciary duties under ERISA with regard to proxy voting.

He concluded that the Department took the issue extremely seriously, and stated that several investigations were under way. One of these resulted in a letter reinforcing the Department's position to the fund manager at Avon Products who had sought guidance on the issue from the Department of Labor. The response became known as the 'Avon letter' and set out the Department of Labor's formal position on proxy voting. The letter was made public and widely circulated. In it the DOL stated that: 'In general, the fiduciary act of managing plan assets which are shares of corporate stock would include the voting of proxies appurtenant to those shares of stock . . . [and] would require the investment manager or other responsible fiduciary to keep accurate records as to the voting of proxies.' The ruling caused a convulsion in the proxy voting arrangements of USA companies. It was grist to the mill of the new industry of consultants and shareholder advisory services. Prominent amongst these was Institutional Shareholder Services (ISS), established by Robert Monks, who left his position as a DOL executive to become an advocate for shareholder activism and a supplier of related services to institutional shareholders.

Since then, the DOL's policy has extended further. The commitment to ensuring that proxy votes are cast was forcefully summed up by the new secretary, David Ball, in an address in 1989:

Our position in a nutshell is:

that fiduciaries of employee benefit plans have a duty to manage plan assets solely in the interests of the participants and beneficiaries of the plans;

that the ability to vote proxies is a plan asset;

and that it would be a dereliction of duty if managers of plan assets did not vote, or voted without paying close attention to the implications of their vote for the ultimate value of the plan's holdings.

The DOL issued further advice on how the procedures governing proxy voting were to be set up, and established a programme of monitoring to ensure that the ruling was observed. The trustees must be able to demonstrate that when voting they are informed, acting independently of company management and solely in the interests of the beneficiaries. Pension funds are required to keep records of their voting activity which must be open to inspection by beneficiaries, so that they can demonstrate they meet the required standards.

As US overseas investment rose rapidly during the early 1990s, the question of voting overseas was raised. Shareholder activists in the USA and UK began to cooperate on proxy solicitations, and to provide detailed company reports in foreign markets. In 1995, the new secretary at the DOL, Olena Berg, ruled that the costs of proxy voting did not outweigh the potential gains over the long term. This meant that American pension funds were given a duty to vote their shares in foreign companies, a factor which may prove to be of increasing significance as US investors increase their overseas holdings.

The development of the DOL's policy over the years is by any standards highly significant, but it is still of limited scope. As we have already noted it covers only a fraction of US institutions—not for instance insurance companies or mutual funds. It does not cover public sector funds either but they have led the field encouraged by state and city mandates. More importantly, the quotations above seem to suggest that the trustees' duty ends with the casting of votes. There is a suggestion that there may be circumstances where more is required. It is simple to see the logic of this, though as we note below there are clearly practical considerations in expressing their obligations more broadly.

The second part of US activism is the prominent role taken by some leading public sector pension funds, who were not covered by the ERISA but felt that there was profit in activity—even in cases where their portfolios reflected precisely the composition of a given share index (index-matched funds) so that their holding of any single company was small.

When CalPERS first embarked on an active policy they conducted a noisy warfare against managements they considered to be underperforming. This produced results—but also hassle, and the Californian politicians were not always happy to see company executives prodded and goaded. CalPERS began to take a more subdued 'British' approach in which they spoke more quietly of their worries to the companies concerned. With this went a public 'sinners' list of companies thought to be underperforming. The CalPERS touch was electrifying—and share prices rose under the glare of their spotlight from a hope that it would wake the sleepiest management from its slumbers. There have been calculations made about the value to the CalPERS beneficiaries of their activist policy, and they are impressive—to the order of $180m. This figure has subsequently been said to be optimistic, but even so, there is no doubt that there has been a massive return on an annual outlay of $0.5m. This policy is conducted with their indexed portfolio which kept to a minimum the basic costs of investment. It sets to rest the 'free rider' argument for a large investor; even if the bulk of the benefits of CalPERS's actions went to others, there was enough benefit to them to make it worthwhile.

EVIDENCE ON PERFORMANCE

There is a growing body of research to indicate that in the USA shareholder activism pays. Voting is as we have seen a part of activism; it is not the whole. The market is thought to appreciate the benefits of action, because it produces a constructive reaction—and to some extent this is a self-fulfilling prophecy; if the market believes that action will provoke a response it will react accordingly. So action will pay (at least in the movement of share prices in the short term). Research is now exploring the link between a 'dynamic' board and corporate performance. The groundbreaking study by Millstein and MacAvoy (1998) is a case in point.

If something is thought to pay, the natural reaction in an entrepreneurial society like America is for others to try to make money out of it—and that is what has happened. Not only is the level of activity growing, but particular funds are being set up to exploit the possibilities inherent in putting a sharp pin into sleepy management. Monks's Lens Fund is a case in point. This is different from the kind of possibility long recognized by managers who set up 'recovery funds' which depended on someone else doing the job of spurring the company into action (and this did not always happen).

The amendments to the Pensions Bill proposed by the Labour Party were important because they did not simply refer to the exercise of voting rights, but to other powers that shareholders have by virtue of their position as equity owners. Voting by itself may in certain circumstances not be sufficient because a company is in a state in which a more positive stance is required. In the UK there have been few cases of shareholders taking positive action which produced a beneficial effect on the company. The changes in management at Rank in the 1980s and Tace in the 1990s precipitated by the shareholders illustrated how heavily a company's future success depends on the competence of its executive management and the board. The institutions' inability to tackle big companies like GEC and Lonrho showed how difficult it can be to effect change when faced with a dominant chairman or chief executive. All too rarely disappointment with the performance of a company results in a long period of Waiting for Godot (in the form of a takeover bid) or quietly selling shares. More recently the ousting of the executive chairman at United Utilities, following his sacking of two chief executives in quick succession, shows that action is possible if led by a tenacious non-executive team (in this case, by a director of an institution in its own right, Barclays Bank, whose fund management wing, BGI, has developed an active corporate governance programme).

Shareholders through the exercise of their voting rights have the opportunity to endorse or reject candidates for the board or to remove directors who are considered inadequate, so as to improve corporate performance. This is precisely the action shareholders took in these cases, and they reaped the benefits in due course. It is not necessary however to consider such activism in a negative light, i.e. as remedial.

There are two sides to the equation. So far we have spoken of improving corporate performance; the other side is not letting it deteriorate, by controlling risk. Shareholders have a legitimate interest in the risks being run with their money. Ensuring that there are checks and balances on the board and accurate financial reporting are essential elements in risk management. The trail of corporate collapses from Polly Peck and Maxwell to Queens Moat has shown the risk which companies run if executive power is untrammelled or incipient or problems are concealed, or both, through the absence or inadequacy of internal checks. Monitoring is an essential element in risk management, and activism covers the range of options open to shareholders to protect their interests. Activism should not generally be negative. It also means the positive endorsement of the present leaders of the company who are running it competently.

If trustees are to ensure that their fund managers are tackling these issues then they need to see that a policy is developed which establishes that voting rights and other powers are to be exercised in the interests of the beneficiaries. Furthermore, guidelines setting out standards of good practice need to be agreed, so that the fund managers are instructed in following a clear and consistent set of principles. This is a vital safeguard to any conflicts of interest which may arise for managers, and provides a framework within which they can best represent their clients' interests. It is also important where the scheme has more than one fund manager—it is not unknown for fund managers with shares in the same company held through two parts of the portfolio to vote in opposite directions, effectively cancelling out the pension fund's impact. A regular reporting system also should be adopted in which the fund manager informs trustees of action (both voting and otherwise) which has been taken on their behalf. As there will be sensitive circumstances at times, arrangements will need to be made to allow for consultation under delegated arrangements, so that if the fund manager needs to come back on a particular issue which falls outside the guidelines agreed, then a procedure is in place to allow this.

With or without a formal policy, trustees will have to weigh up what instructions to give their fund managers about the few difficult cases they face each year. The better their fund managers are the fewer such decisions there will be. What to do must be a matter of judgement reflecting the size of their holdings, the size of the company, the gravity and urgency of the situation, whether others have already shown a similar concern or might do so, and what courses of action are open. Sometimes a letter, a call, or a meeting might be valuable; on other occasions tougher measures may be essential, perhaps in concert with others. At the end of the day the fund managers should be able to face the trustees and say in all honesty that they have done privately or publicly, directly or indirectly, what was reasonable to keep their property in repair. If they wash their hands of the whole affair by selling as is their right, the purchaser, if another institutional fund manager, will have exactly the same question to answer. Only the private holders can ignore the question; as things stand it is their privilege to throw their money away if they choose.

Let us assume that the courts support—or even that there is legislation to support—the general thesis suggested above that trustees who buy equity shares must not turn a blind eye to poor stewardship of the companies in which they are invested. What are the practical consequences? What should they do? How far is too far, or not far enough? Quite properly trustees seldom decide themselves what to buy or sell; this is what they employ managers to do. Inside big firms of fund managers, there will be many dealing in the same shares. Some firms are running funds for themselves alongside funds for others.

The trustee in the days of low inflation and defined contribution pensions could sleep easily without worrying about the safety of US or UK government securities, whatever party was in power. The combination of inflation and defined benefit pension schemes produced a quite different set of circumstances and resulted in the switch to equities, thus causing a change in the nature of fund assets the full implications of which are only now being recognized.

The institutions, as so many of them realize, have to come to terms with a new world, which they inexorably dominate. Many of the old assumptions about trading are no longer valid. The bundle of assets they buy, when they purchase shares, is largely composed of people on whose effective functioning the whole edifice of a modern economy depends. The stock market sends signals which indicate—by the balance between buyers and sellers—what it makes of it, all things considered. But as every transaction needs two parties (presumably informed), with diametrically opposite views, present or potential shareholders must make their own minds up on the basis of the best available evidence before they buy, and check that evidence whenever they have the chance to express an opinion (voting) or at other times and in other ways when the evidence requires it (meetings—general meetings—resolutions—joint action). Not to check that evidence is a dereliction of duty: not to act on it, if necessary in concert with others, does everyone a disservice, not least, in the long run, their own beneficiaries.

Potential benefit exists. It cannot, we suggest, be seriously argued that trustees are entitled to neglect it. We contend that the US DOL is correct in its policy as are the instructions that flow from it as far as they go; but that there is no logic in defining the trustees' responsibilities in all circumstances as simply to respond by voting on management's proposals or nominees. That is a bare minimum. Trustees may be vulnerable to suit *now* in the UK if they neglect to do their duty. Only the legal system protects them because it is so costly to sue.

As to prescribing precisely how trustees and fund managers should act in any particular circumstances, that is for them to exercise judgement; what we are saying is that the role of guardian requires that judgement be diligently made and ensuing action taken commensurate with cost and potential benefit. The law should clarify responsibilities and ensure transparency.

Today's trustees have great responsibility, and will need to be better trained to face it and will have to give more time to it. Training should be a requirement (rather than an option as at present) and some form of accreditation should be introduced.

Trustees, in order to discharge their duties effectively, now need more knowledge than ever before, and this means constantly refreshing and supplementing what they already know. Furthermore their task requires adequate time to be devoted to it. Some trustees may be able to carry out their task in normal working hours for which they are already fully remunerated. In all other cases we feel that they should be remunerated for the onerous responsibilities they bear, and to ensure professional and competent judgement. It is no longer a game for amateurs, however well-meaning.

15

Investment Strategy and Governance

AGAINST the background of existing or developing obligations and the conclusion that many shares are under the effective control of a relatively small group of fund managers, the next question to be asked is what strategies are open to them. If they are in-house, what strategy can they sell to their own management/board? If they are professional fund managers what strategy can they sell to the trustees to whom they look for business or to the consultants advising them? Remember, we are talking only of the proportion of assets dedicated to the equity market, after the asset allocation decisions have been taken in regard to competing opportunities especially in bonds and real estate.

We can identify three main types of strategy which have an impact on corporate governance, though the borderline between the first two is not clear cut: let us look at them briefly in outline.

STRATEGY A: ACTIVE INVESTING

Active investors believe that they can achieve a result above average by picking stock carefully and timing market operations accurately. They tend to want to reduce risk by buying a long list of shares. They are very sensitive to shorter-term market movements and often plan to take full advantage of annual variances, despite the trading costs. Their contacts with companies and intermediaries will be focused on the shorter term. What a company actually does is of secondary importance. They see life through a mirror, i.e. what concerns them is not reality but the market's interpretation of reality.

STRATEGY B: VALUE INVESTING

The principal characteristics of value investing are concentration and depth. Such operators do not enter the market without very careful research, and their holdings are fewer and bigger than A's in proportion to the funds under management. They have far less inclination to trade, except at the margin perhaps, to change the weighting in the portfolio. There is little short-term trading activity. They pay much more attention to monitoring and establish good contacts with their companies.

Such operators sometimes earmark a small part of their funds for special operations, such as venture capital; but again their search is for value based on intrinsic worth and not for profits from the oscillations of the stock market.

STRATEGY C: INDEXATION (TRACKER FUNDS, PASSIVE INVESTMENT)

If the fund decides that A is too risky and B too difficult, or that outperformance cannot be guaranteed and the costs are steep, the answer for it is to buy a slice of the market via a given index, weighting its holdings to reflect, say, the FTSE 100. This means it is locked in to any poorly performing companies that happen to be in the index as well as the best, but it also means it never misses a good company or a takeover premium. This is by far the cheapest strategy to pursue and it keeps the fund up with performance at market levels. In most years such funds will come quite well up the table of comparative fund performance. (Most As will be worse than the index, but then it is of course impossible for everyone to beat the index.) The *Investors' Chronicle* of 13 September 1996 (p. 10) concludes an article on tracker funds thus: 'A random glance at the latest Micropal figures for general UK trusts for example, has three tracker funds among the top ten performers and the leading tracker fund a close second.'

SIZE AND STRATEGY

The size of a fund has relevance in several ways:

1. The bigger it is, the more worthwhile it is to consider the option of managing it in-house.
2. In contrast, the smaller it is, the more likely it is to engage external fund managers.
3. For smaller funds Strategy B would call for more research than they can generally muster.
4. Strategy C is an option for funds of all sizes.
5. A fund can, and many bigger funds do, go for a mix of strategies, e.g. indexing part but not all of the portfolio.

6. The larger the fund the longer the list of shares it must purchase if it wants to avoid acquiring significant stakes in companies (other than the very biggest). For this reason the list is often far longer than would be warranted by the need to diversify *per se*.

7. Some companies are so important that they tend to become 'core holdings' in the portfolio of big funds pursuing an A policy. These funds may buy and sell at the margin to adjust the weighting of the portfolio, but will rarely sell out (and then probably quite slowly so as not to disturb the market).

8. Only the bigger funds can afford comprehensive research and contact programmes. So if in principle they have opted for an A policy, they have the option of using their resources to inform their decisions better *ex ante* and *ex post* on investment decision. So, in practice, what started as an A policy shifts imperceptibly towards a B policy.

We will now look at the implications for corporate governance.

ACTIVE INVESTING AND GOVERNANCE

Active investing is so difficult that in any given year it is unlikely that many will succeed in producing better returns than the indexers—and they will have much higher costs. One of the reasons they find life so difficult is that they probably over-diversify—they buy shares in too many different companies. Obviously they must not put all their eggs in one basket—prudence demands that risk be spread. But there can be too much of a good thing. In terms of diversification there is very little advantage in buying more than thirty or so different shares. (At that level no share would account for more than about 3 per cent of the total.)

Very big funds generally want shares in more than thirty companies simply because they would otherwise hold too much of a company (unless it were very large too). Even so, the point is valid. Every time a fund adds another company to its portfolio it imposes upon itself an extra burden. They know all this, so why pursue such a policy? The answer is safety, or risk aversion. If enough different shares are bought, little damage can be done by the poorer ones and little compensating good can be done by the better ones. This is why it is so easy for an actively managed fund to lag the index; it does not take many poor selections to produce such an effect. The additional dimension is trading. The bigger the position, other than in the biggest companies, the more difficult it is to liquidate it quickly. So, by having a relatively small position in a great many companies, funds think they can trade out of trouble.

What does 'active investing' actually mean in terms of the levels of activity? Some figures for UK equities are shown in Table 7 (the formula is set out in

Table 7. Churning or investing?

	1970	1975	1980	1985	1990	1995
	Mean value of the sector[a]					
Activity	11	25	14	18	37	21
Turnover	28	72	39	41	80	45

Notes: Activity = the lesser of purchases or sales divided by the mean value of
      holdings in the sector.
Turnover = *purchases + sales.*
[a] i.e. it equals (activity) + net investment/disinvestment out of the sector expressed
   as a proportion of the mean value of the funds' holdings in the sector.
Source: UBS Asset Management (1997).

the table). Recent trends suggest that the level of activity has evened out.
Bearing in mind that the financial obligations of pension funds are long
term, and can be actuarially predicted, the levels of activity and turnover
shown in the table seem high.

In his book *What's Wrong with Wall Street?* (1988: 49 f.), Professor Louis
Lowenstein rehearses the principles of efficient market theory—'that competition among sophisticated investors enables the stock market to price stocks
consistently in accordance with our best expectation of companies. Long-
term earnings—or dividends.' And he supports his sympathy for this criticism by a series of telling arguments and a graph of the share price of
General Foods Corporation for a thirty-four-year period demonstrating
that the price fluctuations reflected a great many other things than expectations on earnings. Of course the market is efficient in certain ways—shareholders can buy or sell quickly and easily and get paid promptly, without
having to pay expensive commissions (contrast the costs of dealing in property). In fact what a price tells us is where the balance between buyers and
sellers is struck at any given time—each of whom must have had a valid
reason for wanting to be on one side of the transaction. Everything we know
about market 'experts' confirms that they are ordinary people trying to make
sense of a mass of conflicting data and that they are often wrong: if they were
always right and knew they would be, they would all retire as millionaires
very young.

The use of charts proves the point. Charts are simply a graphical representation of the past movements in a share price. 'Chartists' have been able,
they say, to identify patterns which help predict future movements and they
have developed sophisticated analyses to assist them in their crystal ball
gazing. But charts are by definition about the market's interpretation of
'facts'. Stock prices are, as Lowenstein says, nothing more than a mirror.

To condemn oneself to look at the world through that mirror is to live like the Lady of Shalot.

VALUE INVESTING AND GOVERNANCE

The second policy—value investing—is attuned to trying to discover reality about particular companies on a company-by-company basis. It implies in-depth analysis of the company and its markets (its 'franchise' as some would put it), and a careful assessment of its people. The policy was described famously by Graham and Dodd (1934) and, coming from a different angle, J.M. Keynes (1936). Graham and Dodd (Lowenstein 1988) 'had faith in capital markets over time, coupled with realism about human fallibility in the short run'—'the market is not a WEIGHING machine . . . [but rather] a VOTING MACHINE. Whereon countless individuals register choices which are partly the product of reason and partly of emotion.'

The Graham and Dodd approach—selectivity and careful analysis of fundamentals—was respected then as now, but not always followed. Perhaps it is, as Lowenstein suggests, just too painstaking or boring. It needs patience. Besides, in the short term the share price of the companies chosen may not flourish as well as others and professional managers may find themselves way down the league tables. It would be no consolation to them to calculate in five years' time that their painstaking choice would have outperformed all others, if in the meantime they have been replaced. Graham and Dodd also anticipated the theme of this book by sixty years: they could see no sense in funds making careful purchase decisions and then failing to monitor the business into which they had bought.

Value investing has never been popular but some have done brilliantly well by sticking to it. Its most notable practitioner is Warren Buffet's Berkshire Hathaway fund, which has made fortunes for all who had the wit to invest early in it. Buffet's guide to stock selecting, according to Roger Lowenstein (1995: 325), is: 'Pay no attention to macroeconomic trends or forecasts, or to people's predictions about the future course of stock prices. Focus on long-term business value—on the size of the coupons down the road. Stick to stocks within one's circle of competence. For Buffet, that was often a company with a consumer franchise. Both the general rule was true for all: if you didn't understand the business—be it a newspaper or a software firm—you couldn't value the stock.'

Buffet advises, 'Look for managers who treated the shareholders' capital with ownerlike care and thoughtfulness.' Also 'Study prospects—and their competitors—in great detail. Look at raw data, not analysts' summaries.' Trust your own eyes. But one needn't value a business too precisely. A basketball coach doesn't check to see if a prospect is six foot one or six foot two; he looks for seven footers. The vast majority of stocks would not be compelling either way—so ignore them.' Merrill Lynch had an opinion on every stock; Buffet did not. But when an investor had conviction about a stock, he or she should also 'show courage—and buy a *ton* of it.'

What the value-investing, portfolio-concentrating investor will seek is to get close to a company—not to obtain short-term price-sensitive information, as their substantial holdings may stop them being market traders, but so as to understand it better and evaluate its engine room. Their relationship will begin with sympathetic and constructive dialogue—from which any sensible company will derive much benefit. A good shareholder will, as one CEO put it, 'hold a mirror up to the company'. The company may not like what it sees, but the vision will be a great improvement on ignorance or myopia. Such conversations may be quiet and private, or at times in the glare of publicity, but they will be two-way. They will provide the opportunity for the company to solicit support, as well as for the shareholder to explain why that, and sympathy, may be in short supply.

But for a conversation of this kind to have real value to it means respect for each other. This is another reason why the problem of over-diversification is so important. If an investor has a big holding it will be worthwhile to field an experienced representative and the company will likewise feel it essential to present a senior officer, maybe the CEO himself or the finance director. It goes without saying that in such circumstances intermediaries are superfluous; indeed, it is probably wrong for them even to attend such meetings as their interests are so different from those of the other two parties.

VALUE INVESTING WITH A NEW DIMENSION

There are now funds, especially in the USA and now the UK, like Lens, established by veteran shareholder activists Bob Monks and Nell Minow, which buys in precisely to precipitate improvement by exercising investor influence to improve performance. A similar approach is taken by the Active Value Fund in the UK, which has pursued a range of bruising encounters with companies that have underperformed. This is inevitably a confrontational strategy and will be costly in terms of effort and emotion. Provided the shareholder has adequate resources, and sufficient staying power, and is skilled enough in both diagnosis and remedy, it may be a highly profitable adventure. The more pedestrian approach is to vote critically and on an informed basis as a matter of routine, and to pursue specific courses of action formally only when private dialogue has failed, which is the strategy developed by PIRC on behalf of its pension fund clients.

What we are describing has been called relational or relationship investing, implying as it does continuity and commitment between users and suppliers of capital. Its value to both parties lies in the maintenance of standards it implies: it makes it more difficult for management to be complacent about its own shortcomings, and, just as important, less reticent to take risks. One of the sources of strength in bank-based systems is the knowledge the lender has that he and sometimes she can exert influence when necessary. That system is itself under pressure to reform. A shareholder, however big, cannot be in precisely the same position (unless there is a rights issue in prospect), but the point about influence is valid nevertheless. If one knows one can exert influence when necessary there is less reason to be reticent about risk.

There is little danger of such relationships degenerating into cosiness as the pressures on both parties are too great, and the possibility of a shareholder becoming dissatisfied is always real. When this happens the relationship tautens, especially when the point approaches at which possible board changes come into focus. It is more than possible that there will be flat disagreement, and no certainty that the shareholder will be right. The industrialist will start from the point that any institutional fund manager, be he or she ever so powerful, knows very little about running companies. The same manager may be perfectly mindful of his or her limitations, but nevertheless feel strongly that the evidence points to the inadequacies of the company's direction and management. This will doubtless cause tensions, but far better sooner than later.

Dialogues of the kind described already take place in the UK between some institutions and some companies. For most, though, the holdings are too fragmented to warrant the investment of time and resources, or the holding is passive, and therefore no research is done, decisions are simply made to buy and sell in order that the portfolio will replicate an aspect of the market's composition. What we argue is that they would be of better quality were individual shareholdings fewer and bigger and that it would then be less open to companies to ignore what is being said to them, as they now sometimes do, in the knowledge that the shareholder, although quite well informed, in the end does not know enough to press the point. The alternative is to band together to exert influence, in the way that bodies like the Council of Institutional Investors and PIRC clients have done.

The kind of relationship envisaged makes a shift away from speculation towards investment, and away from short-term trading considerations towards medium- and long-term growth. Of course an investor wants to enter the market at a good moment whether the initial intention is to be there for a week or a decade, but having done so the relationship investor has other things in his mind beside the day-to-day performance of the stock price. But spare a moment of sympathy here for the fund manager being judged by short-term criteria. Even the least sensitive CEO now realizes the incompatibility of his (rarely her) attitude towards his pension fund managers (look at last quarter's league tables!), and towards his own shareholders, who are usually someone else's fund managers.

INDEXATION AND GOVERNANCE

The development of indexation owes much to the growing sophistication of information technology. Index funds are cheap to run but from the point of view of the fund manager intensely boring. Perhaps this is why in the UK indexed managers are prominent among the converts to corporate governance. An alternative explanation is that they have realized the validity of the adage 'If you can't sell you must care'. With their 'exit' blocked, they turn to 'voice'. It is inherent in indexed funds that one has shares in underperforming companies as well as the stars, so action is rational to improve performance.

SELECTING A STRATEGY

Shareholders have before them a wide range of investment strategies. How do they choose? O'Barr and Conley (1992), in a series of in-depth interviews, set out to discover the answer to the question. They concluded it was *not* a rational decision made after careful consideration of the comparative merits of the alternatives on purely economic grounds. They comment,

The evidence we have gathered at nine of the country's largest pension funds suggests that institutional investment decisions are fundamentally indistinguishable from the everyday kinds of decisions made in the most ordinary of social contexts. The trappings of rigorous financial analysis are all around: pension executives' desks are cluttered with reports, strategic options are dissected by committee after committee, outside money managers hawk their services with charts and graphs. But these are not the things that the executives choose to talk about when they analyze how and why they make their decisions. Instead, they gravitate toward such themes as responsibility and blame, the influence of the past, both real and mythic, and an over-riding concern with managing personal relationships.

PORTFOLIO POLICY AND CORPORATE GOVERNANCE

The reason why the style of portfolio management is central to corporate governance is simply that certain types of investment strategy are at variance with any notions of responsible ownership. If at the extreme (and there may not be many funds that would admit to such a policy save in their frankest moments) a fund is solely concerned with short-term price movements and playing the market, it is likely that the skills of the people it employs will be aimed precisely at making the best of that, and it would be unsuitable to delve deeply into the subtler points about the company's place in the market and its medium-term prospects of enhancing it. Investment is not and never will be simply a matter of 'number-crunching', but also of making difficult judgements about people and their capacity to make or seize opportunities, given the 'franchise' their company has created. To make that assessment calls for skills of a quite different order.

THE INTERMEDIARIES

Here we must pause to consider the role of certain intermediaries and in this we identify three main groups: 'sell-side' analysts; 'buy-side' analysts; and consultants.

'Sell-side' Analysts

The 'sell-side' analysts are those employed by intermediaries such as stock-brokers. They tend to organize meetings with company management attended by a group of their clients. They issue assessments which conclude with a recommendation to 'buy', 'sell', or 'hold' the company's shares. Their livelihoods depend on their generating business. If everyone 'held', there would not be much of it. Their firms may act as principal as well as agent; strictly speaking they are barred from front running, or using their recommendations to further their own positions. These analysts are powerful. Companies may not make forecasts (except in the context of a takeover), but analysts can and do both on results and on the level of dividend. These forecasts form the basis of 'market expectations' which no board ever wants to disappoint. Boards therefore strain to satisfy them, sometimes paying out bigger dividends than they would otherwise choose or employing a little accounting elasticity (there is always scope for some). If they fail to do so they are forced to surprise the market (which it hates) or else say something (the importance of which the market often exaggerates). There is a third choice—to tip the wink to the analysts.

  In general the sell-side analysts are not a pressure force for good governance, about which they care little. Boring companies are anathema—the kind that turn in steady unspectacular improvements year after year—though they have to recommend them periodically, especially when the more volatile are in a downturn.

Pension Fund Consultants

The pension fund consultants also have considerable power. Trustees use them to advise on the performance of the fund managers they employ. They do not shy away from recommending change. Their fees do not depend on their suggesting change, but look better value if they do. It may be argued that the pressure on performance that trustees want is all to the good. Certainly some measure of performance over time on fund managers is as reasonable as pressures on others. The UBS survey (1997) assures us that although measurement is taken quarterly, it is rare for a manager to be hired or fired 'without careful scrutiny of at least a three year performance record'.

When a fund manager is replaced his or her successor will invariably switch the portfolio around. What we would like to see measured are:

(1) The cost in fees of consultants' advice + the dealing costs of the changes in portfolio that follow a change of manager;
(2) An *ex post* valuation of the new portfolio against the one it replaced, say two years after the event.

As has often been remarked, the pressures for good short-term performance often come from company directors doing double duty as fund trustees. They have the company's residual obligations in mind (it will have to top up a fund with a shortfall, but can obtain a contributions 'holiday' if it has a surplus). These same people will be first to complain when analysts castigate them for their own company's listless half-year figures, accusing them of taking a longer-term view!

'Buy-side' Analysts

The 'buy-side' analysts working directly for the great institutions are a different kettle of fish. They are not out to promote turnover but to track performance and gauge the potential of existing or possible investments. They are focused on a different time scale. Their employers will conduct regular meetings with a company at various levels (depending on the relative importance of both). There will be a flow of information and opportunities for feedback. A company will often draw great comfort from their support and may on occasions make them insiders on some particular project. The question is often put in these terms, namely, 'Are you willing to be made an insider?' Sometimes an institution will accept, sometimes not.

THE SHIFT TOWARDS OWNERSHIP

Recent surveys suggest that about two-thirds of institutional investors do (or say they do) take corporate governance standards into account when making decisions to invest or disinvest (PIRC 1997*b*; Extel 1997). As a subject, however, it is still pretty low on the agenda for the programme of regular contacts with companies that major institutions now have in place and which puts them in a position to exercise considerable influence. If this is of a corrective nature—say the board looks thin in independent directors, or the succession looks particularly insecure—this may be rebuffed. The directors, not the institutions, are responsible for running the business and must therefore have the last word. What the institution then does will depend on how strongly it feels, how important the issue is, and how tough the management turns out to be. As much as possible will be resolved in private. The institution would prefer to avoid public conflict because:

- it would not want to tip off its 'competitors' by making its concerns public;
- news of its disquiet could adversely affect the share price;
- it dislikes publicity—it is not its style;
- it is costly in top management time;
- if it is to win it will need allies and it is reluctant to court 'competitors';
- it is reluctant to unsettle the market as it may reduce its own scope for manœuvre;
- it does not want a reputation for aggressiveness;
- it may have internal conflicts of interest if it is part of a group that includes corporate finance;
- the risk of failure may be high and outcome uncertain.

It is quite impossible to gauge accurately how effective and useful an institutional shareholder's influence is. To do this would require an analysis of how much management had been deflected from or indeed encouraged on a course on which it was doubtful. The mere fact that meetings occur regularly may of itself induce a degree of self-discipline that makes the exercise of influence—let alone power—quite unnecessary. Managements do say 'Our shareholders would never wear that'—and employ expensive advisers to tell them whether they are likely to do so. Good business opportunities might be missed if the relationships with shareholders induced excessive caution, but our experience is that shareholders who trust what a management tells them will go along with its risk taking provided it appears soundly based and that the quality of the management's judgement is perceived to warrant it. All the parties believe that such meetings add value, as they would not otherwise take such trouble to attend them, often at a very senior level. The challenge is to bring corporate governance higher up the agenda to ensure it is fully integrated into routine meetings.

The Institutions: Combined Action

INSTITUTIONAL shareholders in the UK have a variety of trade associations to represent their interests: among the longest established are:

the National Association of Pension Funds (NAPF);
the Association of British Insurers (ABI);
the Association of Unit Trusts and Investment Funds (AUTIF);
the Association of Investment Trust Companies (AITC);
the Institutional Fund Managers' Association (IFMA).

Subcommittees of the main trade associations, variously called investment committees, investment protection committees, or case committees, were set up (in some cases many years ago—the ABI's in 1933 and the NAPF's in 1963) to issue general guidance but also to handle particular issues.

Those who have been concerned with the running of trade associations know that it is a difficult task calling for great tact and diplomacy as well as firmness—because of the need to reconcile leadership with the representation of the differing views of a wide range of members of disparate size. Getting consensus may be difficult and time consuming.

It is therefore no surprise to find these particular associations more adept at dealing with general issues than particular cases. General issues can usually be taken at a more leisurely pace, so that there is time to reconcile divergent internal views; more of the membership (if not all of it) will feel themselves involved. By contrast, cases which involve particular companies may only be of interest to a handful of members. The issues may be far more intense and contentious: handling them will generally require urgency—and discretion.

The kinds of general issue that the institutions dealt with—and in some cases continue to handle—are:

• The gradual elimination of non-voting shares, which have virtually disappeared among new issues. The way this was handled, incidentally, saved the Stock Exchange from the awkward spot in which its New York counterpart found itself. The NYSE had ruled against companies issuing more than one class of common stock, but was then faced with a company that intended doing so and threatened to take its quotation elsewhere. That is the trouble with delisting as a weapon; it hits the wrong target—shareholders. The wrong people are penalized and the Stock Exchange itself loses revenue.

- Pre-emption rights. The principle is that if a company wishes to raise new capital it should first approach existing shareholders so that their proportion of the outstanding equity is not reduced (dilution). The institutions have fought to preserve pre-emption rights not only to prevent dilution, but also because many of them get a cut of the profits of raising the new money. Rights issues as they are called are cumbersome and may be relatively expensive. Some companies can raise money more cheaply by other means, e.g. a placing, in which shares are issued directly to purchasers, generally institutions. An accommodation has been reached in which companies can raise a limited amount of equity capital without having a rights issue and the institutions have published guidelines on the limits—currently not more than 5 per cent of issued ordinary share capital. A third reason for the institutions' wish to preserve pre-emption rights is to exercise some control over management, through the purse strings, so that management that needs new money must listen.

There is a wide range of areas of general interest in which the institutions have formulated policy, sought changes, or imposed rules (including the two above). The process by which the standards have arisen is opaque, and there has been sharp criticism of some elements as reflecting outmoded attitudes. In some cases their ideas have been adopted by other bodies such as the Cadbury Committee or have culminated in guidance (as in corporate treasury policy). Some contributed to changes in legislation (e.g. insider trading), or listing rules, whereas others went into areas which might reasonably have been the subject of legislation, and some have been largely ignored by companies (such as guidance on R & D expenditure). The associations have produced statements on a wide range of issues. The list includes guidance on the following (Stapledon 1996):

pre-emption rights;
non-voting shares;
enhanced scrip dividends;
major transactions/acquisitions;
own share purchases;
management buyouts;
pre-bid takeover defences;
equality of treatment on takeovers;
disclosure of financial information;
corporate treasury policy;
disclosure of R & D expenditure;
disclosure of non-audit relationship with auditors;

rotation of audit partners;
insider dealing;
election and removal of directors;
board composition and structure;
executive remuneration and service contracts;
regulations affecting general meetings.

A further level of coordination between the trade associations was established with the formation of the Institutional Shareholders' Committee
which was set up at the instance of the Bank of England in 1973, under
prompting from the then Prime Minister. The ISC has provided a forum
for the various constituent bodies to discuss matters of common interest,
and from time to time to make policy statements on particular topics. The
original idea was that ISC should itself monitor individual companies, but its
machinery was too cumbersome and it cut across too many other interests
for many to want to make it work better—so it failed to do so despite the
efforts of various people over the years.

To some extent IFMA has become a parallel organization to the ISC in that
it too draws its membership from right across the board: the members of
IFMA join it individually, however, whereas ISC is composed of trade associations. IFMA also considers general issues, though in the context of the
particular interests of its members as fund managers. It does not have
provision for case committees to deal with particular companies and does
not see itself collectively in that role.

Although the trade associations have collaborated successfully on establishing minimum general standards, there have been areas of disagreement,
between organizations and also with members of the trade bodies, who do
not always agree with the stance taken. An example is the liaison between
the ABI and NAPF, generally the two largest and most important institutional
investor trade bodies. The ABI published guidance on what it considered
acceptable by way of performance targets for share option schemes, namely
earnings of 2 per cent in real terms. The NAPF disagreed, preferring share
price appreciation as its chosen measure, and considering that 'sustained
underlying improvement' should be the standard for accepting a particular
scheme. With disputes over the establishment of share option schemes, even
further disarray was prompted by the arrival of long-term incentive schemes,
which the Greenbury Committee suggested should consider taking total
shareholder return (share price appreciation plus dividends reinvested) as
the measure. By the time the Hampel Committee issued its preliminary
report in August 1997 it was clear that some negotiation between the trade
bodies should begin on the issue, and the Institute of Directors made a plea
for the institutions to agree just what was a 'stretching' target as a general
rule, or abandon the hope of general definitions.

The publication of the Cadbury and Greenbury reports prompted a wide
range of institutions to develop their own internal policy on corporate

governance issues. A survey (PIRC 1997*b*) of the largest 150 investors representing 36 per cent of the UK equity market showed that the majority were prompted to develop a corporate governance policy by the publication of the Greenbury Report and general row on executive pay. Whilst there was express support for both the Cadbury and Greenbury committee standards, there was little indication that the trade association standards required specific endorsement. The development of market-wide standards of best practice has cut across the different trade associations' remit. The Institutional Shareholders' Committee (which largely reflected previous documents of the ABI) set out in *The Role of Directors* (1991*a*) a number of issues directly picked up by Cadbury. Similarly, their statement on *The Role and Responsibilities of Shareholders* (1991*b*) provided an important background document. Other bodies, such as PRO NED, which was not a trade association, but a ginger group supported by such associations, had issued guidance on, for example, the establishment of audit committees, remuneration committees, and appointment process for non-executive directors. These too were given broad endorsement by Cadbury.

Meanwhile other bodies have emerged to provide guidance, especially Pensions & Investment Research Consultants Ltd. (PIRC), which was set up by a consortium of public sector pension funds in 1986 to provide advice to them and other institutional clients in respect of individual companies on a wide range of corporate governance and ethical issues. Although PIRC's client base, particularly for its research services, has now broadened to include corporate pension funds and investment managers, the public sector funds continue to play an active role through a linked body, the Local Authority Pension Fund Forum, which is advised by PIRC but has a separate constitution.

PIRC's approach to corporate governance is based on a set of principles which are revised, normally biennially, in consultation with clients. PIRC examines individual companies' compliance with these principles, discusses its conclusions with the company concerned, and publishes its view of the line shareholders should take. In some respects, for example the independence of directors, their criteria are more stringent than those of Cadbury. Companies are given a chance to see and comment on PIRC's advice before it is given to their clients. Sometimes a difference of opinion may emerge between PIRC and a company, but in many cases a company has quietly modified its plans. The voting decision in all cases rests with the client; PIRC only advises.

THE BANK OF ENGLAND

No account of the role of the institutions would be complete without mentioning the interest of the Bank of England. In a narrow technical sense it is difficult to see why the Bank should have any responsibility towards industry beyond keeping its normal fatherly eye on the workings of the City. It is naturally concerned with the efficiency of the financial system in producing funds for industry whether through the banking system or the markets, and it has a proper concern for the relationship between that and the macro-economic situation.

Beyond these particular instances it might have been supposed that if there were to be a body in Whitehall taking an interest in all angles of the prosperity of commerce it should have been the Board of Trade (that is the Department of Trade and Industry), possibly aided and abetted by the Treasury. In some aspects of policy there was a void, and that is why Prime Minister Heath turned to the Bank to do what it could to stimulate constructive supervision by institutional shareholders. The Bank meanwhile, through its Industrial Finance Division, played its part in helping troubled companies by holding the ring whilst its bankers attempted to see whether a rescue was feasible and desirable.

The severe downturn in the UK economy in the 1970s meant much more activity at the Bank as numerous companies—including some well-known major ones—faced difficulties. The Bank's success was and is due in no small measure to its objectivity and dislike of publicity. The firms and banks concerned in the various cases knew it had no hidden agenda of its own. Public money was not involved and there were no charges for its services. What the spate of cases did do was to provide it with an insight into the causes of distress and it concluded that the fault often lay with the board; management had failed to take grip of problems in good time and the remainder of the board, usually dominated by executives, were too weak to force it to do so, or bring in new blood. The Bank's response, under the leadership of Sir David Walker, the relevant executive director, Sir Henry Benson, an adviser to the Governors, and with the blessing of the Governor himself, Gordon Richardson, was to marshal support in the City and industry for a scheme to promote the wider use of non-executive directors. This led to the birth of PRO NED in 1981 with the backing and financial support of the Bank, the Stock Exchange, the clearing banks, the Confederation of British Industry, the Scottish bankers, the British Institute of Management, the Institutional Shareholders' Committee, Equity Capital for Industry, and—with great reluctance—the Accepting Houses Committee. Sir Maurice Laing was its first chairman, to be followed four years later by Sir Adrian Cadbury (both were at the time directors of the Bank). Charkham was its first director.

PRO NED ran its promotional campaign by holding seminars and conferences up and down the country and issuing a stream of booklets and guidance on the role and functions of NEDs. At the same time it ran an agency to help companies find suitable NEDs. By the time Charkham moved to other functions in the Bank in 1985, it was assisting in about fifty appointments a year. PRO NED's work over the eleven years 1981–92 was an important precursor to the work of the Cadbury Committee, because it consolidated a trend that had been in place for some years, echoing developments in the

USA, where NEDs had in practice been mandatory from the end of the 1970s. After the Cadbury Report (1992) recommended that quoted companies have non-executive directors, PRO NED's 'missionary' role was completed; the sponsoring bodies did not feel it essential to remain involved in its residual agency function, and this was accordingly left to find a new home, which it did, with a firm of international search consultants.

The Bank could see by the mid-1980s that although its policy on boards was slowly succeeding, its earlier parallel policy of encouraging greater activity by the institutions as shareholders was not. In general terms the Bank perceived that the basic problem of institutional reluctance to intervene was that costs would be concentrated and benefits spread (the 'free rider' problem). It suggested informally to the leading firms of fund managers (of every kind including pension funds and the insurance companies) that coordinated action might be facilitated in the occasional case where there was a consensus that it ought to be considered. And it opened the prospect that it might itself do the facilitating, in much the same way as it handled troubled company cases, i.e. holding the ring but not forming a judgement itself—it was not for the Bank to assume a general supervisory role. Informal discussions produced a positive response, but nothing ever happened. With the benefit of hindsight, we now understand better the long list of reasons against joint action, given at the end of the last chapter. Even so, joint action did occasionally take place, organized ad hoc.

In its 'London Approach' the Bank of England fulfils a role no one else is as well placed to do, because it stands, independent, at the crossroads between the financial and industrial worlds. UK industry will hope that the breadth of vision that has marked the direction of the Bank for many years does not contract.

PROBLEMS OF COORDINATION

As an example of how difficult it is to secure cooperation between institutions, we can quote a 1992 report which commented: 'X (a major institution) hold 15% of Midas (which was in difficulties) and had found it extremely hard going either to influence the board or to get other shareholder support. X doubted that shareholders would ever act in concert unless they were really incensed by something.' We have noted before that emotion is underrated in financial affairs.

A real issue is competition between fund managers, who are vying for the task of managing pensioners' or insurance policy holders' funds. They will only retain their management contracts if they do at least as well and generally much better than others. Their motivation therefore is never to help their competitors. That is one of the reasons why cooperation between fund managers is so rare. Indeed there are sound commercial reasons, not just pure *schadenfreude*, for hoping their competitors will make mistakes. So if fund manager A's careful (and expensive) research tells him that a company has problems of which it is itself unaware, or which, more likely, it has concealed, he has a double incentive to unload the shares without saying a word—it will save his portfolio and drag down those of the purchasers. Unfortunately in such cases it is the purchasers' ultimate beneficiaries who suffer. In time, if those purchasers continue to make mistakes, their contracts will be terminated and will go to the victorious A. A meanwhile has the resources to obtain a level of research the others cannot match. We would expect that the As among the fund managers will take an increasing proportion of the market. On whom will they offload shares then? Is it right that, when the knowledge exists within the market (but is not general), one set of beneficiaries should suffer as a result of their portfolios being managed by a particular manager? The beneficiaries have no control over events at all. They cannot replace the manager or the trustees who appointed him or the consultants who advised the trustees, even if they wanted to. The trustees may in any case have been very careful in their choice and not in any breach of their duties. This is a sad case of the logic of the market injuring the helpless.

Institutions have long acted in accordance with the 'free rider' theory—that they should not initiate action the benefit of which accrues mainly to others: however, if their own holding is big enough and the benefits big enough, there is an economic case for acting irrespective of whether others benefit too. CalPERS certainly take this view and reckon to have profited substantially by their activities. They do not seem to mind that others who are carried along in the same tide enjoy the ride too. The more institutions club together the fewer 'free riders' there must be and the greater the sum of the benefit the activists will enjoy (as well as a spread cost), but it still leaves the 'steal a march' argument intact. Competition by all means, but never at the expense of the interests of the beneficiaries.

Some commentators have advanced the idea that the institutions might set up a secretariat to coordinate action. The problems with this are that

- if it depends on being brought into play by individual institutions, they will continue to display all the reluctance they have hitherto done, to bring to the attention of others weaknesses they themselves have diagnosed, as this might weaken their competitive position; if compelled to join, the initiative would be bureaucratic;
- if the secretariat were given an initiating role it would need to have at its disposal the fruits of in-depth research, without which it would generally be impossible to move in a timely and effective way.

Even so, some kind of timely concerted action is clearly a vital alternative to allowing corporate decline, collapse, or the expense of takeover. The next stage in considering how to coordinate effective shareholder pressure is now in hand, with discussions regarding the merits of establishing an organization similar to the Council of Institutional Investors in the USA, which provides a forum in which individual investment institutions (originally public sector funds and industry-wide pension schemes) come together to develop a common approach. Informal networks exist in the UK—such as the Corporate Governance Forum convened by Standard Life, and the group of clients associated with PIRC. This may provide the basis for development of an institutional forum.

The Hampel Committee did recognize the problems of divergent views and the need for coordination, calling upon the ABI and NAPF to coordinate their views in order that a common approach should develop. This looks unlikely. The different approaches reflect the range of interests each body represents. As individual shareholder networks have become more influential, via American activists stealing a march on UK shareholders, Lens and funds such as the UK Active Value, and the coordinating role of PIRC, the institutional trade associations have been challenged to develop a more comprehensive approach in order to maintain their influence. Both the ABI and NAPF have taken steps to devote more resources to research and advice on shareholder issues in general and specific outcomes at particular companies. The competitive pressures in the growing market for corporate governance research and advice reflect the increasing recognition that the exercise of influence over shareholder power is highly sensitive, contested, and of vital importance to all institutions. We do not see a bland uniformity of approach emerging, but further development of a variety of views. Beyond this period of rapid innovation, there may well be convergence around common views, but for the moment, even on the hot topic of executive share schemes, the institutional bodies do not agree on how they should be designed, what should be paid out, or even the key indicators of acceptability. The stage is therefore set for further lively debate and exchange of views between institutional bodies, and although the complexity of the issues and differences of opinion may be frustrating for companies, it is a great improvement upon the passivity of recent years. However, as shareholders get more involved with considering particular issues, and thereby closer to companies on particular issues, the question of commercially sensitive information is raised.

INSIDER TRADING

A further, important, consideration is insider trading. Not many years ago it was considered perfectly respectable to take advantage of inside information when buying or selling shares—much as it is today when backing horses. Everyone was deemed to know that such practices existed. Using such information often proved unprofitable. Sometimes the information proved to be wrong, or else it was in the market already and the price moved in the opposite direction to the one expected. By and large serious long-term investors got little advantage from inside information, because any modest gain they might have made by good timing became, over the years, insignificant compared with a share's performance. Few people who have constructed a really sound portfolio can remember whether their timing was perfect, although the performance measurement consultants specifically consider this point in assessing success. Most shares fluctuate substantially during a year and inside information is unlikely to be significant in normal circumstances for a long-term holder (absent catastrophe or a takeover bid). The principal opportunities to make a profit from insider information arise from knowing that a bid is in the offing far above market price, or that a company's results will so disappoint the market that a sharp drop in price is likely. (In the latter case the practice has grown of warning the market in advance, but even so there may be opportunities for those in the know before the warning is issued.) The market is sensitive to minor issues too, and can be jerked by such matters as an unexpected resignation or the announcement of a new product. It is often easy to guess that particular information will move the market and if the market is thin the movement may well be pronounced; it is however not always easy to tell which way it will move.

The modern drive to protect the untipped purchaser (or vendor) stems from an underlying notion of 'fairness', suitably dressed up in economists' underclothing (integrity of the markets etc.). The professionals are generally assumed to be able to take care of themselves by detecting trends and being party to any significant information, but even they are often uninformed about a bid or indeed a collapse—as holders of Polly Peck demonstrated. Even so, it is the small holder, the private individual, who is felt to need protection, so that he or she can trade without disadvantage.

The insider trading law is not designed to protect shareholders, nor the company. Indeed, we have come to believe that it may inhibit sound relationships for reasons we explain below. In the balance sheet of advantage to the community as a whole the imperfect protection afforded to a few for a limited disadvantage, imposed by a law which it is expensive to police and difficult to enforce, may be outweighed by the disadvantage to the many because a deeper relationship between company and its major shareholders becomes more difficult.

EFFECTIVENESS

We are doubtful whether the law works well. There have been so few prosecutions and those mostly minor. New civil penalties and fines from the FSA may help tackle this. We find it difficult to believe that the financial world has suddenly become so honest when fortunes can still be made by exploiting information; the temptations are too great. We do not believe either that the surveillance systems, thorough though they are, are totally effective. Professionals that really want to trade can do so by devious means, covering their tracks. Many *are* in receipt of price-sensitive information, simply because companies that do not want to upset the market or the analysts by leaving their inaccurate forecasts uncorrected tidy them up by judicious winks and nudges or more specific statements. This much was confirmed by a study conducted by the University of Northumbria and others in 1991/2 which demonstrated that a substantial proportion of the respondent companies admitted commenting to the analysts about their forecasts, and often guiding them. It is of course possible that no one has ever taken advantage of this information to buy or sell, or adjust their book.

Take costs first. The London Stock Exchange has to bear the costs of monitoring trades. Individual firms have compliance officers and extensive surveillance procedures. No costs 'disappear'. All costs are transfers. In the end the public pays.

INFORMATION

Information which has no use, or is not intended for use, is just gossip. It must be assumed that when any existing or potential shareholder obtains information about a company it is with an intention to act (a researcher may have no intention whatsoever to trade, but nevertheless has a purpose). We therefore dismiss the proposition that being an insider is fine, but trading on the information is not. The mere obtaining or holding of the information is in itself a crucial fact. Take an example: the manager of the Xanadu Pension Fund which holds Amalgamated Differentials PLC in its portfolio is minded to sell the shares. As a result of inside information from the management she decides to hold. Note that the information may very well have been received on the basis that it made her an insider, so that she could not trade! That is not insider trading under any definition. But it is using 'information'.

We think 'information' can be too narrowly defined. It is thought of in terms of gamblers' 'tips' as well as news of a bid or impending disaster. In fact a meeting with a company's top management at which no material fact is divulged that was not already in the market can provide information of the highest quality. Is not the assessment of the ability of the company's leadership important?

In this regard the system is already unequal. The private shareholder with a minuscule holding has virtually no chance of meeting a company's management on the same terms as an insurance company with 5 per cent of the equity. Nor should they have, for if all shareholders claimed such a right, management would have no time for anything else.

What is absolutely desirable for the small shareholder is that big share-holders should get close to management. A close relationship between a company and its major shareholders is an advantage to both. The counter-balance must be to ensure accountability for the exercise of that influence. A close relationship puts major shareholders in a position to exert influence should they need to; and if they know this is possible, they can afford to give management the confidence it needs to plan long and take the attendant risks. *Confidence* comes with the ability to exert influence. So what the small shareholders should pray for is that the big shareholders' relationships should be sound. They should recognize that just because things are unequal they are not necessarily unfair or unprofitable.

It is therefore unfortunate to have laws which may actually injure the very people they are designed to protect. By inhibiting big shareholders and company executives nervous of having full discussions they are doing no service to the company, to other shareholders—large or small—and others dependent on the company's prosperity.

Does the law help markets? The market seemed to work pretty well before the law came into existence and we have seen no evidence about liquidity, even if that were the ultimate criterion. Lack of liquidity does not seem to stop gamma stocks seeking a quotation. Does it make the cost of capital cheaper? The cost of capital is related to risk and risk to information. The absence of insider trading means that by definition all the information is *not* in the market. (If it were there would be no inside information and no need of a law.) This leg of the argument must rest on the proposition that there will be a peak propensity to use a market in which no insider trading occurs. We would like to see hard evidence of how significant this is. The provisional conclusion we draw, unpalatable though it is to admit it, is that from the market's standpoint it does not matter much. The principle on which it rests is a moral rather than an economic one—that of fairness. Fairness in itself will underpin confidence in the market.

It is not an unworthy aim nevertheless. There are two types of occasion when one party to a transaction might contend that he would not have concluded it if he too had possessed the same insider information as the other party. The seller may lack information that would push the price up (a takeover bid for instance) or a buyer may lack information that would depress the price (like an imminent profits warning). In the one case the seller loses the possibility of profit; in the other he faces a loss. The loss of profit or actual loss is pecuniary—and it is suffered by the party to the transaction and by no one else.

A civil remedy would be much more appropriate than a criminal one. As we have already noted it is difficult to make criminal charges stick; the burden of proof in a civil case is lighter. Compensation to the injured party would seem more to the point.

The expense of litigation and the log jam in the courts suggest it might be worth thinking of a special tribunal perhaps under the auspices of the Stock

Exchange itself. The Tribunal might be empowered to award multiple damages. That would be a more powerful deterrent than a criminal law that is not enforced. The expense of a case should be kept low so as not to deter litigants from pursuing claims that were prima facie reasonable.

There are already stringent laws about directors dealing in their own company's shares. There are other classes of connected persons for whom dealing on the back of information they have received by virtue of their position or relationship amounts to a breach of faith (as well as a crime). We can understand why the criminal law should bear down on them—if the offence be proven, but it seldom is. We offer no opinion on where the borderline should be drawn between a criminal offence and a civil remedy but consider it bears re-examination together with a better means of achieving the latter. Perhaps, if the burden of proof were shifted altogether in a civil action where one of the parties might be assumed by virtue of office or connections to possess or have access to inside information, the precise drawing of the line would matter less.

There is at the moment a constant trickle of inside information from companies to analysts whose forecasts are significantly awry, in order to correct the market's impression. This is wrong, as many companies realize which have the courage to issue a profits warning. A much better and fairer way would be for chairmen routinely to issue a third-quarter statement to update their pronouncements about trading given at the halfway stage. The fact that it was routine would take the sting out of it; they could often simply say, 'I have nothing to add to what I said three months ago.'

17

Remuneration

OTHER people's money has always been a subject of endless fascination so it is not at all surprising to find directors' remuneration in the headlines. Setting aside the noise and entertainment value of the various skirmishes, what part should shareholders play—if any—other than to foot the bill?

What a company's employees are paid does of course have a direct effect on its prosperity. Where management owns a business it can take the view that every penny paid to employees comes directly from its own pockets; even then its pockets will suffer in the long run if poor pay means second-rate employees. Where managers are hired hands, as they are in virtually all UK quoted companies, they know they have to strike the right balance between parsimony and generosity to attract and retain staff of sufficient calibre to assist competitiveness. There are no agency costs here— everyone is in the same boat: they must find and keep that balance or it will sink. That is one of the skills shareholders trust the board to identify in its executive directors, as part and parcel of their management expertise. This has been the formal position from the beginning, and very sensible too. Imagine Unilever's share-holders trying to doubleguess local management about pay rates in Poland or the prairies. As far as we know, no shareholders in a modern UK PLC have essayed such a thing. However, shareholders are right to want to know what the policy is, and whether it is consistent with best practice in those markets. Currently, they have no way of knowing what the company is actually doing on pay and conditions, in their broadest sense, for the 'human capital' at home or abroad. This is a clear gap in reporting, and one which should be addressed in the growing trend towards disclosure of non-financial issues. The Fabian Society has proposed a format via a working party of business and trade union advisers, as has the Institute for Personnel and Development in its submission to the Hampel Committee. In the United States, the Depart-ment of Labor and a number of large investors are pursuing the notion of 'the high performance workplace' in which shareholders use their influence to ensure that the company's human capital is effectively managed.

A mean or short-sighted remuneration policy (for that matter an over-generous or lax one) may be one of the factors that contributes to poor results, but it would be almost impossible for shareholders to know how significant that particular issue was. Even boards may find such a judgement difficult to make. Occasionally a scandal may surface—a sweatshop policy for instance—that makes the headlines, but otherwise on current disclosure shareholders have little option but to trust that the managers to whom the board has delegated authority act wisely. As every chairman will attest that the company's greatest asset is the workforce, some information on the management of human capital is surely in order.

Despite the importance of these issues, they have not attracted anything like the attention devoted to executive directors' pay—and for all the ink spilt on top pay it has not been effectively dealt with. The pay of the top people is part and parcel of a company's general pay policy, even though it is convenient to pretend otherwise. Indeed, the success of a company's general remuneration policy is far more important to its shareholders than the sums paid to the top man or a handful of colleagues. This is certainly true arithmetically. One or 2 per cent on the total pay bill is a huge sum in a big company—much more significant in cash terms than the odd hundred thousand pounds too much paid to the CEO. The general re-muneration policy is far more important than the CEO's pay for another reason—a workforce that is not dissatisfied is far more likely to lead to profits than one that is. (In putting it in those terms we follow the Herzberg thesis that pay does not satisfy, but that the 'wrong' pay dissatisfies.)

If shareholders want to give practical recognition to the contribution that employees make to performance, they should be giving equal consideration to employee schemes which can reward and motivate staff. Somehow remuneration committees have now been locked into a set of assumptions about the need for particular kinds of rewards that seem built on executive demands rather than any objective measure of justification.

TOP PEOPLE'S PAY

Nevertheless in concentrating on the top executives' pay, the shareholders are addressing an issue of some importance because

- whether or not a company has a remuneration committee, the board's attitude to pay at the top will be taken as an indication of its integrity. If the board is seen to milk the company for all it can, no amount of verbiage on ethics will cut much ice. It is comfortable to pretend there is no such thing as morality in company life in any way that hurts the pocket. But there is and this is a prime area. The 'market' is imperfect, and the ethics lie in not taking advantage of its imperfections;

- particularly in smaller companies the sums involved may be disproportionate to the profits;
- unusually large sums may set a poor example within the company, and
  this may have repercussions at other levels and in the general tone of the
  attitude towards the company's funds;
- too great a differential with average pay may lead to tensions and strains,
  inside the business and in society more generally. The multiples in which
  such differentials are sometimes expressed have increased dramatically in
  recent years for no obvious reason;
- if the wrong kind of scheme is in place executives may be focused on a
  time scale or set of targets that are not in the best interests of the business
  long term.

Graef S. Crystal wrote of the USA in terms that could to a lesser extent apply
to the UK (1992: 26, 27 f.):

a finding that manufacturing pay has been flat for twenty years, while CEO pay has
risen more than three times, is plenty damning enough. Where that typical CEO
earned total compensation (excluding perquisites and fringe benefits) that was
around 35 times the pay of an average manufacturing worker in 1974, a typical CEO
today earns pay that is around 120 times that of an average manufacturing worker and
about 150 times that of the average worker in both manufacturing and service industries. And US tax policy during the past twenty years has just made matters worse. The
total tax load on highly paid executives has declined substantially at the same time
that the total tax load on the average worker has increased—though only by a little.

The same is generally true on a smaller scale of the UK. When the top tax
rate was dropped dramatically after 1979 and settled at 40 per cent the view
was taken that there would be less pressure for increases in executive pay as
they would benefit from a big increase in take-home pay without the company laying out another penny. It was not so. When the top rate had been 85
per cent (not counting unearned income) there had been little point in
chasing rises; now that they could keep 60 per cent, there was, and the
explosion followed. Crystal continues:

These huge gaps at home between the pay of a CEO and the pay of a worker might be
less reprehensible if the same huge gaps could be demonstrated in our major competitors—Japan, Germany, France, and the United Kingdom. But my research reveals
that only the UK shows signs of catching the US executive compensation virus, and it
has only a mild case. In contrast to the 160 times by which the pay of an American
CEO exceeds the pay of an average American worker, the corresponding differential in
Japan is under 20; and even in the UK, it is under 35.

The gap between the top and the bottom in the USA and UK has since grown
further, although the US scale dwarfs our own local problem. The TUC
published its own report on pay arguing that average salary at the top of
companies had expanded from 12 times the average pay of employees to over
16 times, within a three-year period (TUC 1998).

THE 'RIGHT' RATE

Why is it necessary to pay the top people so much? We want to explore some of the issues, since this is the ground that shareholders' thinking must traverse. We start with the concept that there is a 'right' rate for 'the job'. There is not. An organization whose findings confirmed this was the government's Pay Research Unit (*floruit* approx. 1956–80; now disbanded). It is difficult to imagine any body tackling the task of pay comparisons more thoroughly and objectively. It started in every case with a careful analysis of a job and then sought comparisons. It was well known both to management and unions that some industries paid far better than others so there was always a struggle to pick a sample that would produce the most favourable results. When a list was agreed the Unit went to the various companies, found comparable jobs, and noted not only the pay but also all the other terms and conditions. Some were open to argument and formed the basis of lively negotiations between management and unions. At the end of the analysis, the Unit produced 'league tables' showing what the external analogues received (all adjustments for terms and conditions having been calculated). Even then there were the unquantifiables. How do you price relative security for instance? The research showed that the labour market is imperfect and that the rates actually paid for virtually identical work vary far more than most would suppose. The difference between the top and bottom numbers in a league table could easily be 50 per cent or even more. If this is so for basic and middle-range jobs—and it is—how much more difficult is it to assert there is a 'right' rate for a complex job where true comparisons are very difficult indeed to make? And for the very top jobs of all, which are virtually unique?

Sir Christopher Hogg, addressing a NAPF conference in February 1995, put the argument with his usual clarity:

One might think that, given the importance of judging top executive performance, the ground rules for measuring it would be such as to enable broad agreement between all interested parties. Unfortunately, that is far from the case. There are just too many variables and too much is unknown, including to the executives themselves. For example, even inside a company, it is seldom clear what happens because of the CEO, what happens in spite of him, and what happens independently of him. Of course, probability tells you that if a company's financial performance keeps going downhill over time, it has something to do with the management; and vice versa. . . .

But what about when it comes to translating that judgment about *performance* into a judgment about appropriate remuneration? I have to say that in this translation, like a performance measurement, is anything but cut and dried. There are some clear starting points in the form of cost of living indices, the previous year's remuneration and internal relativities. When it comes to market comparisons, there is a paucity of really accurate and comprehensive information except for what can be arranged through *detailed* information exchange with other companies of roughly comparable size and complexity. And even with such an exchange, it is difficult to judge relative risk and true job responsibility. In addition, one knows what one has had to pay recently to recruit executives from outside. One also knows something about the recent offers made to one's own executives to entice them away (which can, by the way, be profoundly upsetting to calm and rational judgment about remuneration). Most larger companies will also have to factor in international comparisons of one sort or another. All this is greatly complicated by additional performance—linked remuneration and the issues surrounding that, i.e. its relationship to base salary and possibly to pensions, its total quantum, the basis of it, the emphasis as between short-term and long-term and so on. You will see I have not even mentioned service contracts . . .

It is possible to invest the whole process with a spurious aura of analytical accuracy, as if all factors tended to a given answer. In practice, particularly at the top of a company, every situation is unique as to a person, his responsibilities, his performance and a particular period in time. What one tries to do is to use a mass of facts, a few basic principles and a lot of experience and judgment to sculpt an appropriate outcome.

COMPARISONS

It follows that when a company has to decide the pay of its top executives it should be chary of the information it receives about 'comparable' rates. Non-material conditions vary hugely, such as pride in the organization, satisfaction with one's work, the pleasure of working with agreeable colleagues, a sense of being valued, and a feeling of relative security. If all these are present, and they often are, the executives concerned will not generally be amenable to the blandishment of higher offers elsewhere unless the advancement is considerable and the prospects inviting. In a company where they are not present—some to a marked degree—the 'coefficient of stickability' will drop sharply. The point is that comparisons that do not take all these elements into account—and they are notoriously difficult to assess—will be of little real value. They will tend to ratchet upwards partly because they depend on the point in the pay cycle that both companies have reached, but even more because no one likes to tell a company that they already pay enough or too much! Comparisons across industries are of course notoriously unreliable, since some have always paid much better than others—oil for instance. To be of any real value comparisons must take all the unquantifiable factors into account, measure them, and put numbers to them. There is no way in which this can be done with scientific accuracy, since we are deep into the realms of the behavioural sciences. When people change jobs they often say that 'pay' is the main reason. It may be, but as often as not the reason can be something quite different, which not even the person can identify accurately. A sense of dissatisfaction may derive from many causes, some of which people are more comfortable burying in their psyche or else concealing.

MOTIVATION

From this analysis we conclude, as many others have done, that remuneration is not the only force at work. Even if some economists believe so, the actions of people are not solely dictated by maximizing economic returns. Many of the ablest staff in business schools could make far more money from practising what they preach, for instance: and whole battalions of nurses and teachers would get better pay elsewhere (not to mention the clergy). Remuneration is important, to be sure, as we all like to live decently, but it is not after a certain point the be-all and end-all. As ambitious people ascend the managerial ladder—often against strong competition—what they relish as much as anything else is status, power, and recognition.

To the extent that pay motivates, it motivates everyone. Indeed, it is probably more powerful further down the organization than at the top, since increases represent a greater potential change in the level of comfort. In logic therefore incentive schemes should have breadth and depth within a company, as indeed they sometimes do. By the very nature of its responsibilities top management ought to start each day fully 'incentivized'. It ought, at its level, to be giving its all anyway. It is a ludicrous idea that a manager will sulk in a corner and hold back without a juicy carrot; if it were true it should lead to dismissal. As to rewards for achievements *ex post facto*, we are all for them provided they are spread widely enough. It is true that top management has a leadership function, but that is precisely what it is paid for. The teams that respond to this leadership (without which it could do nothing) up and down the business have as much claim to share in its prosperity as the leaders themselves.

AN AMERICAN VIEW

The Council of Institutional Investors in Washington, DC, represents a huge weight of US institutional money. Its executive director, Sarah Teslik, wrote acidly in the April 1994 newsletter, 'Tell me again why Akers got a bonus?', commenting, 'The first gem is the observation, complacently repeated at conferences by CEOs and institutional shareholders alike, that it is OK to pay CEOs amounts that truly make them not just well-to-do, but make them some of the wealthiest people on earth, as long as the pay is linked to performance.'

This begs many questions. Everyone agrees that, at some level, pay becomes too high: it would be too much to pay an executive all corporate profits, for example, leaving none for shareholders. But the standard wisdom is that, for big companies at least, the cash flows are so large that a little larceny at the top will have next to no effect on the bottom line. So it cannot be bad, and it is also assumed that (1) large amounts 'incentivize' (apparently in a way smaller amounts do not) and (2) 'incentivization' will improve productivity. The problem is, huge amounts of pay may not have these good effects. They may, in fact, have significant harmful effects instead.

Probably the single biggest problem with paying executives lavish amounts is the potential for a negative impact on corporate productivity through hitting employee morale—their willingness to give a little extra, their interest in conserving and enhancing corporate assets, their long-term loyalty to the company. There is no way any theoretical additional motivation created in the CEO by mega millions can offset this huge corporate-wide negative effect. It does not take soldiers long to figure out whether their leaders value their lives like their own; it does not take employees long either. So giant payments to CEOs, regardless of form, may have a greater potential to harm corporate performance than to enhance it.

The other main casualty is the reputation of the directors concerned and, thereby, the company. Lack of judgement in this arena may be an indication that the board has lost its touch. Integrity and the ability to lead by example are priceless intangible assets in any company's board.

MARKETS

The market in remuneration is imperfect, and it is so partly for technical reasons and partly because there is no general and uniform system of valuation across industries, regions, and countries, and there never can be. What exists is a means of testing the market for a certain post at a particular time. At senior levels this is a chancy business anyway. A heavy disruption premium is generally payable for someone already in employment (and the more contenders there are, the higher the premium is likely to be), unless the buyer is running a perceived risk—by for instance employing someone at a level higher. The market for CEOs is somewhat like the market for Van Gogh paintings—the price depends on what a given purchaser will pay to cover a particular space on the wall—the main differences being that no CEO is irreplaceable whereas every Van Gogh is—and there is no effective auction. Those who offer very high 'packages' for a CEO should recall that graveyards are full of the indispensable.

Comparisons are often made between entertainment stars—cinema, sports, stage, pop music—and the leaders of business. We agree that it says something—and something not always agreeable—about a society that keeps its pop stars in the lap of luxury and treats its teachers meanly. It is partly, indeed mainly, a function of the market and it will last until people have different views of where they want to spend their money: if they were not so keen to watch football the income from the gate, sponsorship, and television would drop dramatically and with it the stars' earnings. Even in present circumstances the number of highly paid stars relative to those who eke out a living is very small, and their position is always fragile. Football salaries are becoming a real burden on clubs; even sport is not immune to concern about the merits of high pay. Society as a whole tends to regard these people as *sui generis*, and so they are. As far as business salaries are concerned they are irrelevant. Indeed, some sporting stars turn into businessmen and make fortunes (think of O'Reilly at Heinz or Leschly at Smith-Kline Beecham). We do not know of any CEOs who have moved successfully in the opposite direction!

THE PROFESSIONS

The majority of lawyers and accountants make their living from their business clients. Private clients butter few parsnips for either. The top lawyers and accountants are well paid by business standards—much better paid than most people know, because there is little public information about what they get (unlike business). This has begun to change for accountants—and not only for those who incorporate as companies and have to disclose; their openness deserves credit. It is an article of faith among those who worship market mechanisms that competition ensures a clearing price that reflects the balance between supply and demand. If no one knows what the prices are, or there are structural rigidities, the market does not work.

If industry is to attract sufficient recruits from university it must compete with the professions, however they come by their wealth. So we are not against good pay for top executives whose performance, over time, justifies it. This seems to be the widely held view among shareholders, judging by the large number of companies in which they have never thought it necessary to comment. But they are entitled to turn their minds to the matter, and they can only do this if they know the facts.

DISCLOSURE

Both the Cadbury and Greenbury reports emphasized the need for disclosure, the latter in some detail, and the complexity of its requirements has caused some trouble. PIRC published a report (1997*e*) which demonstrated that 86 per cent of the companies in their sample made a statement of compliance either with the Greenbury Code or the Stock Exchange listing rules which covered some aspects of the Greenbury Code for the period in question. According to PIRC's definition of independence rather less than a third of the companies' remuneration committees were wholly composed of independent directors (which weakens further our confidence in them). How do shareholders assess this information? What are the costs?

TOTAL COSTS

Life at PRO NED was enlivened in its early days by the tales—and confessions—of many directors from companies of all sizes. The proportion of what directors actually cost a business visible to the outside world is greater than it was, but is still incomplete. What now has to be disclosed (Greenbury 5.8) includes salary and bonuses (calculated in all manner of ways), benefits in kind, and pension benefits. But benefits in kind are not a precise concept, and not as meaningful as total costs. These include the cost of a car or cars not assessed as a benefit in kind, but incurred by the company nevertheless—as well as cars for the family. In one case the business, a public company, paid for a car for the vicar! Also included should be support staff, chauffeur(s), staff who assist domestically, and all entertainment at the company's expense of whatever kind. Expenses may be 'wholly or necessarily incurred for the business', but they are expenses just the same, even if not a benefit in kind. They may include a great many Concorde flights, all doubtless fully justified. Also included are donations in the director's name and financial assistance of various sorts: e.g. help with a mortgage or loans for other purposes or the increasingly common practice of paying for tax advice to help the fortunate individual on the other end of such generosity to plan out the minimum slice for the Inland Revenue.

All of this makes for a complicated remuneration picture. When John Clarke, former CEO at BET, took Rentokil Initial to court, suing for compensation, a lush and varied range of claims was made, including use of the company car plus driver and potential earnings under bonus schemes which would pay out after he had actually left the company! He was awarded £3m. by the court, tripling the award offered by Rentokil Initial on the basis of the main points they considered warranted compensation in his contract.

A NEW DISCLOSURE FORMULA?

The current format for disclosure needs reform. There is a blizzard of detail, but shareholders are often none the wiser. We believe that the way forward is for the report and accounts to include a relatively simple piece about each director covering the salient points in both graphic and narrative form. The information should be divided into two parts. Part A would go into the report and accounts. This would be a statement which requires totals to be provided, including a valuation of shares or options awarded, in addition to a graph showing a five-year trend on pay for the board set against the company's performance relative to competitors and the market. Part B would be lodged with Companies House for public inspection and made available to shareholders on request. This would provide full details, such as rules of bonus and incentives plans and contracts. The onerous nonsense of inspecting the details in person, without being entitled to a copy of the documentation, would be ended. More companies now have web sites and such information could easily be posted there to save administrative time and effort on the part of both shareholders and companies. These statements should provide full details, and should be certified by the auditors.

SEC RULES

The SEC has responded to the row on executive pay in the USA by requiring clear disclosure. Rather than seeking the statistical detail which the Greenbury Committee has requested, in true American style, the big picture is what is required: the top five earners in the company (regardless of whether they are on the board or not) must see their remuneration set out in graphic form and set against the performance of the company, against both their industry and the market as a whole. Not only must pay, bonuses, and other perks be valued but also share options and any other stock plans. The idea is that shareholders should be able to see at a glance whether pay and performance are parting company. Linda Quinn, then director of SEC's corporation finance division, commented that 'The idea behind the new rules was to give shareholders a more comprehensive picture of how top executives are compensated so that the market place could provide active oversight.' These rules were introduced in 1992. The SEC also ensured that shareholders had the tools to intervene on pay if they felt the matter was getting out of hand. Previously it had been considered that decisions on pay were 'ordinary' business—in other words, shareholders should keep out and it was an issue for directors to resolve. In 1993 they reversed this ruling and allowed shareholders to lodge resolutions on executive pay. As shareholders can requisition proposals at little cost and with a low threshold of shares owned, this has become an effective route to intervention. A resolution at the Centerior Energy Corporation in 1994 to limit the CEO's salary to 150 per cent of President Clinton's salary attracted 32 per cent support! Since then a number of shareholder resolutions have been passed seeking to limit or restrain pay, and won a majority of the votes. This has not necessarily resulted in the changes sought at the company as unlike special resolutions in the UK, they are not binding on the directors. Clearly the mysterious formulae of the remuneration consultants have not persuaded US shareholders, even if companies are still able to get away with it. Finally, the Clinton administration added its own sting: in the 1993 federal budget all executive compensation paid by companies over $1m. could no longer be claimed as a business expense. It was a below the line item, making high pay more expensive for shareholders. In response many companies have put a cap on the gains that can be made from salary and stock option plans.

REMUNERATION COMMITTEES

The concept of the remuneration committee sounds attractive, especially if it is genuinely composed of independent directors. In practice it contains many flaws. First, the directors on it may not all be independent. Secondly, they will bring with them peer group norms as most non-executives are current or former executives. Thirdly, they do not necessarily have all the facts about the 'total cost to the company.' Extravagances may well be concealed from them. They may not know the costs of the trips the CEO took and how much home and other entertainment he charged up. How many shooting parties, opera, and theatre trips does the company pay for? Fourth, they are faced with a subtle conflict of interest—they have to work with the chief executive afterwards and it is easy to take the line of least resistance when faced with the able but greedy. Finally, quite properly they will be inclined to defer to the (chairman or) chief executive's advice about his colleagues (who are also his subordinates). They are in principle no different from all the other executives under his command who are not on the board and we would argue that it is part of his task to see that the remuneration system that covers them all works to the company's benefit as well as theirs.

As long as their members are genuinely independent remuneration committees do their best to reach 'fair' conclusions, i.e. those which reconcile the interests of executives and shareholders—it is just that their best efforts appear so often to be unsatisfactory that it appears there is a systemic reason. To talk of 'reconciliation' of conflicts of interest by remuneration committees is misleading—it is not in the shareholders' interests to pay as little as possible. In their minds will be some vague concept of fairness and its very imprecision has led to complex and varied performance criteria.

One practical innovation to try and solve this difficulty has been the invention of performance-related share schemes. It is not clear whether such schemes *actually improve* performance. The evidence, such as it is, seems inconclusive, and bonus schemes may distort decision-making in ways which involve the taking of additional risk which may not be appropriate or may focus upon a horizon (the standard is three years) which cannot possibly be right for all companies.

It is inherent in the acceptance of the responsibility at the top of a company that the executives will give it 100 per cent effort and skill. It is possible that schemes may actually deflect effort to produce the results necessary to manipulate great rewards into a time frame that may suit the executive's pocket but not the company's long-term interest.

The NEDS may themselves be highly paid elsewhere and if so they will be conditioned by what subconsciously they have learnt to believe is 'reasonable'. The chairman at British Gas who oversaw the company's controversial increases for the chief executive, Cedric Brown, was himself formerly the highest-paid man on a British board at BOC. In the days when there were serious discussions about a maximum wage, it was said that most people pitched it at one and a half times their own. The story is illustrative not of the numbers but of the element of subjectivity and personal experience that inevitably colours people's approach. It is not an accident that the stoutest defender of the pay changes at British Gas had a history of high earnings himself; this is not to impugn what he felt to be correct, but simply to say that personal experience always colours judgement. The cross-connections between committees and board membership demonstrated by a network produced by PIRC for *The Times* illustrate some of the cross-linkages that condition pay determination at the top. The same newspaper included a piece by Mervyn Marckus on 5 March 1994 which started by quoting the then Chancellor of the Exchequer Kenneth Clarke, 'I disapprove of some of the high executive salaries paid by British companies and I wish more of our business leaders showed a decent level of restraint,' and concluded by saying:

All of which serves to reinforce the belief that the Cadbury Committee's faith in the ability of non-executive directors to enforce restraint, via remuneration committees, is ill-founded. Since when has the presence of the great and the good in Britain's board rooms (hardly a new phenomenon) heralded a clampdown on remuneration.

The thought that remuneration committees might not be the safeguard shareholders hope receives some support in the work of Main and Johnson of Edinburgh University (1992). The evidence is not clear cut—but at the very least such committees appear not to have been able to hold back the pressures. A more worrying interpretation is that they could well facilitate greater increases by legitimizing them. Remuneration committees can provide a fig leaf to hide embarrassing pay decisions. There is a question also of whether the trend to establishing remuneration committees allows executives to hide behind their decisions, and not be held accountable as a whole board for the expenditure. For that reason the Hampel Report revised the status of remuneration committees from 'determining' pay to 'recommending' to the full board.

AFTER KNOWLEDGE, ACTION

The shareholders already have a picture of what is actually happening. There are some outstanding issues on the valuation of pensions benefits, share awards, and no real feel for total costs. Most of the time they may feel that what is occurring is reasonable and that there is therefore no need to comment, much less to intervene when they next meet representatives of the company. But how do they maintain routine oversight?

The concept of the shareholders being invited to endorse remuneration directly has been opposed on the grounds that it would be impracticable. Boards, it is said, have to award increases during the year, without waiting for external approval; besides, new recruits to the board would be deterred from joining were their remuneration subject to ratification. Besides, what would happen if shareholders turned a proposal down? Would this executive receive nothing at all (if a recruit) or his formal remuneration? Such arguments are a *reductio ad absurdum* and quite specious. Shareholders could propose an amendment to the resolution of the 'not X but Y' variety. The fact that they could and indeed might do so would stop boards tempting providence as they currently do by paying patently excessive sums (especially in the back of poor performance). The Lex column in the *Financial Times* (not noted for revolutionary ideas) endorsed the idea of shareholders voting on remuneration in these words (27 Sept. 1997):

But imagine that such a right existed. In the vast majority of cases, where the remuneration committee had clearly done a sensible job, its proposals would rightly go through on the nod. And in the few cases where salaries were a matter of controversy, a shareholder vote would surely be a good idea. At present, the decision rests with a committee of company directors; they may be non-executive, but in the public eye they rarely look entirely independent. And it is not their money at stake. By contrast, shareholders ultimately bear the cost of employing an executive; a clear vote from them in favour of a controversial high salary would have a great deal more force than anything directors might say.

This view (long held by bodies such as PIRC) made a surprise leap into the mainstream with the National Association of Pension Funds' argument for this form of shareholder voting in its submission to the Hampel Committee. The President of the Board of Trade stated in March 1998 that government wanted to see this become common practice. The two brave companies Siebe and Premier (with a director in common notably) have put their committee reports to the vote, although their example has not been followed, despite Greenbury's suggestion that if there were controversy or a major change of policy the remuneration committee should consider seeking approval from shareholders. By mid-1998 only two other companies (United News and Media, Cox Insurance Holdings) had sought shareholder approval where a director, Clive Hollick, was a special adviser to Margaret Beckett at the DTI.

How can shareholders avoid the problems of remuneration committees? One possibility would be for shareholders to appoint a committee who were not directors to recommend the pay of the chairman and chief executive. If the board disagreed with their proposals, it could put counter-proposals and shareholders could choose between them. This would avoid conflicts of interest and would settle the awkward yes/no choice—new rates would have been fixed. The proposal is open to the objection that the members of such a committee would not understand the company and its people well enough. It also undermines the current board structure in the UK, by removing a key responsibility from the directors and introducing third parties to the debate. The TUC has argued that employee representatives should sit on executive remuneration committees in order to bring balance to the discussion. Shareholders (but which and appointed how?) would have a direct interest. On balance, putting the report of the committee to shareholders for a vote, however it was constituted, would give some spine to those responsible for poor decisions. There would be no legal consequence to the report failing (as with the report and accounts) but it would send a signal to the directors that could not be ignored.

THE REMUNERATION OF THE NON-EXECUTIVE DIRECTORS

One other area which needs tackling by the remuneration committee is the reward for non-executive directors. Their task is by common consent becoming more onerous, especially because of the committee work they must undertake and its demanding nature. As they comprise the remuneration committee, they ought in logic not fix their own, but in principle they should be subject to a proper objective procedure. The amounts are not insignificant. The 1997 Top Pay Research Survey suggests that in companies with a turnover in excess of £500m. the median was more than £32,000. Also, the Companies Act provides a direct shareholder role in setting the cap for these fees. Most companies have an article which states the maximum payable by way of fees, and authorization must be sought if the ceiling is to be raised. This appears wholly sensible and some have argued that the principle should be extended to the executives (Plender 1998). A more thorny issue is that of finding other ways to pay non-executive directors. Some have argued that they should be paid in shares, for example, Hermes. The argument is that the non-executives need motivating to think about the company's share price, and if they were paid in shares this would be brought to their attention. We do not think this is the central issue. Arguably if non-executive directors do not have proper regard to shareholders' interests they should not be on the board anyway; we do not believe that paying them in shares rather than money will make much difference. A much more difficult issue is quantum. The more NEDs are asked to do, the more they deserve. At what point may independence be prejudiced? In this respect we have serious reservations about paying NEDs in options. This gives them a pecuniary interest in short-term share price movements which can undermine objectivity. For

Lucas Varity, defeated in 1998 in its efforts to seek a new listing in New York, the options held by NEDs were viewed as fatally undermining their independent judgement.

It is clear that unless shareholders wish to continue handing over a blank cheque for board pay, they do need some vetting process that works better than leaving it all to a remuneration committee. There seems to be no satisfactory process other than to require a resolution to be put each year, in the same way as one is already put for the auditors, and to give shareholders a power to amend. The prospect of effective shareholder scrutiny with a better means of registering disapproval would quicken the pulse of remuneration committees.

Let the last word rest with Sir Christopher Hogg (who was addressing NAPF in 1995):

Your support for non-executive directors does *not* always have to be uncritical and acquiescent, any more than the support by the non-executives for the executive has to be. The right relationship is bound to involve challenge and disagreement—even replacement—from time to time. You must face up to the hassle, cost and effort of doing this properly. If I have any criticism of investing institutions over the years, it is their tendency to pass by on the other side of the road when they see someone in the ditch. Remember Burke's words to the effect that all it requires for evil to triumph is for enough good men to do nothing.

All proposals on remuneration are matters of judgement and 'evil' seldom comes into it. The hallmark is more often folly. But the judgement of a remuneration committee is not infallible. We are content to believe that they do their best, often in complex circumstances, and their best generally has an appearance of reasonableness. This being so we cannot set a sound argument against shareholders having a voice in regard to directors' remuneration.

18

Disclosure

STANDARDS of disclosure internationally vary dramatically. However, in a world of global capital markets, the trend is towards greater transparency. It is increasingly accepted that shareholders (and others with a legitimate interest) are entitled to a comprehensive flow of information and that the board should reveal as much relevant material as possible, holding back only to protect commercial confidentiality.

In the past it was not always so. There was a widespread feeling that shareholders were not entitled to know more than a minimum; that the board should be trusted to protect their interests; that almost any information (even turnover) was valuable to competitors; and that if shareholders did not like the secrecy or were dissatisfied with their dividends, they should sell their shares to those of greater faith in the stewardship of the business. Furthermore, in self-protection, the less one said or wrote, the fewer the hostages to fortune.

Secrecy and openness have long battled in the English psyche. Charles II's cabinet was distrusted for its secrecy and its members produced the word CABAL for the language (Clifford, Arlington, Buckingham, Ashley, Lauderdale). On the other side of the scales the English legal and parliamentary systems are open, and secrecy in them is suspect.

The civil service provides an interesting example of the conflict—well illustrated in the Scott Report (1996)—and the principles and practice are directly relevant to business. Briefly they are as follows. In government the country's security obviously needs protecting and vital information must not be made available to foreign enemies, real or potential. In commerce the same is true about crucial information that might be of value to a competitor, actual or potential. But—and it is a large 'but'—what starts as a legitimate exercise in protecting what is in the country's or the firm's interest can soon degenerate into an exercise to save a minister or a director (or group of them) from embarrassment. Numerous attempts have been made to stop over-classification of documents in Whitehall by persuading the originators not to label them 'Confidential' unnecessarily or to call them 'Secret' when a lesser classification would suffice. Such efforts only have a temporary effect, which is why they have to be made so often. The reasons are not hard to discern. People feel more self-important if they are involved in 'secrets'; their ministers should be protected from any kind of possible embarrassment; accountability interferes with their exercise of power; there are no penalties for over-classification—and no medals for openness. Even in the USA where 'sunshine' was deemed the best disinfectant, there are dark corners like the Iran Contra affair.

Business is similar. Directors do not want 'failures' exposed if possible, and may go to great lengths to make the facts inaccessible in the report and accounts even if they cannot altogether escape mention. Commercial confidentiality is a convenient cloak to draw round shortcomings to protect them from the critics' blast.

Professor Louis Lowenstein (1996) provides a short history of the dawn of the age of disclosure in the USA after the crash, starting with the Securities Act 1933 and the Securities Exchange Act 1934 which created the SEC and the reporting and disclosure framework for the day-to-day trading markets. He states:

The financial disclosure system, while intended to permit investors and creditors to make rational decisions, and to make markets fair and efficient, in fact has the quite independent effect of forcing managers to confront disagreeable realities in detail and early on, even when those disclosures have no immediate market consequences.

In the UK the tide, in business, has turned. In financial matters a whole industry has grown up devoted to getting disclosure right. Disclosure was one of the foundations of both the Cadbury and Greenbury reports. Yet still there is reticence to tell all, as was shown in the way the directors of British Gas gave evidence to a Select Committee of the House of Commons, where some members of the Committee felt that the directors giving evidence provided an overly flattering picture of what the company was doing with its remuneration policy. The chairman and chief executive were later recalled to explain themselves. Some of the problem is due to poor timing. The board of GEC could have handled the appointment of George Simpson and the terms on which he was engaged with greater frankness. The chairman Lord Prior explained that the terms of the appointment had not been agreed when he was appointed to the board, hence the lack of disclosure in the report and accounts. A row still ensued. A similar frustration occurred for shareholders in the same year at ASDA where the accounts were already issued and published before the board changes were announced to the Stock Exchange, meaning that the description of the directors' various responsibilities (including the chairman and chief executive) was already out of date. Perhaps there should be introduced a governance equivalent of the concept of 'going concern' so that when a company goes to press with its report and accounts, shareholders can have reasonable assurance that the company is not about to transmogrify at board level into a dramatically different body.

The accounting profession has been busily engaged in improving standards of disclosure. Their interest is to ensure that reporting gives a better picture of the company's position and progress, and thus prevent the concealment of the unpalatable; the auditors are better placed than they were, thanks to audit committees, to hold the line in support of consistency, disclosure, and integrity. There is still much to be done. Even in the UK there is no requirement to provide shareholders with a 'warts and all' biography of each director. The pressures for ever more disclosure are becoming relentless, and are growing to include new issues such as environmental standards, workplace policies and practice, terms for creditors, and prices, and it will not be long before these are joined by new governance concerns such as board assessment and future strategy.

All these are matters which arguably affect performance and thus the shareholders are entitled to know. This should help them evaluate the relative and absolute competence of the company's management. At the same time there is absolutely no point in providing information unless it serves a useful purpose. The OECD convened a working party on the issue in 1997, recognizing that comprehensive disclosure of information was essential to the efficient workings of the capital markets, quite apart from the wider public interest in the issue. Companies need to strike a balance between information which is provided to all shareholders, and ensuring full details are available on request or made readily accessible to those with a special interest.

Private shareholders with small holdings seldom have the patience to study the comprehensive information already available or the understanding to interpret it (there are always retired business people or professionals with time on their hands, who have both, but they are in a small minority). The professionals, usually acting as fund managers for trustees, ought to have the capacity to do both, or they have no business to have bought the shares. 'Buy knowingly' must surely be their maxim—and that does not mean old-fashioned insider 'knowledge'.

Despite generally delegating investment functions to their professional managers, even trustees will find that on occasion they need to study the report and accounts of a particular company—perhaps in the context of a takeover where they have not delegated voting powers to the fund managers, or in connection with the support for a shareholders' resolution.

The way things are moving, the professionals will find themselves sorting through even more facts. Disclosures can obscure as well as illuminate, and one of the skills they need is to distinguish what is important given more verbiage, a task with which they will become increasingly proficient as time progresses! These professionals may be as inclined to tap into the company's web site as to seek lunch with the chairman. Perhaps it is time for shareholders to become more demanding about what they need in the report and accounts. Companies could establish a small review committee from among their shareholders with the simple remit of providing feedback and keeping costs down as much as is consonant with the adequacy of disclosure. And what a lot of money could be saved by cutting out the unnecessary illustrations, so beloved of firms of public relations specialists. As Gilbert and Sullivan advised,

> and when the client proves refractory,
> show him pictures of the factory.

When Burtons floated off Debenhams, the chairman, Sir John Hoskyns, set up a competition among shareholders, employees, and customers to find a new name for the company. The winning entry was 'Arcadia', which nicely combined a notion of a shopping arcade with classical utopia! Diageo by contrast was a name dreamed up by consultants paid several hundred thousand pounds and met bitter criticism at the meeting from shareholders upset that the merging of Guinness and Grand Metropolitan had produced at great cost a name which meant nothing to anyone. *The Times* in due course announced it was a South American rodent.

But above all there are two golden rules. If information is material it should be disclosed, and as succinctly and clearly as possible; this means that the format must allow relevant comparison between companies and against the benchmarks; eventually this will mean internationally. Secondly, the criteria for suppressing information should only be strict grounds of commercial confidentiality; there should not be exclusion of matters merely on grounds of potential embarrassment. The Institute of Chartered Accountants, with the Tomorrow's Company team, have developed a model annual report which reflects this, for 'Prototype' plc. Such experimentation is welcome and should prompt a healthy re-think on the quantity and quality of information provided by the companies. The Shell group of companies is setting the pace with a suite of financial, social, and environmental reports, backed up by detailed specialist data for those who need it. The reports are benchmarked, globally integrated, and externally verified. They surely represent the future for reporting by transnational corporations.

INFORMATION WITHIN THE COMPANY ITSELF

There is one haunting question that is often asked after some catastrophe has affected or engulfed a company—'What was the board doing . . . ?' The question presupposes that the board itself knew what was occurring. It is clear in many cases (from subsequent evidence) that it did not. Ferranti and Atlantic Computers immediately come to mind. A more recent example was Reed Elsevier where the board belatedly found that publication figures of certain publications were being exaggerated to keep the advertising revenues buoyant. The reasons why this was so are unclear—a misplaced sense of loyalty perhaps or the desire to shield senior management from bad news.

The increasing obligation on directors to broaden and deepen disclosure to shareholders places an additional burden on them to ensure that the information systems *within* the company do not let them down. The price of failure can be high; it cost Reed Elsevier £250m. in compensation, to say nothing of what it did to their reputation and share price. Disclosure in other words is the public face of an adequate system of internal information and control.

WHAT INFORMATION?

What shareholders and others need to know falls mainly under what we have dubbed the four Ps. Two speak largely for themselves: Performance: how the various parts of the company have fared in the basic financial reports and non-financial measures that underpin the bottom line; Position: how the company stands in terms of its strength, resources, and situation in relation to the various industries in which it is engaged. The third 'P'—People— requires some enlargement. We have already stressed the need for shareholders to be told more about the functions of the directors; and, in the case of new directors, their past track record (with blemishes) and their qualifications. To this we would add some basic information about the firm's investment in people. But the most important is the fourth P—Prospects.

PROSPECTS

Most of the material in the report and virtually all the numbers in accounts are backward facing. Prospects or looking to the future are more difficult to handle since by definition they rest more heavily on judgement and are most susceptible to fraud in the hands of crooks; consider all the ridiculously over-optimistic prospectuses of a hundred years ago (Kynaston 1994: ii. 176 f.). They are also dangerous in the hands of honest optimists. In its report of September 1995, entitled *Lifting All Boats*, the US Capital Allocation Sub-council of the Competitiveness Policy Council devoted a whole section to 'Improving the quality and availability of information on firms' prospects'. The discussion is conducted in terms of amendments to present US law and regulation, and is not directly applicable to the UK. But the principle is: 'Efficient capital allocation depends on the availability of accurate and fundamental information about companies and their prospects.' The problem is how to achieve this without misleading.

Responsible managers are naturally disinclined to give hostages to fortune (even discounting external surprises over which they have no control like central government economic mismanagement, wars, civil disorders, or freak weather). But management does make judgements, and budgets are the form in which they are generally quantified—though these are for internal use only, and firms would be nervous—understandably—of making them available to the capital markets. If, however, a takeover bid is launched it is generally countered *inter alia* by a profits forecast.

Management is understandably reluctant to signal its commercial intentions too precisely in case competitors move to frustrate its plans. Even so, 'prospects' are far more than a set of imprecise profit figures for the next six months—they cover all aspects of the way the company is preparing for the future. Arguably, disclosure should cover all the main categories of investment for the future, including, vitally, training and retraining policy (and expense) as well as R & D and the more usual items of 'hard' investment in plant and premises. Some companies are in fact good at supplying such information, but the ISC recommendations are still not being universally followed. Whether all this is better presented in a lump or allocated to the sections dealing with various bits of the business is a matter of choice in the light of what is more meaningful. We would include in this section a mention of long-term relationships with suppliers and the firms' payment policies and prices. We would also cover marketing costs as these are part and parcel of investing for the future and it is only too easy to improve the bottom line in the short term by cutting back on them. This is easy to forget about during a bull market.

WORDS AND NUMBERS

There are many reasons for placing emphasis on the virtues of disclosure. Not least among them is the self-discipline it imposes. People are more solicitous about what they are obliged to reveal than about things they can conveniently conceal. Will it on that account make managers more risk averse on the grounds that the less they say, the less there is for which they can be held accountable. We think not. Besides, the directors have a duty to present a 'true and fair' view in the accounts, and this should extend to all information provided in the shareholder circulars.

Companies have long recognized that shareholders' needs and wishes vary according to their own skills, interest, and position and no formula would please all of them. For the most skilled and assiduous even the most detailed accounts and obscure statements are only an obstacle course—a challenge to be surmounted. At the other end of the spectrum, even the most simplified accounts are like Greek. Can 'Sid' understand them?

What seems to have happened over the years is that the numbers have beaten the words. Numbers look accurate; words are vaguer. Numbers speak for themselves; words speak for their authors, frail as they may be. The dividend is reckoned in numbers; words pay for nothing. The auditors can get their teeth into numbers, the judgemental world of words is far more difficult for them. Yet if truth be told all numbers are the subject of judgement. The foundations are built on sand. It is the words that can tell the story best, because the numbers look backward and the words can put the past into perspective with the present and the future. Management discussion and analysis is an example of what can be done if words and numbers are reunited. The numbers give some measure of quantification to the narrative, rather than the words qualifying the numbers. Judgement needs words; and shareholders peering into the future above all need to know how themselves to make judgements. The complexity of operations need not be matched by obscurity in presentation.

The market has long appreciated the importance of qualitative information—witness the yawning gap between book and market value in the UK and elsewhere which indicates how much more there is to valuation than simply adding up the numbers. The reputation of management, quality of corporate governance, and employee and social relations are increasingly priced by the market. Yet disclosure on these qualitative and non-financial aspects of corporate performance can be patchy or non-existent (Brancato 1997, PIRC 1998a). There needs to be a review of reporting requirements to establish a clear format for ensuring such information is consistent, comparable, and verified. This has been partly achieved via the Cadbury Code on board structure and governance; the same is needed on a host of other issues, cited above, where disclosure is poor.

Even if we take today's world as it is, there are some odd features. Management may not make forecasts, but analysts do even though they know less about the business. And although we disagree with the practice, management often moves surreptitiously to amend the analysts' forecasts to bring them into line with what they would themselves present if they had to do so.

The UK is heading in the right direction. No one suggests pulling back, and helpful noises are made from time to time—for instance by the RSA's inquiry into 'Tomorrow's Company' which is making efforts to develop reporting formats on non-financial indicators of performance. It is also debating new formats for the report and accounts under the heading 'Sooner, Sharper, Simpler'(RSA 1998). Much work remains to be done about what shareholders should get, bearing in mind their different needs and skills. The solution is to have a longer menu from which to choose. Some might want a postcard full, others a telephone directory, but whatever the form and length we consider the narrative vital and the section on prospects of the greatest importance.

One final question before we move on. The UK has no organization comparable to the SEC which has 'active oversight' of companies' annual reports and other filings. Lowenstein (1996) reports that in 1996 there were 120 accountants at the SEC engaged in this task. Their value is seen as helping to maintain high standards in financial reporting as much as it is in identifying matters where the reports are misleading or inadequate. Would the quality of disclosure improve if there were some similar screening in force in the UK? Would the cost and burden be worth it for companies who deal with them and investors? Probably. The Stock Exchange has various listing rules requiring disclosure of relevant material, but it has extremely limited monitoring capacity and few sanctions beyond the overreaction of delisting. The solution must be for shareholders to have full and ready access to material information (both financial and non-financial) in a timely manner, but then to be provided with the tools to address problems, rather than simply watching any bad news filter through into the share price. For all the general agreement that disclosure is vital, standards are patchy and access is poor. Notwithstanding the requirements of the listing rules, much can be improved in the type, format, and availability of information.

19

....

The International Dimension

THE great multinational company has become so familiar that it is almost a cliché to comment that of the world's largest 100 economic organizations, less than 50 are nation states and the others are corporations. The multinational serves customers round the globe, employs people in many countries, brushes up against regimes of all sorts, and may have shareholders in many countries whether they invest directly or through a trust or mutual fund.

THE SHAREHOLDERS

The risk of owning shares denominated and trading in a foreign currency adds exchange rate risk to company, political, and market risk; that is one dimension too many for some investors. Besides, electronic trading has not removed all the hassle from owning shares in companies abroad, at least for the private individual, if only because of the tax complications. None of these problems has deterred the professionals as the steadily rising proportion of UK shares in foreign hands shows; it is now around 20 per cent. Paris has 30 per cent or more. Spreading risk geographically is seen as another dimension to asset allocation. It sits alongside the alternative strategy of buying shares of indigenous companies that do a high proportion of their business abroad. A Swiss shareholder in Nestlé is buying into a company that does 97 per cent of its business outside Switzerland. The 1996 IFMA survey shows that their members managed £530.1bn. for overseas clients.

The greater the stability of international currencies the less deterrent there is to holding foreign shares on account of that particular risk. So if the common currency is introduced successfully in Europe the risk will be eliminated in the participating countries, and cross-border holdings seem likely to increase. The 1998 convulsions and capital flight across markets put into sharp focus the hazards of global investing. For the nation states watching footloose capital leave their borders at high speed, it has placed new and urgent emphasis upon the need for common standards to underpin global markets.

TECHNICALITIES

The simple goal of diversification through international investment poses a number of challenges. The mechanics of dealing with foreign reports and accounts may be complex. In the first place they may be in a language that the fund manager does not understand, though increasingly major companies publish an English version. Then the accounting conventions may be different and the figures difficult to compare for that reason. Thirdly, even if the first two obstacles can be crossed, it simply takes longer for the documents to arrive, and there is less time to respond to them than the indigenous shareholders have. Finally, even if a shareholder is minded to take action (and presuming he or she understands the legal requirements in the country concerned), the costs and complications of mounting operations abroad may be a major deterrent. Small wonder therefore that any disposition shareholders have to be active may be undermined by these Grand National fences. There are various trends which will erode such barriers over time—international accounting standards, internet delivery and electronic voting, cross-border alliances of active investors. If the OECD succeeds in its task of establishing minimum corporate governance standards, the global market will be transformed.

VOTING

Private shareholders are as usual in an even weaker position to exert influence. They have sometimes had a rather a poor time of it in indigenous companies as well, so it is not surprising to find organizations springing up in various countries to protect shareholder minorities. Eurotunnel provides an example of the problems faced by small shareholders on both sides of the Channel. The company's shares when floated were heavily promoted by the French government and the majority were bought by private investors. Some invested their life's savings, and, ill advisedly, even pension provision. Only 10 per cent of the shares were sold in the UK, and not much of that to small shareholders. As the company ran into default on its debts, eventually a major restructuring was put to shareholders—many of whom had seen the value of their holding plummet. The matter was complicated by the dual incorporated structure of the company which was listed on both the London stock market and Paris bourse. In the UK the company was making efforts to conform to the governance norms of the stock market, in France, the company was being investigated by a commercial court to determine whether the shareholders were being roughly handled by its banks—a notion unheard of in the UK. Meanwhile, disgruntled private investors in France were banding together under various alliances of varying hues of radicalism, and one was eventually joined by a Bermuda-based fund manager representing Americans. The stage of the 1997 AGM looked set for a classic international confrontation with a potential alliance of private French investors linking with US institutions to scupper a restructuring of the company's debt. The stakes were high as bankruptcy loomed. In the event, there was a surprise volte-face from the Americans and militancy ebbed among the small shareholders. Ironically, under UK law the company's creditors could have pulled the plug long ago and only the protection of French law to the company (over and above its creditors or shareholders) gave the Americans the prospect of anything to squabble over in the first place. Similarly in Korea, private investors made a serious impact at Samsung with the support of overseas institutions. Their determination and imaginative tactics broke new ground in Asian markets.

FUTURE DEVELOPMENTS

There will inevitably be further convergence on accounting practices; the more firms seek to raise capital internationally or seek quotation on overseas stock exchanges, the more likely this becomes. If tax is simplified too, so that expenses are reduced, another obstacle will be easier to surmount—as they should be to assist the most efficient flows of capital. All this may lead to foreign-held stakes growing in significance and if so the incentive for foreign institutions to monitor their investments will increase. There will be circumstances when they find themselves with the pivotal votes—for instance in a takeover. They may wish—as may companies—to develop regular contacts as they would for indigenous companies.

All this leads to two conclusions. The trends to globalization will not lead to an erosion of differences in domestic markets, other than what is absolutely essential for transparency of information and protection of shareholder rights to attract international capital; but beyond this, nations will cherish their special emphasis on particular aspects of corporate purpose. The Germans are not about to abandon the two-tier board just because Americans do not have it; what they will do is harmonize their accounting standards and probably raise dividend payments to satisfy a global audience of shareholders. This will also lead to growing shareholder activism internationally. The disposition of UK voters to abstain may invest foreign holders with an influence out of proportion to their numbers. International shareholders will no doubt form working relationships to exchange information, either via informal networks such as the International Corporate Governance Network, inspired and currently somewhat dominated by 'Anglo Saxon' members, through to the OECD corporate governance working parties which reflect a more diverse constituency in which shareholders are viewed in different ways in relation to the company and others with a legitimate interest. Nations will continue to define their own view of the purpose of the company, and this inevitably leads to a different emphasis upon the role of shareholders. Change will come at a rate dictated by the need to raise capital internationally, and restrained by domestic pressures to retain local features which are valued in particular jurisdictions. With multilateral agencies seeking to establish minimum standards, and local investors forming alliances with overseas shareholders, the stage is set for the liquidity of the global capital markets to be given depth by more secure governance standards. That can only be to the benefit of both domestic and international investors.

The AGM

PERHAPS at the prompting of the seasons, all kinds of regular activity from prehistoric times have been punctuated at set intervals by special events. Many events had and still have a religious connotation; Christmas is a good example—the overlay of Christianity on pagan rites, themselves connected with seasonal change. One of the elements of the prayers and rituals tends to be a kind of formalized stock taking, sometimes coupled with prayers for the next period, accompanied in olden times by propitiatory sacrifices.

In the secular sphere, many kinds of political organizations—like the Athenian democracy or Roman Republic—translated this rhythm into political terms by making provision for the transfer of power at special intervals through regular elections. In the Roman Empire, the form survived long after the reality had changed. Elections are a form of 'stock taking' based on assessment and judgement, coupled with choice for the future.

Such patterns are now so much part of our way of thinking that they generally escape notice. Yet a particular rhythm is not an essential feature of political or economic organization, as history attests. There were many kingdoms or empires like Rome, where (even though reforms might have suggested otherwise) the ruler was not accountable and stayed in office until death or forced removal. The monarchy survives in the UK, and elsewhere in Europe, though its lack of accountability is rendered unimportant by its lack of power. Hitler and Stalin, on the other hand, abolished the electoral calendar in order to maintain power.

The general rhythmical pattern permeates the social milieu. There are few organizations in any part of society that do not have a general meeting on an annual basis at which the leadership render some sort of account of their stewardship. This is true in many social, political, and educational milieux. It is not true of the UK judiciary, in order to protect them from pressure.

THE ANNUAL CYCLE

The choice of a year as the period between company meetings is a reflection of the world of nature and the tyranny of the seasons, rather than any particular logic dictated by the needs of any organization that is not subject to them. This is recognized in the political world by having elections at various intervals: in this the UK has itself varied and to this day does not have a uniform period between elections for all levels of government. As far as companies are concerned, there is no particular reason, especially in these days of overflowing information, why the cycle should be a year long. It might be a half-year, or a quarter, for that matter eighteen months or two years. Of course, taxation has a bearing on the choice of period and most governments raise taxes on an annual cycle. But even this is not necessarily immutable and the accounting period does not have to be twelve months either; indeed companies do from time to time have a different period when they are changing their financial year end from one date to another.

The point of questioning the seeming inevitability of a specific and familiar pattern—namely one year—is that it does not necessarily coincide with the most sensible intervals for assessing the performance of an enterprise either internally or from outside. In commercial organizations there are in fact simultaneously various cycles. An organization needs to review its aims and objectives from time to time—the apotheosis of introspection. It does not serve to do this too often. To become over-introspective is to risk doubt and uncertainty; to live without it is to risk becoming aimless. The process of monitoring is however continual, irrespective of the intervals between rendering account. The processes of management review and decision-taking are both short and long term depending on the issues.

This leads to two conclusions:

1. The periodic general meetings are and always have been about stewardship—in any kind of organization. In those with an economic purpose like a company, accounts are an indispensable way of quantifying the competence of the stewardship, though they are not its only measure. Most employees and shareholders want to feel proud of their companies or at the very least sympathetic to them. Accountability increasingly extends beyond it, very obviously in environmental matters, and as 'stakeholder' thinking develops, it will get broader.

2. The cycle of business operations, which by no means fits into regular cycles of precisely one year, is made to adapt to it by accounting alchemy—accruals and deferrals, depreciation, and all that. What the accountants can do for a business is what photographers with an ordinary camera can do at a football match. Even so, business is a movie and accounts are snapshots.

THE ROLE OF ACCOUNTS

Accounts are the chief exhibit at annual general meetings and the main evidence of stewardship. They put numbers to the chairmen's narratives; to their excuses; but not, because of the conventions, to their hopes (unless a bid has been launched). Those who analyse the company's performance will look at the numbers rather than the words, because they appear to facilitate comparisons with past performance, with other firms in the sector, and with the market as a whole. There is relentless pressure to replace judgement with formulae, so as to be able to replace the skilled by the semi-skilled. This rests in part on the fallacy that numbers are more precise and accurate than words. As anyone who has compiled a set of accounts knows, almost every number is a judgement. Who knows what the stock is really worth, which debtors will fail, which dire contingencies will reduce the value of a project? The values in the balance sheet are often virtually meaningless, as the periodic collapse of property prices demonstrates. All the conventions affecting accounting and valuation may tend to curb optimism and induce prudence, but they cannot ensure accuracy. There are bound to be grey areas about treating particular expenses or costs as if they enhanced capital values rather than writing them off as incurred. Management has to exercise judgement in preparing the figures. However honest it is and however much it may rely on past experience, the judgement may in the event prove wrong. Most of the time it will be near enough for general purposes, but wrong enough in retrospect to show that figures are less precise than they appear.

COME THE DAY

Viewed from the inside, the AGM is a nuisance, interrupting the normal flow of business for the executive members of the board and a great many of their supporting staff. Management is used to having to squeeze the normal rhythm of business into the ill-fitting corset of annual accounts, but the job will have been done (not without disagreement on some points with the auditors). During the year, the main shareholders have, if the company knows which side its bread is buttered, all been seen, to keep them in touch with the company's general progress and plans, in order to convey a sense of competence which will inspire confidence from shareholders.

The chairman will, at great expense, be well briefed on every conceivable question that might be raised at the AGM. He (there are few female chairmen among listed companies) may well have in front of him a volume of notes as large as the London telephone directory, but far less readable.

Few companies nowadays pick obscure venues for their AGMs on unlikely days: Christmas Eve in Wigan is not a regular date for companies, although Costain was criticized for holding its meeting over the holiday period when being challenged by environmental groups. There is no conspiratorial arrangement to hold meetings on the same day, as there is in Japan, although there is substantial clustering of meetings, meaning that five or six large companies may be holding their AGM on the same day, making it impossible for the assiduous shareholder to attend them all. Many companies make efforts to broaden participation, by rotating the venue of the AGM around the country (as BT and British Gas—now BG and Centrica—have done) in order to allow regionally based shareholders to attend.

The style of meeting varies, and not just with the size of the company, or the spread of the shareholders. A locally held company, meeting in a hostelry in the heart of its business area, may encounter a lively and informed audience wanting hard facts, not soft options. On the other hand it may find that only two shareholders have turned up and one of these is the retired sales director, so the whole process including resolutions is concluded in six or seven minutes.

A major business may hire a huge room at a hotel, only to find a tiny and mute audience. Some, particularly those that are, by accident or design, in the public eye, may anticipate or be used to lively proceedings, and deal with them by stage managing a set piece of theatre designed to dazzle the audience. There may be formal presentations—or none at all. Some chairmen take the view that if the figures are good, they say it all; and if they are bad, the least said, soonest mended. *Qui s'excuse s'accuse.* The chairman may occasionally arrange to deflect questions to other directors or more usually handle them himself. Cadbury and Greenbury broke new ground by suggesting that chairmen of audit and remuneration committees should have questions referred to them. The chairman's general objective in meetings may be to break the record for brevity and he may be firm about achieving it.

The provision of refreshments or other goodies varies according to taste. The better they are the more likely small shareholders are to be attracted (which the chairman may not relish); on the other hand, there is nothing like the scent of gin to make the body of shareholders impatient with the garrulous. Some chairmen enjoy the challenge of a confrontational meeting, in a similar way to an able minister at the dispatch box at Question Time in Parliament. Others fear losing face, temper, and control.

AGMs may be enlivened by professional nit pickers who know how to make awkward points; by disruptive single issue groups, who have slipped past the increasingly heavy-handed security arrangements; or by eloquent and informed campaigners with a serious point to press with the board, which other shareholders may even support in the meeting. Apart from these, who at the least are articulate, there is the occasional eccentric contributor pressing some obscure point with great vigour; representatives of the institutions who may look grave but stay silent; former employees who know the company well; and even those with a personal grudge. Finally, the media may be allowed in to observe proceedings, but usually only if the company is fairly sure it will not get a rough ride at the meeting.

There are many people who might want to attend the meeting, and hear what the directors say, but who are not shareholders. These have no right to attend. In this group are included employees, members of the local communities affected by the company's operations, bankers and debenture holders, or key suppliers. At first sight they may appear to have much in common with the shareholders. For debt holders, their interest is in the company's capacity to repay a specific debt when due, but not perhaps in any other matters dealt with at the meeting. Suppliers are in a similar but not identical position, in that the capacity they dedicate to the company may not be easily transferred elsewhere if they lose its custom. An issue to consider is whether employees, who have as great, if not greater interest in the company's prosperity than shareholders, should have some presence at the AGM as observers or participants. For service industries with low capital requirements and a highly skilled workforce, arguably the employees are of more importance to the company's prosperity than the shareholders.

EMPLOYEES AT AN AGM

There are two different possibilities, the first of which is far less controversial—some employees attending as observers. The rationale for their doing so would be to involve them in the company's affairs more closely. The arguments against it are that unless they bought a share or two they would be barred from contributing (by definition), and they might feel frustrated. Besides, they might well fear to ruffle management, and would need to take time off. In a big multinational group it could be difficult to decide what constituted an appropriate balance, and costly to implement it. It cannot however be seriously argued that only members should attend as so many non-members already do so.

The second possibility would be to let some chosen representatives attend as if they were members and participate in the proceedings. If the formalities had to be observed they might attend as proxies or on the back of a single share. The main objection to their presence would be the diffusion of accountability. A management that had to answer both employees and shareholders, whose interests are not necessarily identical on a particular issue, might well end up satisfying neither. Not all employees have the same interests. Supposing a firm had four plants, one of which was dragging down the whole enterprise. The employees of the other three plants might take a different view of its closure from those employed there.

Rather than inviting representatives of the employees to participate in general meetings, it would be preferable to concentrate on improving arrangements within the company for information and consultation to make people feel they are part of the same team—a far cry from confrontational modes but something which the more enlightened management and unions of modern Britain have shown can be done. The introduction of works councils may help this process, though many large firms already have satisfactory arrangements in place. The key to solving this is to boost employee share ownership, and, rather than simply handing the shares over to a trust, to allow employees to have rights to attend as beneficial owners.

It will increasingly be the case that employees hold shares personally or through some collective scheme and if so, it is right and proper that they should attend general meetings *qua* shareholders. Would this compromise confidentiality? It is hard to see how. In general concerns over 'confidentiality' are too often used to conceal what one is ashamed to disclose rather than what it would be genuinely damaging to reveal.

Our conclusion therefore is that there would be no damage, and perhaps some benefit, to employees attending as observers at the AGM, and for those employees who hold shares, arrangements should be made to encourage them to attend and vote. Among many of the collective vehicles (such as ESOPs) this issue has barely been addressed, although one reason for giving employee share ownership schemes tax privileges was to encourage employee participation in the company. Currently it is extremely difficult to arrange this as the shareholder rights rest with the trust and not with the employees who own the shares. This needs reform.

ABOLISH THE AGM?

This makes us enquire whether when the last torn-up agenda has been binned, and the last coffee cup borne away to be washed, we should ask— what is the value of the AGM? Could more be gained from them? Or, to adopt the modern style of zero budgeting, what would we lose if the AGM were abolished? It is one test of the value of any institution to consider what its abolition would mean.

AGMs are of little moment if the company is prospering and the shareholders have no complaints. They provide an opportunity for compliments, but as a cynic put it, 'The only place one finds "gratitude" is in the dictionary.' It certainly does not figure at the AGM except in perfunctory form. The silent applause comes from those who held on to their shares or bought more. The better a company performs (on all fronts) the more boring the AGM. Only when times are troubled, and the company has done poorly, or the directors' greed is abnormal, or there has been a scandal, can a flicker of real flame be seen, and felt. This is all perfectly sensible—up to a point—and it provides a possible clue to a different course of action. There are two possibilities: make the AGM a working meeting, or abolish it unless extreme circumstances require it to be convened. The first proposition has generated various suggestions for reform, which we consider below. First, though, the alter-native—if the AGM is not being used, why not abandon it?

As meetings are most needed in times of trouble, there is an argument in theory for abolishing the regular AGM, but making it easier for shareholders to call a meeting if they have complaints. The circulation of the report and accounts could continue, as at present, with the accompanying resolutions; proposals for the election or re-election of directors likewise. All votes would be postal (or electronic). If shareholders wished to convene a meeting they could have an expanded set of powers to their current right to call an extraordinary general meeting. We could call this new form of meeting a 'special general meeting'. This would allow shareholders to convene a meeting, table resolutions for the agenda, and have the right to circulate material. Shareholder resolutions for an SGM would be accompanied by an explanatory text, and a response from the directors. The threshold for calling an extraordinary general meeting by shareholders currently is 10 per cent, which is too high.

The purpose of the law allowing shareholders to convene a meeting is that it caters for those issues which fall outside the normal cycle of the AGM. The timing of the AGM only fits pressing need by accident. Judging by the poor attendance at most AGMs the present system is out of touch with reality. Even so, we judge that the abolition of such a venerable procedure would be the corporate governance reformer's Arnhem—a bridge too far. So rather than try to capture it we turn to the alternative strategy: reform.

MAKING THE AGM MORE EFFECTIVE

Those who defend the AGM point out correctly that whether shareholders take the opportunity or not, it is an annual opportunity to see the whites of the directors' eyes, see them debate questions in person, and take them out of the secluded environment of private briefings and PR groomed perfor-mances. Seeing the directors on the platform and hearing them answer questions may provide some valuable clues about the company's leadership. It is also an opportunity to hear the views of other shareholders.

Even so, most will contend, out of habit and tradition if not logic, that a year is so embedded in our subconscious that it is the natural period for rendering account, and that account should be rendered in person. They will stress the discipline it imposes within a company, at least in theory. Few will however defend the AGM in its present form; if it is to be retained it should be made more effective. In this there are a number of issues to consider.

WHO SHOULD ATTEND?

The general meetings of companies are generally viewed as private occasions for members and no one else has a right to attend. This even applies to directors unless they hold shares or the articles permit it. In practice, especially for bigger companies, the AGM has become a public occasion, at which the media may even be welcome. It is a PR opportunity. Many companies provide tickets for guests, shareholders, proxies, and corporate representatives which are different colours to allow the chairman to know who is who.

Every individual shareholder in a company has the right to attend the AGM. This could provide practical problems for companies, and indeed some utilities have seen several hundred, or even thousand, shareholders turn up for the meeting. Companies have in recent years been seeking amendments to their articles to allow shareholders to attend via video links in overflow rooms (such as Shell) and even by ticketing arrangements to restrict access (such as GUS). With the development of new technology, the problem of physical attendance at the meeting will no doubt soon be resolved via 'on line' meetings or the use of cable television (as Scottish Power has done).

A simple way to solve any potential attendance problem would be to restrict access to all shareholders who did not hold a certain proportion of the equity (for example, a minimum of 0.001 per cent). This has been canvassed as a method of excluding special interest groups who have bought a share in order to raise their particular cause at the AGM (such as environmental groups and campaigners against the arms trade). However, to restrict access inevitably impinges upon the rights of current shareholders. One benefit of such a rule would be that all attending would be seriously interested in the business, by dint of representing a substantial investment in the company. The restriction suggested above would limit attendance to a maximum of 1,000 (by definition). Those with smaller shareholdings would have to club together to ensure their attendance. Another possible form of restriction would be to limit rights of attendance to shareholders who had held their shares for a certain period of time. This would deter 'bandwagon' campaigners and fly-by-night speculators. Even under these arrangements, all shareholders would still receive the report and accounts and could vote by proxy as at present. We do not support such proposals. The principle of equal access for shareholders regardless of size is one to be cherished. Often it is the small holders who have raised the important questions, or campaigners with one share who have brought a serious issue to the attention of the board, and other shareholders at the meeting.

However, this is running ahead. What is the problem with the AGM which reform is attempting to solve? Is it lack of interest by shareholders, or too much interest from a certain group of shareholders? Can both of these problems be tackled by the same reforms, and are they even linked?

Although some have argued there should be restrictions on attendance at the AGM, we do not overall consider them to be practical or desirable. The real problem is not those who do attend, but those who do not. This means considering the nature of business at the meeting, and why the majority of shareholders (and usually most of the institutions) do not consider it worth their while even bothering to attend.

The AGM should be the high point of the year. The directors present the report and accounts which sets out the fruits of their efforts on behalf of shareholders, they offer themselves for re-election (assuming all stand down), and the auditors must be approved. Would it be possible to make the AGM a working meeting in which shareholders exercise their powers effectively?

What are some of the problems which shareholders currently face? Leaving to one side for the moment the cultural baggage which means the AGM is relegated as an event of little importance, upstaged by preliminary results, private meetings with institutions, and analysts' briefings—for the AGM to come centre stage, some of this competition, off stage, needs to be rethought. For example, why shouldn't briefings happen at the AGM rather than in a separately staged event for the media and analysts some weeks beforehand which inevitably means the financials are 'old news' and the probing questions on strategy have already been put forward and reported? The Hampel Committee suggested in its report (1998) that the directors make a business presentation at the AGM. We consider that unless something new and worth hearing is announced by the company, there will be little to tempt the institutions to attend.

There are some signs of life at company meetings—they regularly feature in the City news columns, as not only private investors, but protesters, and even active institutional representatives such as PIRC, attend to ask questions, call polls, or hear what the company has to say in response to shareholder criticisms. An example was Farnell, a medium-sized engineering and catalogue company which bid for a much larger company, Premier. The bid attracted some controversy, with opposition not only from PIRC but also Standard Life, a leader in governance issues in the UK. The company had booked a small upstairs room at its offices on an industrial estate near Whitby racecourse, far from any public transport. No doubt the expectation was that only a handful would attend. In fact not only were leading institutions present at the meeting, but former employees and executives, advisers, and even the national press. The small crowded room heard a tense debate about the virtues, risks, and financing of the bid. This and other occasions show that far from being moribund, the AGM is actually coming to life.

Let us assume that companies intend to treat the AGM not as a formality to finish off the paperwork, but as an occasion on which to secure the shareholders' support for their regime and the board's future strategy. What changes need to be made to the arrangements in force under the present legal framework?

THE TIMETABLE

Consider first the timetable. Under the Companies Act, an AGM is obligatory. It must take place not less than seven months after the end of the financial year. The shareholders are entitled to receive the report and accounts, which are prepared according to statutory requirements (profit and loss, balance sheet, directors' report, and so forth) and required resolutions, such as appointment of the auditors, election of new directors, alterations to capital, and any amendments to articles. Along with the report and accounts the company must circulate a summary of resolutions (for the full text of proposed changes to the articles, the hapless shareholders must visit the solicitor's office and take a pen and paper—they are not entitled to a copy). The law does not provide that full information should be made available to shareholders, although the Stock Exchange does require that all information should be provided which is necessary to a voting decision. It is up to companies to interpret what this might mean. Shareholders wanting to consider diligently a new share incentive plan for the directors, or an amendment to the articles, will have to go to considerable lengths to view the necessary documentation. By law they may inspect a number of documents, but are not entitled to a copy. When PIRC wanted to inspect the minutes of the AGM at EMAP, this entailed a trip to Peterborough. This is merely inconvenient for shareholders based in London, but for overseas investors the situation is impractical.

For all material or relevant matters, shareholders should be entitled to information in a readily accessible form. The Stock Exchange rules only provide that the documents should be made available for inspection fifteen minutes prior to the AGM. One can imagine that the queue from shareholders would rival that for the cloakrooms if the documents contained controversial issues. For documents such as the articles to be displayed like holy relics in the antechamber of the meeting is ridiculous. Simply filing past these documents is hardly sufficient.

The notice must be dispatched just twenty-one days before the meeting. There is no mention of whether it should go by first or second class post, and whether weekends and bank holidays should be taken into account. This has quite an impact on those companies (of which there are many) holding their AGMs over the Easter bank holiday period, following a 31 December financial reporting period.

Shareholders first need to have established arrangements to receive the material. In the case of private shareholders, this means doing a deal with the nominee holder of their account, and in the case of the institution, ensuring that the holder of the shares refers the material to the body responsible for making voting decisions. This procedure must then be put into reverse once consideration of the material has been given, and the institution then instructs a complex chain of command in order to ensure that the custodian holding the shares casts the vote in accordance with their client's wishes. It is not uncommon for custodians (or subcustodians) to require eight days' notice for this. The proxy must arrive forty-eight hours before the meeting at the company's registrars. Again, there is no requirement at law for companies to make their proxy deadline a day with postal services. A Tuesday AGM means a Sunday proxy vote, with another day sliced from the timetable.

The date of the AGM will for practical reasons be set well in advance. It should therefore be notified to shareholders much earlier, either by announcement at the prior AGM, or, at the least, announced with the interims. Furthermore, the materials for the meeting should be sent out earlier, to allow shareholders time to consider them carefully. The Institute of Chartered Secretaries and Administrators has suggested that twenty working days should be the minimum notice, and the Hampel Committee has endorsed this. At certain times of the year, this would be particularly useful, due to the bank holidays. It ought also to take account of days without a postal service.

The 'clustering' of AGMs on the same day would ideally be dealt with via cooperation between company secretaries (perhaps via the ICSA) to ensure a 'fixtures' list which would allow shareholders to attend all meetings if they should want to. For the largest 350 companies, which make up over 90 per cent of the portfolio of most institutions by value, this would at least coordinate morning and afternoon meetings within the same broad location.

A full copy of all relevant documentation should be available promptly on request.

A further anomaly on the timetable also needs to be addressed: shareholder resolutions. These are important, but little used, powers which allow members to put forward an item of business for the meeting. Under the Companies Act, six weeks' notice must be given to the company by the shareholders intending to requisition a resolution. As the company only has to provide three weeks' notice, the shareholder must either have prescience or inside knowledge to work out what the deadline is for filing a resolution.

PIRC has argued that shareholders should also be able to propose a resolution after the report and accounts have been published. This would mean in effect that the agenda for the meeting, containing the resolutions, would be dispatched after the report and accounts. This would further extend the timetable, and allow shareholders to respond to the information in the report and accounts (PIRC 1997a). Too often shareholders, on those rare occasions of filing a resolution, have drawn up their proposal with only a broad indication of what the board intends to disclose in the report and accounts. Electronic delivery will in due course cut down the costs of such an exercise, which is the main objection companies might have to these proposals.

INFORMATION DISCLOSURE

Despite the premium which the market places upon the timely disclosure of full information, there are still areas in UK corporate governance where current practice is woefully inadequate. Take the example of the directors who must be elected at the AGM. There are no requirements under the Companies Act for biographical details to be disclosed, simply the person's name and their date of appointment to the board. There may be provisions in the articles which modify other Companies Act rules such as the requirement to be given special notice of a director aged 70.

The Stock Exchange also makes only a lame gesture in this direction. It requires that 'brief biographical details' should be provided about the non-executive directors. There is no reference to the executives. This is clearly not appropriate. Brevity may conceal information of importance which may not be flattering to the individual concerned. Hampel made a half-hearted effort to improve this by saying that the directors who retire for re-election should provide biographical details. This is inadequate as shareholders need details for the full board. The old legal maxim *suppressio verio, suggestio falsi* is apt (suppression of the truth creates a false impression).

Leading companies in recent years have published their report and accounts without including full details of all the directors. In most cases there was clearly no suggestion that the candidates concerned had skeletons in their cupboard that should be declared to shareholders. However, the same principle applies; a full 'warts and all' biography should be provided. Where the director has been on the board or at senior level in a company which has failed this is surely relevant.

To vote at the AGM on a director, shareholders are entitled at the least to a full biography, a statement of all current and recent directorships (as per the Companies House return required for all directors), public and other significant appointments, plus, dare we say, a full account of any former convictions, DTI investigations, bankruptcies, disqualifications, regulatory sanctions, and referrals. For candidates to specialist committees such as audit or remuneration, special reference should be made to the qualifications or training received by the candidates which suit them for the post in question. It is notable that prominent corporate collapses and scandals have not prevented non-executives who were on the board at the time of the troubles in question from reappearing without a blush as candidates elsewhere.

With so inadequate a picture of the candidates, it is understandable that shareholders treat the approval of directors as a formality. They have no opportunity at the AGM to quiz candidates on their suitability, calibre, and proposed role, though the chairman may respond to questions; however, the latter are, in politburo fashion, viewed as disloyal and 'no' votes are viewed as almost treasonable.

SHAREHOLDER RESOLUTIONS—AND AMENDMENTS

Let us imagine that our shareholders have become restive and are concerned to read in the report and accounts that a poor performance in some important part of the business, or some policy development, might imperil its future or that inappropriate and substantial sums of money are being paid to the directors which they consider an expensive waste of money, and damaging to the company's reputation and employee morale. The first step is to raise the matter in question at a private meeting, if they can secure one, or otherwise in correspondence. Neither bears fruit.

They consider the AGM agenda. There is no vote on the particular issue. If it is a matter of remuneration, shareholder approval is not required, and the individuals in question (either the recipient or the decision-maker from the relevant committee) may not be standing for re-election. They may be exempt under the articles from retiring by rotation, or it may simply not be their turn under current UK practice, under which approximately (and sometimes very approximately) one-third of the board stands down each year.

We gave an account earlier of the different types of shareholder resolution. They are rarely used but they provide an important protection under the law. They are a potentially useful means of resolving disputes over major issues, without the 'nuclear' option of voting the board out, or selling the shares in question. They also pass the disputed matter for judgement to other members of the company.

The shareholder who wants to requisition a resolution faces a practical dilemma. Although the resolution is an essential tool in the kit of the active shareholder, it is particularly tricky to use. The first requirement is that the shareholder hold 5 per cent of the equity. This is a high target for large listed companies, where the UK's largest beneficial holder, the Prudential, will typically have 3 per cent of a stock on a market weighting. However reasonable the resolution, without this substantial stake, it is not possible to move forward. This is the Brobdingnagian solution. Only giants can intervene.

However, the law does provide for a Lilliputian solution. Here 100 shareholders owning not less than £100 on average may requisition a resolution. This may seem straightforward enough. However, there are few shareholders who are on speaking terms with 99 others in the same company. For shareholders who wish to identify 99 others, the task is not made simple due to the use of nominee accounts. The shareholder is entitled to inspect an elderly copy of the share register lodged with Companies House. These can be horribly unusable documents. Shareholders may be listed by size, alphabetical order, or any other sequence which the company considers satisfactory. There may simply be a paper register with hundreds of thousands of references, or a computer screen scrolling endless numbers of account holders.

The share register only lists the nominee accounts, not the ultimate owner of the shares—known as the beneficial owners. More than one shareholder is probably using an account provided by his fund manager or custodian. It is equivalent to looking for a plumber in the Yellow Pages with all references to plumbing removed!

Account number 1234TT nominees will tell the shareholder nothing about the name, identity, or address of the real owner. If the shareholder is sufficiently enterprising to consult a directory of nominees or use a database service, this will only tell who the nominee account is registered by, not who uses it. A further improvement to disclosure would be to require at least a quarterly updating of the share register for public records, identifying the ultimate owners using individual nominee accounts and beneficial holders.

In the rare event, let us imagine that our diligent shareholder has managed to identify 99 others and they have agreed to requisition the resolution. The next step is to lodge it with the company. It may already be too late. Although the shareholders only receive their report and accounts, with the notice of meeting, three weeks before the meeting (or thereabouts if the post is reliable), any resolution must be lodged six weeks before the meeting. Obviously, it means shareholders cannot lodge a resolution in response to what they read in the report and accounts, which dramatically narrows the purpose of such an instrument. Of course, they can always wait until next year . . . PIRC's pension fund clients faced just this situation in filing a resolution at British Gas. Meetings with the company, Select Committee hearings, and an inspection of contracts indicated that a controversial policy on remuneration had been agreed. However, the resolution had to be filed 'blind' in order to meet the timetable, in this case a practical one, for including the material in the print run for the AGM.

For the purposes of this example, though, let us suppose that the shareholder wants to address an issue which is not contained directly within the report and accounts, for example, it relates to an issue which has arisen over the year, perhaps through close press attention to the company's activities.

Even if they have managed to dodge the difficulties of the timetable, and identify sufficient numbers of others, our doughty shareholders have another problem to confront: costs. When the directors put forward a resolution (even if it is not required by statute) the company foots the bill. When the directors want to mount a public relations campaign in order to promote their views, again, the company pays. There is apparently no limit to the shareholder resources which can be deployed by the directors, if they consider they are in the right. When the directors disagree on a course of action, the recourse to company funds can become a vexed issue.

The company does not automatically pay for shareholder requisitions. When a shareholder resolution is lodged, the requisitionists must provide an undertaking to bear the reasonable costs incurred by the company in relation to the resolution. No doubt the courts would have a field day with this. Is it reasonable to ask the requisitionists to pay for the typesetting, the printing, the paper? Should it include postage and envelopes? A proportion of labour costs? The costs of postage alone for a share register running to half a million shareholders or more could be crippling. This may not be all. What about the time involved with the company secretary, board directors, and legal advisers in considering the resolution? The total costs, though reasonable, may be prohibitive.

It is no surprise therefore that shareholder resolutions in the UK are rare and greeted with alarm by most boards of directors. In the USA the shareholder is not bound by red tape, or deterred by prohibitive costs. Not surprisingly, the average US AGM is substantially more interesting, as the agenda is likely to contain at least one proposition put forward by the owners for consideration.

QUESTIONS

It is no surprise that the typical AGM will not contain a single item of business proposed by shareholders, even though the company may be at the centre of controversy, failing badly, or generally in the doldrums financially. However, those who bother to attend have the opportunity to ask questions. They are not entitled to an answer. Chairmen are not required to answer questions and some are skilled at brushing them aside. The modern method for large companies is for the meeting to provide microphones which are under the direction of the chairman, or even stands where the chairman may simply cut off the shareholder from being heard by the rest of the meeting. The heavy security presence at some AGMs means that shareholders who do not cooperate face the prospect of being carted off by men in uniform, though in some cases this has been to calls of 'shame' from other shareholders who consider such interference to be heavy-handed. Where the directors have faced verbal and even physical attack at the AGM, such measures are understandable, though not excusable.

If the AGM has any purpose it must be to encourage critical questioning and informed debate among shareholders. This means investors themselves need to make more effort. The Cadbury Committee suggested that companies should ask shareholders to write in with questions in advance, which would therefore allow the directors to give a considered response. The practice, though generally welcome, can be abused. Spin doctoring at the AGM is an art. The carefully planted shareholder question, which combines to praise the chairman and ask a leading question allowing an answer which flatters the board, is reminiscent of the sycophancy of Question Time in Parliament when the trusty supporters of HM Government can use an enquiry regarding court luncheons to exude compliments in the hope of preferment.

However, there is a serious potential use to such a procedure, not to prevent tough questioning of the board on the spot, but to allow full preparation of a decent answer. Questions could be considered by a committee of NEDs who would eliminate the trivial or personal, and group similar questions together. Such questions could be incorporated into the order paper circulated to the meeting. Supplementaries should be allowed, and, of course, minutes of the meeting should be circulated to all shareholders with the next convenient mailing, rather than allowing such an account of the meeting to moulder at the solicitor's office. The Hampel Committee has suggested that companies should circulate a 'résumé' of the meeting; better still the minutes, which are a formal document, should be circulated. This entirely sensible suggestion was dropped in the final report.

THE AUDITORS

The auditors rarely have more than a bit part at the AGM. They may be called upon to read out the audit report in sonorous tones and to smile pleasantly upon accepting the proposal that they be reappointed and the directors are authorized to remunerate them. They are appointed by the board, but their responsibility is to the shareholders. The shareholders, however, simply ratify the appointment of the auditors and authorize the directors to pay their fees. The Companies Act allows shareholders to seek the removal of auditors, but such a course of action is virtually unknown. There are other concerns. Shareholders have little information about the consultancy work done by the firm and under UK disclosure rules do not even have to declare non-audit work outside the UK. Sadly their role in reviewing corporate governance has been curtailed by the Hampel Committee's recommendations.

The auditors have the right to attend the AGM; and may be invited to read out their report or qualifying comment. Otherwise, they must stay silent. The chairman may in his wisdom ask them to respond to a comment or question, but he can refuse a request by shareholders to question the auditors. The purpose of the auditors' attending the AGM needs to be clarified. If they are there, it must be for a reason. The Cadbury Committee recommended that the chairman of the audit committee should be available to answer questions at the AGM; the Auditing Practices Board has endorsed this.

MULTINATIONAL DIMENSION

UK companies are among the world's most international businesses. Likewise, the London stock market is one of the premier global markets. Whatever is done to improve the AGM must take account of the fact that a substantial proportion of the company's business may be conducted over-seas, and also that its shareholder base is not necessarily in the UK. The company itself may have a listing on more than one international market. Overseas investors can only benefit from an improvement to the timetable in the UK market, fuller information, and more practical access to the agenda of the meeting via shareholder resolutions plus a proper account circulated afterwards. The most important issue for overseas (and absent) shareholders is the UK voting system, which requires a thorough overhaul.

VOTING BY PROXY

As described earlier the UK has a bizarre voting system. Shareholders have the right to vote on a range of important issues. Their views are solicited, and, via appointment of a proxy, even those who do not attend are asked to cast their votes for or against each proposal. Shareholders may therefore imagine that by filling in their proxy card, and ensuring it is delivered in time for the meeting to the correct address, they have in fact voted. In fact, they have not. This is what actually happens.

The general practice at the meeting takes place on an entirely different basis. Shareholders who attend the meeting will have had a number of resolutions put before them. The chairman will invite questions from the floor, and then will respond. The board may answer, adequately, or not. The platform may be wholly worsted in the argument. However, the matter will eventually be put to the vote. At a normal AGM, there may be no questions and debate, and the votes will be taken in quick succession allowing max-imum time for refreshments immediately afterwards. The chairman at this stage will have no interest in the votes sent in to the meeting by absent shareholders, even though they will overwhelm the votes of those present. The vote will be taken on a 'show of hands'. Hence, the resolution is passed (in most cases) by a majority of those present at the meeting, regardless of what the proxy votes might indicate. However, this is not on a system of one share, one vote. Each shareholder has the same status in the meeting; regardless of the number of shares each owns, each shareholder has only one hand to raise in the meeting. This transition from 'one share one vote' to 'one shareholder one vote' means that farcical situations arise. Occasion-ally due to the ire of the meeting, or close questioning, or a heavy turnout from interested parties, the chairman may not win the vote on a show of hands. If he decides in advance that victory is unlikely due to the restive nature of the meeting, he may be able to circumvent the show of hands altogether. Those who have bothered to attend, and consider they have pressed their point effectively, are about to be out-manoeuvred. The chair-man may call a poll, when he considers fit. Hence if he loses a vote on a show of hands, he can turn to the proxies cast beforehand, which, almost by sleight of hand, become the votes which determine the business of the day.

It is not all the chairman's prerogative on this issue. A shareholder who is confident that proxies will show some opposition, or even a principled proponent of one share one vote, can seek to call a poll. However, the shareholder must have the backing of others at the meeting for this procedure to be valid. The Stock Exchange limits the number of supporters a company may require. Whereas articles of association traditionally stated that two members of the company must seek this course of action (effectively, a proposer and a seconder, whereas the chairman could act alone), the upper limit is now five. This means that four other shareholders attending the meeting must support the call for a poll.

Even at this point (and four are not always willing or available) the chairman can (and often does) plead inconvenience and delay caused by the procedure as an excuse for not going ahead; the shareholder will usually be requested to withdraw the call for a poll. Persistent characters will prevail, backed by the number specified in the company's articles (which will also be frighteningly precise about the timing of such a request, otherwise it may be ruled out of order).

At this point, the proxy votes, representing those who are not at the meeting, and who have not heard the debate, are brought to bear on the business of the day. Those who have bothered to attend, press their questions, and hear the reply may be understandably infuriated if the proxies then prevail on a poll. Of course, any shareholders who have voted by proxy, but then decided to turn up, can countermand their voting decisions.

There is therefore a tension between the evident democratic merits of the one share one vote system, and the problems of 'absentee landlords' determining the outcome simply by completing the proxy form in advance of the AGM itself. We are persuaded that shareholder democracy is best served by allowing one share one vote. The advent of electronic voting procedures and potential for participation in debate would make proxy voting efficient and effective.

Whilst this voting system prevails, the AGM will remain largely a theatrical, or procedural, event, with too little of substance to interest the large and long-term investors which determine the company's fate. Reform is necessary—to the timetable, the right to introduce resolutions, and the conduct of meetings to ensure the AGM is a working meeting, rather than a ritual.

21

The Obligations of Significant Ownership

So far we have considered the duties of some shareholders that arise from their duty to the beneficiaries. We have argued that this duty includes as a very minimum the obligation to see their shares are voted. The actions they take may well improve the running of a business, but their obligation to that business derives from their fiduciary position. The private shareholder has no such obligation. What though of other shareholders who may have a significant holding? Is it acceptable to continue with a view that they owe no duty to the company at all, or do their rights also incur responsibilities? We would argue that rights incur responsibilities for these investors also, even though they are not fiduciaries. The following arguments apply to private investors, who will be investing alongside the institutions whose main role has been explained earlier. The reason is that wider society is entitled to expect responsible ownership from those upon whom the law confers substantial rights.

AN OLD PRINCIPLE RENEWED

The proposition that shareholder rights incur shareholder responsibilities is a more general and broader proposition based on quite different criteria. At first glance it may look radical, but closer inspection shows that it is not; it is the logical development of an idea that is, in different spheres, wholly acceptable (and sometimes enshrined in law). Put simply it is this: the ownership of a significant proportion of a company's shares imposes obligations. We will first of all address the basic principle and then consider what we mean by 'significant proportion' and 'obligations'.

THE RESPONSIBILITIES OF OWNERSHIP

In an earlier chapter we examined what 'ownership' meant and its connection with control. There is no precise general meaning, but the rights vary according to the particular circumstances. Now we look at the other side of the coin and see that this is true of obligations too.

The doctrine of significant ownership imposing obligations is deeply embedded in English law and history—as far back as the feudal system. It was recognized by enlightened industrialists throughout the industrial revolution, with the Quaker firms shining examples—Cadbury's, Fry's, Lever Brothers. It has been recognized by enlightened landowners throughout the ages *Noblesse oblige*. To be sure the majority did not honour—and may not have accepted—such obligations. But few will dispute the principle—not least because it has so long found expression in the tax system. The idea that people should pay the same tax irrespective of wealth now strikes us as ludicrously unfair (and was one of the main objections to the way the poll tax worked in practice). Obligations attach to the owners of Grade I listed buildings that do not apply to a terraced house in the Rhondda. There is a huge sense of unfairness when rich people dodge taxes by devious accounting devices; the jobbing gardener or decorator who 'includes himself out' of VAT or income tax suffers disapproval but to a far lesser degree. There is not only one rule for the rich and one for the poor, but also a shading of moral attitudes to breaches of the rules.

Our proposition is that the inequality of obligation in the tax system (the more you have the more you pay) applies to ownership too, and in the context of this book specifically to the ownership of shares. It is unreasonable and indeed impractical to load obligation on 'Sid' or 'Aunt Agatha'; and we do not suggest it should be done. If they want to band together to exercise influence and power so much the better, but it would be quite wrong to try to force them to do so.

Before we go further, we must repeat the reason why we believe an obligation is necessary. It is because the good working of the market-based system demands it for economic, social, and political reasons. The economic reason is that there needs to be a mechanism for controlling boards that do not work well so as to prevent unnecessary waste of resources; the social reason is that listed companies are a crucial and integral part of the fabric of a modern society and their success reduces alienation; the political reason is that the limited liability company has achieved its far-sighted originators' aims beyond their wildest dreams, of producing concentrations of power and resources, and that those who exercise these powers must be effectively accountable for the way they do so. The power and influence of the leaders of companies in domestic politics—and indeed internationally—are considerable.

We are left with the inescapable conclusion that the best available guardians of companies—and because of that the system as a whole—are significant shareholders who alone have the necessary combination of power, influence, and interest to warrant bearing modest obligations. These obligations are intended to override the conflicts of interest, costs, and systemic efficiencies which lead to passivity by shareholders individually and result in collective lack of oversight over companies. Some would argue that imposing duties on fiduciary investors can act as a proxy for introducing a more general shareholder obligation as they hold a majority of listed companies' shares. Yet it is simply an accident of history that we are in this position and could give rise to arbitrary results; one company may have the bulk of its shares owned by institutions and therefore be subject to routine oversight via voting, another may not and consequently will not be monitored as carefully. This is neither economically nor socially desirable.

What precisely do we mean by 'significant' ownership? For practical purposes we relate this to two measurements—the proportion of equity held and the total investment. There can be argument about how to define 'significant'. Let us take as a starting point 0.5 per cent of the equity. This would imply that no company could have more than 200 significant own-ers—and in reality there would often be far fewer as there will be holdings bigger than that. In terms of the size of the investment, 0.5 per cent of a company with market capitalization of £200m. is £1m.; and £5m. if it is capitalized at £1,000m. We would also argue that intermediaries, such as fund managers, should aggregate the holdings for the purpose of determin-ing whether they are significant. We would also encourage smaller share-holders to band together in order to act effectively. It could be viewed legally that if smaller shareholders have the power to pool their holdings and exert influence, then they have a responsibility to do so.

If a company has a large market capitalization—over £1bn.—it becomes less likely that there will be many shareholders with as much as 0.5 per cent. So we suggest that an alternative approach would be to consider a cash sum in relation to either the investor or the company. For the sake of example here, £25m. could be considered as a yardstick for companies in the largest of the stock market indices in the UK.

The precise definition of significant is open to further debate. The reason we have selected these levels is to create a simple, fair, and practical approach. It is no use trying to impose obligations on those too weak to bear them; nor would it be right to confine the obligation to too few. If the principle is accepted that significant ownership implies obligation, then the details of where to set the level can be elaborated elsewhere. We can take as an example the RTZ Corporation PLC, a big company by any standards. The 1995 Report shows that its top twenty shareholders at 15 March 1996 held 31 per cent of the equity. The smallest holding among them was 0.66 per cent.

What we propose goes with the grain of market practice. Although we have drawn a distinction between private and institutional shareholders, we might have put the dividing line in a different place—between small and large shareholders. The point is simply that the larger shareholders have the resources the others lack—and the interest too. That is reflected in the move towards active and well-informed monitoring already under way among some of the larger institutions. The imposition of obligation in relation to size is already reflected in the UK via the disclosure requirements for investors with a 3 per cent stake or more, and Takeover Rules which apply to holdings over 29.9 per cent.

The modest obligations on significant shareholders (of all kinds) comprise for the most part those that are already recognized—especially voting. There are occasions—not many—when significant shareholders should do more than vote. Votes are infrequent and limited in scope. If a shareholder has 0.5 per cent of the equity or more than £25m. invested, it is most likely that he or she will be keeping a close eye on the investment. We do not propose a programme of unparalleled activity, of micromanaging a business or of inappropriate intrusion. We do propose a duty to take or participate in any action that the circumstances seem to demand. If for instance a company's record is poor *and* its board looks badly structured in one way or another, or it has consistently taken a series of bad decisions, it would be up to significant shareholders to do whatever was appropriate—that must be a matter of judgement in the circumstances.

We advocate *an enhanced duty of care* expressed as a duty to vote in these companies. What needs to be done will depend on the circumstances, on an assessment of the facts and their relative importance. In other words it depends on the intelligent use of discretion; we already expect that of our non-executive directors. There is no book in which they can look up instructions on how to deal with particular circumstances. We rely on their intelligence and courage and sense of where their duty lies. So it is with shareholders. No one needs to prescribe how they vote or exercise their powers: it is enough they should accept that they do have the general responsibility. And this goes for significant holders whether or not they are fiduciaries. In parallel to fiduciaries, significant owners should be required to vote, and to state their policy.

In all this we have excluded smaller shareholders—on policy and practical grounds. A lesser responsibility is theirs, but even so their interests too are best served by vigilance and voting—and making any other contribution they can to the common cause of efficiency and prosperity. And their contribution may be far from negligible.

SANCTIONS AND REMEDIES

If new requirements are introduced the question arises whether there should be sanctions or remedies to enforce them. The common law definition of negligence and the way this has been interpreted over the years have been skilfully adapted to modern situations. At its heart lies the notion of a duty of care; and a remedy is available if it can be established that a duty of care was owed to the plaintiff, that it was breached, and that damage ensued. (The classic definition was by Lord Atkins in *Donoghue* v. *Stevenson* 1931 AC 562.) Trustees, as we have seen, owe a duty of care to the beneficiaries, but we are moving beyond that to ask whether significant shareholders should owe a duty of care to the company that is in some way enforceable at law. We might note in passing that directors do owe such a duty to the company, but are rarely sued unless the company has failed or changes hands (consider the Caparo case). Should the Department of Trade, in extreme circumstances, have the right or duty to sue shareholders for total dereliction of duty? Our view is that this would be impracticable and inhibiting.

There is one sanction that would be easy to apply in respect of one class of fiduciaries—to remove from a pension fund its tax advantages if it did not vote. True, this would leave all other significant holders in a different class, but even so it would cover a large part of the UK market. And it is something they should already be doing. A move in this direction would amount to a penalty imposed by the state in the public interest at no cost to the company. But this is not in our view necessary or probably the most effective way to proceed. It is notable that the Inland Revenue already has this sanction if pension funds are viewed as 'trading' shares rather than 'investing'. It would be a simple extension of this to remove tax privileges for pension funds which did not exercise a proper duty of care. We do not advocate such a course however. We would not wish to see the fund's beneficiaries penalized just because its managers had failed to satisfy their obligations. A requirement to disclose policy and regard voting rights as assets would in our view achieve the improvements sought.

Part of our reasoning lies in the fact that capital is international and that we do not want to impose such obligations on shareholders in UK companies that either shareholders or the companies move offshore. On the contrary, our aim is to secure a better corporate governance system so that more investors take shares in UK companies and benefit from having done so.

If there are no sanctions, does it mean that our principle is doomed to destruction? Far from it. Attitudes have changed greatly in the last decade and best practice is already being redefined in the way we advocate. As it becomes general, the need to consider the terrible twins of legislation and litigation falls away. But there is another approach altogether.

CARROT OR STICK? INCENTIVES

The lawyer's approach to a problem is to consider rules; what constitute breaches of the rules; and the remedies and penalties. We have been through that process in the paragraphs above. The economist's approach is to consider incentives—what induces people to act in certain ways? We now examine the problem in that light. If the process of voting is valuable to a company as well as to the owners individually, it is worth something. It may be worth little to each shareholder—its value lies in the aggregate. Might it therefore be worthwhile paying for it? This is not as complicated or expensive—or as curious—as it first sounds. It might work as follows.

Dividends would include a bonus for those who had voted on the *last* occasion on which it was possible to do so (normally one year to the next). The aggregate amount to be distributed, pro rata to the votes cast, would be *n* per cent of the declared dividend—say 5 per cent of it. This would be the 'voting bonus'. It could by definition only apply to shareholders on the register last time round and only in respect of their then holdings. And if they had sold in the meantime it would be extinguished.

It would be difficult for institutions to argue that a voting bonus was not worth having: they might indeed be in breach of their duty not to earn it. And this would include people like stockbrokers who were holding shares in nominee names (or indeed those administering Crest). Administratively it could be dealt with by a holder of record who would simply fill in an extra paragraph on the voting form as he or she completed it to claim the bonus.

Looked at from the other end—the vantage point of shareholders—a private shareholder, with a gross dividend of £500 for the year, would find it enhanced by £25—not much perhaps, but worth voting for. And an institution with a dividend of £10,000 earns £500—certainly worth the trouble.

Should companies in principle pay to have themselves monitored more effectively? We all do, constantly: that is part of the price we pay to sleep peacefully in our beds. Would the receipt of a voting bonus affect behaviour, or would shareholders just tick the boxes and collect the cash? We cannot be sure, but at least the registering of votes would make people think about the company. But disclosure of voting records might highlight woodenness or perversity—transparency therefore is essential.

A further obligation which we consider should be embraced by significant owners is disclosure, not just of their holding, but voting policy. Companies should know who ultimately owns them; so should other shareholders know who the members are. This in itself could affect investment decisions.

AN ALTERNATIVE

German commentators reading these arguments would reflect that their ancestors had anticipated them a hundred years ago. They knew that diffuse shareholdings made the supervisory role almost impossible and that the power entrusted to management made some kind of supervision desirable. Their solution was to introduce the concept of the supervisory board; in those days it had nothing to do with employee representation (which was only introduced in its modern form after the 1939–45 war). The Germans realized that in the normal course of events shareholders (especially in those days) knew and could get to know very little about a company. By creating a supervisory organ, which was entitled to be consulted on major matters and to have the necessary supporting information, they intended to bridge the gap of ignorance and to lessen apathy.

The clue about the main purpose of the German law lies in the definition of the companies to which it applies. It does not cover companies/groups with fewer than 500 employees. It does cover all the others whether or not they are quoted. The reasoning is clearly that after a company grows to a certain size the effects of its success or failure on the community are such that the state is warranted in prescribing its structure. This is not quite the same as the principle of the responsibility of significant ownership enunciated above, but it is based on a similar rationale.

The supervisory board (*Aufsichtsrat*) in Germany in its present form is far from perfect, as German commentators accept. Manifestly it does not always work well. No system or structure can keep a company going for ever, but there is little excuse for a supervisory board not knowing what is going on and in some cases the *Aufsichtsrat* has clearly been taken by surprise. It does not hold formal meetings more than four times a year—at most—though its work may be supplemented through informal committees. There is talk of introducing audit committees on Anglo-US lines, though how this would work with codetermination is unclear; presumably such a committee would include employee representation. Similarly, the US has tackled the voting issue through two routes: a regulatory obligation for fiduciaries and a voting quorum set at 50 per cent which means companies have an interest in ensuring a majority of all votes are cast on resolutions. UK court meetings of shareholders have similar provisions, meaning that a majority of share-holders (not just votes) is required for business to be carried. The result is that companies cannot be ruled by the minority, even if the majority acquiesce by apathy.

There has been discussion in the UK and elsewhere about forming share-holder committees to help in the monitoring task. This is an idea that is not wholly without merit, and one variation of it would be to brigade such appointees as a supervisory board but not on German lines. If we follow the inescapable logic of the responsibility of significant ownership such a body would comprise the appointees of major shareholders (appointees, not representatives, as members of the board should have regard to the interests of the company and not just particular investors).

Would a two-tier system be advantageous in the UK in terms of the effec-tiveness of companies? We leave aside all political considerations in trying to answer this question, which has suffered in the past by being intertwined with other issues. Our conclusions are as follows.

1.   The question of whether places should be reserved on a supervisory board for employee representatives must be put on one side and considered separately. It is a separate issue.

2.   At present in the UK the supervisory task is entrusted to the directors, among whom there should now be enough non-executives to bring to bear a

reasonable degree of detachment. The shareholders 'manage by exception'—and that is all we ask of them. To impose a new structure to corral a few poor boards seems a cumbersome remedy and we much prefer the lighter one we propose. Our views are strengthened by observing what actually happens in Germany. In principle there the shareholders appoint the non-employee members of the *Aufsichtsrat*, and it in turn appoints the members of the management board (*Vorstand*). In reality the *Vorstand* usually has a great say in the choice of members of the supervisory board and its own composition. The way the system works reflects the relative strength of the personalities concerned.

3. We can see no reason to object to UK shareholders having the option, as they do in France, of voting in favour of their company having a two-tier board rather than a unitary one. To introduce such an option would require a definition in law of the functions of the management board and of the supervisory board. (Definition is long overdue in any case even in our unitary system.) There are circumstances in which the French have found the alternative useful; so might the UK. We suspect however that just as the two-tier system is rarely used in France, it would be generally ignored in the UK. There is no evidence of any yearning for it. But there are many kinds of company and many different sets of circumstances, and choice is always useful.

4. What finally persuades us that a two-tier system is not the answer to problems of monitoring is that even the existence of a supervisory tier would not extinguish the need for shareholders to be alert and active. No system yet devised can entirely offset human frailty and incompetence.

Our conclusion is that the principle of the responsibility of significant ownership can be implemented in various ways which we have described, and there may well be others. The essential principle is that ownership confers responsibilities, and not just for institutions, but any holder of a significant portion of the voting stock. There are economic, social, and political benefits to be gained in improving the oversight provided by shareholders over limited companies. Ensuring this through distribution of a voting bonus would provide the appropriate incentive, rather than sanction, from which both domestic and international investors could derive benefit. Power confers responsibility, and this should be recognized. To reward responsibility, in part at least, addresses the 'free rider' problem which has dogged debates on shareholder activism.

Guarding the Guards

THE power that the institutions possess is evident. Its potential is vast. The fate of most quoted companies could be decided by a group of people who would fit comfortably into a decent-sized room—and sometimes into its antechamber. The Takeover Code assumes that holding 30 per cent of the outstanding capital of a company is sufficient to produce effective control. The analysis of shareholdings in company reports will confirm how few institutions this implies.

What the institutions control is the nation's savings. The economy depends on their effective deployment. For this reason we consider that institutions and other investors with a significant holding in a company should view their role as guardians—within the limits of the powers at their disposal. The next question is naturally: 'Who will guard the guardians?' This question has a long honourable history certainly as far back as Plato and probably beyond. Classicists will recall the Latin version *Quis ipsos custodies custodiet?* To put the question in corporate governance terms: 'To whom are the various classes of institution accountable? Is this accountability effective?'

It is sometimes suggested that the market for fund managers itself ensures accountability, that is to say that because they work in a highly competitive environment, they are under appropriate pressure to ensure performance. In the market for fund managers, for which the league tables provide the main signal of relative performance, the relatively poor performance of a particular fund manager may have many causes. It is a matter for those who engaged him or her to see what these are. Just as for shares, a market and its processes may help to sharpen accountability, but they do not provide it. A man swimming for his life in a teeming sea is right to be afraid of hungry sharks, but he is not accountable to them.

Whether fund managers are active towards the companies in which they invest or not, the question remains: is there an adequate line of accountability from the fund managers to those who appoint them? This is not so easy to answer, because it takes us back to the structure and dynamics of each type of institution. All have one function in common, namely people actually running funds, making the decisions about what to buy or sell within the parameters set them. Their constitutions, however, differ. Suitable arrangements will depend upon who the client is. If it is a unit trust, an insurance company investing life funds, or a fund manager acting for a pension fund the requirements will be different.

There should be a number of principles which guide the process for accountability in each case: effective regulation, transparency, reporting to those with a legitimate interest.

PENSION FUNDS

Here the fund managers are appointed by trustees. It is the trustees' task to 'guard the guardians', and they already have a clear responsibility to do it under trust law and the Pensions Act. What mechanism is there for ensuring the trustees themselves fulfil their role? After all, many may have conflicts of interest (as employers or even as employees). Since our system now loads so much responsibility on trustees we ought to ascertain beyond peradventure whether it works properly and if not how it might be improved.

As a minimum it should be a requirement of every fund manager's contract with his or her client for a corporate governance policy to be specified. This should include an agreed overall framework for the exercise of shareholder rights and powers in the interests of the beneficiaries. There should be guidelines for routine voting activity and detailed reports with clear record keeping. There should be arrangements made for consultation on urgent issues with the clients.

The accountability of the trustees is a separate matter. The trustees can only be held accountable if they are required to report to the beneficiaries on corporate governance issues. The Pensions Act has a number of badly drafted measures which attempt to tackle this issue. Trustees have the right to training and independent advice, but it is not required. Likewise, in principle accountability to the beneficiaries is established via allowing one-third of trustees to be elected by members of the scheme. In practice, the rules are a mess due to complicated consultation and opt-out provisions. Few companies are expected voluntarily to relinquish the power to appoint (and remove) trustees who have powers over large sums of money. Current best practice among large companies is to allow trade unions to nominate up to 50 per cent of the trustees' members—but the formal power to hire and fire remains with the company. Pension fund democracy still has a long way to go, and for corporate governance the implications are profound. Whilst companies retain direct control over the administration of the bulk of the nation's capital via their control of trustees, there will only be halting efforts to stir shareholders into life. The conflicts of interest raised are too great for companies to surmount. One trustee commented frankly that 'none of the member trustees liked rolling contracts, but it was impossible to issue a statement on this whilst our own employer offered these to the directors'.

A growing number of public sector pension funds hold an annual general meeting to which current contributors and pensioners are invited. There is usually a presentation from the chair of the trustees, fund managers, and advisers, with a question and answer session. An occasion such as this could also be the time for electing any trustees. At Kent County Council the annual meeting is usually a packed affair, with keen questioning of the investment firms and lively debate on the fund's policy, be it asset allocation or voting.

All pension funds could be required to hold an AGM and provision made to allow contributors and pensioners (i.e. the beneficiaries) to propose items of business for discussion. The debate on the Pensions Bill considered the question of general meetings for beneficiaries along with other related issues. Pension fund democracy needs to be addressed if we are to improve governance.

LIFE OFFICES

The web is tangled. Life offices such as Legal and General or the Prudential are quoted public companies in their own right. The big life offices manage funds for others. Profits come from many sources and the shareholders cannot easily reach a straightforward conclusion. The share price of an insurance company reflects many things of which its fund management efficiency is only one. It would not have been helped for instance in recent years by any ill-timed foray into personal pensions and other areas. We conclude that the shareholders of the life offices cannot realistically be seen as 'guardians' of the way they conduct their investment operations and their attitude and behaviour towards companies. There is a vacuum— ironical because the history of recent years shows that they have been among the most active shareholders. Accountability to policy holders needs to be considered after demutualization.

The 'mutuals' belong to a strange genre in the UK like building societies and housing associations, where in theory the policy holders or depositors or members act *qua* shareholders but in practice do not, because there are a myriad of small holders, none with a significant stake. There is no effective accountability outward by the board (or committee) in any of these cases because there are too many small holders with too small an interest, and they are immune to takeover. The recent efforts of carpet-baggers at the Nationwide and elsewhere to put forward directors to pursue incorporation were defeated, but show that life could be injected into the democratic process at the mutuals without too much effort.

Significantly all have regulators (the DTI; the Registrar of Friendly Societies; the Housing Corporation), but the DTI does not monitor the insurance companies' discharge of their corporate governance responsibilities, whether they are quoted companies or mutuals. The FSA now picks up this responsibility for regulation, but details on corporate governance requirements have not been specified. They should be.

UNIT TRUSTS

Unit trusts are run by management companies, which may themselves be quoted, and the management function is farmed out. The fund managers are answerable to the management company and the board of the management company to its shareholders. The chain of accountability stops there. Would it be effective if, say, a major mutual started to throw its weight about with companies in its portfolio? It is not so far fetched. One UK unit trust caused a stir a few years ago by making aggressive noises about the need for companies to maintain their dividends come what may. Paddy Lineker at M & G was aware that their income would be threatened. The correspondence with companies was enlivened by Gartmore's (mainly investors of pension fund monies) writing that investment should not be cut at the expense of dividend payments. There was much commentary in the press at this and not a little criticism. It is by no means clear that the line of accountability is effective, though the market in which these companies operate is very competitive and itself requires strong discipline as the funds are open ended. There is a need to ensure accountability to unit holders and currently the framework does not ensure this, or even allow for it. This needs to be addressed to ensure accountability to the ultimate investors.

INVESTMENT TRUSTS

These are the 'closed end' funds run by professional managers—who may charge handsomely for their services. The capital is fixed and investors buy and sell the shares in the market like any others; there is no pressure on the managers to deal whatever the market conditions. Despite their name, they are in fact formally constituted as public limited companies. They are subject to the same disciplines as others (except that they have a special tax regime and may not distribute capital profits). The line of accountability is the same—and it may well end up with the other institutions, with the same considerations. Recent pressure from shareholders concerned with independence on the board, management fees, and contract length for the investment firm has begun to stir life into the sector, showing that shareholders have the potential to make accountability real.

DISCRETIONARY FUNDS

What we are covering under this heading are the funds managed by stock-brokers and the trust departments of banks etc. for private clients. Generally the question of accountability for the way they exercise power only applies negatively, i.e. they do not use it at all. We referred earlier to the 'black hole' into which votes are sucked. The owners have lost them and the managers have not made arrangements to do anything about them. The answer is to cover the question in the managers' contracts. Then they could be held properly accountable. As it is, 'nothing comes of nothing'.

REGULATION

Regulation plays an essential role in ensuring accountability. All investment managers come within the ambit of the Financial Services Act 1986. Some are directly supervised by the Securities and Investment Board—now Financial Services Authority—whose primary concern is to ensure that conduct towards investors is fair and represents best advice. Under the Securities and Investment Board, each individual regulatory agency had responsibility for drawing up a detailed rule book. The system was essentially self-policing and viewed as failing in maintaining public confidence in an effective system of regulation. In addition there is a regulatory regime linked to the Pensions Act, with a Pensions Regulator, who has extensive powers to investigate and issue judgements.

Regulation on corporate governance issues is virtually non-existent. The stock market can only monitor (scantily) its own listing rules, and there is no companies regulator. Ultimately, beneficiaries could pursue their case through the court, arguing that there had been a breach of trust, if they considered insufficient care was paid to corporate governance issues in the portfolio and this led either to losses or to unacceptable risks. Indeed, the IMRO booklet *Protecting Investors* is explicit about the limits of its authority, and they do not include the selection of investments, much less *ex post* monitoring: 'It is up to investors to weigh up an investment offer and decide whether the level of risk is acceptable, or indeed whether the investment is suitable . . . The fact that your investment has performed badly will not normally be regarded as a valid complaint.'

The intermediaries that come under the aegis of the Stock Exchange must likewise satisfy it of their competence; some of its members do possess great power, but providing they stick to the rules there is no check on its use.

THE MEDIA

In all this we must not lose sight of the fourth estate. The press can be relied upon to report and comment upon the actions of investment managers in their monitoring role, in so far as it reaches the public eye. It is a topic of continuing interest—especially if there is controversy. The row at British Gas (1995) produced headlines on the front pages of the *Sun* and the *Financial Times* on the same day—no mean feat. Corporate governance is an increasingly lively subject in both the City and business pages of the press.

Pressure from the media should not be underestimated; in a controversial case they may very well contact leading institutions to ascertain their intentions and the climate of opinion they establish can sway votes. Columnists regularly provide their own advice on what shareholders should and should not do to tackle a particular problem. The media's attention has done much to heighten a sense of accountability by both companies and institutions.

AN AWKWARD EXCEPTION

We discussed earlier the vulnerability of shareholders in unquoted companies; their remedies are sparse, especially if the cause of their problems is that management is poor rather than dishonest. What of quoted companies where the original family or its descendants still control it, and may still be heavily involved in management? They are no doubt highly motivated to succeed, but as we saw earlier motivation does not ensure competence. Besides, they may be greedy too, and take a disproportionate slice of what is available. Minority shareholders may not even have a vote, because of the voting structure. A CBI spokesman was relaxed about this (*Investor's Chronicle*, 22 Nov. 1996: 19): 'What about companies where the directors hold more than 50% of the shares?' he asked. 'There's plenty of those about. You may have a vote, but in practice it makes no difference.'

In all such cases the controlling shareholders' role as guardians is potentially compromised by their interests as managers. Caution is needed. The boards may be superb and they may therefore be fortunate enough to participate in a wonderful success, but such businesses can decline at an alarming rate so that the option of escape through what is frequently an illiquid market anyway may be unattractive. It is a high-wire act with no safety net. For this reason, there should be reform of the percentage of shares which a company must issue in a public offering. The present requirement is for a minimum of 25 per cent control to reside with the board—they cannot only win any ordinary resolution, but can even block a special resolution; if one vote was missing, they could be guaranteed to win even these.

It is not just founding directors and families where these structures prevail. Companies as diverse as BSkyB, Telewest, and Rentokil Initial are effectively not accountable to shareholders in the market because so much of their share capital is controlled by one or two large investors. Sometimes the directors appointed by such controlling groups are not accountable to other shareholders as they do not stand down for regular re-election or have special privileges on board committees. This should not be acceptable in a company which is offering shares to the public, and reflects the type of stacked insider system which the UK and US markets view with horror in the French and Korean markets, because 'outsiders' who buy in the market are effectively powerless to effect change. Such shares notionally carry votes, but the outcome is never in any doubt because the board has an inbuilt majority on any contentious item. The solution would be to require a majority of shares to be issued in a public offering, with the removal of special voting rights or committee powers for certain categories of investor.

TAKEOVERS

In takeovers many institutions will have a holding in both bidder and target so they will be anxious to take the most responsible decision. No one can tell after a successful bid whether it would have been beneficial, all things considered, for it to have failed. Academic work suggests that successful bids do not generally result in much value being added. An institution may well be proved wrong in the view it took by subsequent events—but so may any other human decisions. Guardians are not gods.

Takeover bids force shareholders, including institutions, into action. These may lead to increased communication between institutions and companies and a gradual sharpening of their monitoring role, but an extreme reluctance to use heavy pressure for all the reasons we set out.

It is not over-enthusiastic action by the institutions as guardians that is to be feared—that is most unlikely given the forces of inertia and modesty—but timidity and inaction. The expression 'guarding the guardians' seems to conjure up a picture of a power-hungry Praetorian Guard running amok in the Emperor's palace as happened from time to time in Imperial Rome. That is the wrong image. Despite all the 'noise', even the massive pension funds in the USA target relatively few companies. In October 1996 TIAA/CREF, which then had about $160bn. under management, targeted between 15 and 30 companies in a year out of the 1,500 in their portfolio.

What the United Kingdom has to fear in the twenty-first century is that the guardians will fall asleep on the job, or look the other way, or wash their hands of the problems and leave it to others to find solutions. We do not believe that on balance it should be a matter of concern that institutional shareholders will abuse their potential power. They are more prone to masterly inactivity. They too rely heavily on the prosperity of companies in the UK for the benefit of the beneficiaries whose savings they administer and society which needs the stream of taxation from earners, owners, and companies. They are the best available guardians in whose good judgement reasonable confidence can be reposed, providing only that they accept the limited but crucial responsibility we have suggested should be theirs and do not believe that neglect is benign. The exercise of their power can only be acceptable in a democratic framework if those guardians are in turn accountable to those on whose behalf they invest. This requires: effective regulation to ensure the public interest is represented, transparency, a duty to exercise voting rights and other powers, and reporting to those with a legitimate interest. This applies to fiduciaries, but also to all significant owners of shares.

23

A Summary of Proposals for Reform

In reviewing the history of shareholding in the UK and setting it into its historical perspective, we had in mind that what might emerge would be a series of practical adjustments that could be made—some of which might involve legislation. Other commentators have made suggestions, some of them similar in purpose; the Law Commission and the Department of Trade and Industry have been grappling with some of the issues and now there is to be a thorough look at company law—a development we warmly welcome. Our own thinking has developed over many years and we freely acknowledge our debt to others. Our proposals for reform are intended to draw together a range of ideas to modernize the framework governing the role of shareholders in the interests of competitiveness and accountability. A full account is given in each of the relevant chapters. In summary the main reforms we propose are as follows. We argue that the active role of shareholders is key to effective governance and thereby to competitiveness, the accountability of the corporation, and the cohesion of wider society.

A DUTY TO VOTE

More than two-thirds of UK equity shares are now controlled by fiduciaries. They already have an obligation to exercise oversight over the assets in which they choose to invest. There is evidence that many are already taking more seriously the duties of ownership as far as shares are concerned. We hope that this trend will continue. We do not accept the arguments against there being an obligation to vote. We propose: that fiduciaries should be required to see that all shares are voted (the duty to do this would normally be passed to fund managers subject to an agreed procedure for referring back in specified circumstances); that records be kept of votes; and that reports should be made periodically to the beneficiaries on their steward-ship. Thought might be given to rewarding shareholders who do vote. The duty to regard voting rights as assets should extend to all shareholder powers. We consider that similar reforms should be introduced to ensure accountability by other institutional investors such as insurers, unit trusts, and mutuals.

THE ROLE OF TRUSTEES

Trustees, by whatever means and procedures they are appointed, have a responsibility to supervise the fund managers to whom they entrust business. For this they need training, which should be a requirement, not an option. They must not only understand alternative possible strategies in changing external circumstances, but also keep abreast of the managers' reports on their investments, and any changes in the law and accounting conventions which affect the way in which they discharge their duties. Some will be full-time paid employees of the company and able to discharge their duties in normal working hours. In all other cases we feel that the responsibilities laid upon them (and the time involved) warrants their being paid.

THE OBLIGATIONS OF SIGNIFICANT OWNERSHIP

Although most major shareholders are fiduciaries, we do not believe that their responsibilities rest upon this fact alone. We feel that the power that comes with a major holding itself imposes an obligation to share the burden of ensuring that the direction of the company is being adequately conducted. We call this the doctrine of significant ownership. How this obligation should be discharged will vary according to circumstances. (Directors themselves owe duties to the company well established at common law, but how these should be discharged will itself vary.) The important thing is to recognize the obligation. Voting is a requirement but sometimes, and we hope rarely, more is required. We suggest an incentive, rather than a sanction, to ensure votes are cast, by way of a voting bonus.

PUBLIC OFFERINGS AND MINORITY SHAREHOLDERS

The current requirement is only for 25 per cent of the equity to be offered when a quotation is sought. This leaves minority shareholders obviously vulnerable in such cases especially where the board contains a controlling shareholder. There are various ways of dealing with this from insisting that a majority of shares be made available to modifying the rules governing the lodging of resolutions by shareholders. Certain categories of shareholder should not be accorded special privileges, in appointment of directors or board committees.

SHAREHOLDERS IN A RECONSTRUCTION

When companies are threatened with dire trouble and some kind of reconstruction is in the wind, a place should be found at the table for shareholders with the creditors wherever there is a possibility that they might contribute to a solution.

SMALL SHAREHOLDERS

The encouragement to 'wider share ownership' is in our view misguided. 'Deeper share ownership' is a better policy. Even with all the supervisory arrangements it is difficult for private shareholders (other than the experts) to know how to pick their way through the bewildering choice that faces them. This is an area that the government could with advantage address.

When they have invested in a public company private shareholders will find they have little influence and less power. They can enhance their influence by judicious correspondence and questions at AGMs. If they feel they need power, the only answer is for them to band together. Some groups exist already. It can only be beneficial if they improve understanding and play a constructive part. PRO SHARE is helped by government; perhaps the time has come to look at the subject more broadly to facilitate the growth of shareholder associations.

The pressure for the private investor, accentuated by Crest, to put shares into nominee names for administrative convenience has meant that unless deliberate steps are taken, the shareholders' rights get sucked into a 'black hole'. They are not exercised by anyone. This breaks one of the main principles upon which Companies Acts have rested from the outset. A way needs to be found for the link between shareholder and company to be restored as a matter of course.

MODERNIZING THE AGM

The annual general meeting is still the main opportunity for the generality of shareholders to see the board and question it if they wish. We have outlined our proposals for improving the way it works. The timetable should accommodate those living abroad in this more international world and this would help shareholders at home too to take a more considered view. By the same token the timetable for lodging resolutions needs amending so that the proposers have the latest report and accounts in good time. The terms on which they can be lodged should be less penal. The double voting system in which the principle may swing in a trice from one man one vote to one share one vote is a farce; the latter is the only sound basis and if that means relying solely on proxies, so be it. There should be a system for lodging questions with the company beforehand, for grouping them together, and for circulating the responses. This would not prevent supplementary questions or emergency procedures. Our aim is to make the AGM a working meeting, rather than a ritual.

DIRECTORS' REMUNERATION

Shareholders should have some opportunity to register their views about executive directors' remuneration. We accept that giving them a simple right to vote down the board's proposals on directors' pay is too blunt an instrument. It is undesirable for a board to feel it must treat any criticism as a vote of confidence. Nevertheless, the shareholders do have an interest, not just because of the numbers but because of the general message they send about the company. A solution would be for the shareholders to vote on the report of the remuneration committee and to be able to lodge amendments to the board's proposals if they wished. The procedures could ensure it was done in such a way as to avoid its being frivolous or vexatious. We see the debate on whether non-executives should be paid in shares as a red herring. If they need such an incentive to think about shareholders' interests, they probably should not be on the board in the first place. They should definitely not get options.

DISCLOSURE

Every report on corporate governance stresses the importance of disclosure—and we fully agree. There are many proposals for increasing what is available, for instance concerning the systematic reporting of risk. We ourselves would like to see a greater concentration on 'prospects'—everything that is forward looking, investment, training, how the directors set about assessing the board itself and the contributions made by individual directors, and so forth. We are however very much aware that there are many classes of users for the information a company provides and we cannot see therefore why it should be necessary to assume they all want the same. It would be helpful and might save money were a company to be able to offer a range of formats to suit the users' needs. It would be useful to shareholders to know what information was available should they desire it and the ways in which they might obtain it (by mail or fax or electronically). Certainly we are averse to the over-complex material produced on the principle 'never mind the quality, feel the length'—into which category some of the accounts for pay arrangements unfortunately fall. The perceived need to correct analysts' forecasts would diminish if company chairmen routinely made a third-quarter trading statement. The quality of reporting on non-financial performance, from human resource management to environmental and social policy, needs dramatic improvement.

THE BOARD

Finally there are our concerns about the board. There seems to be a somewhat grudging acceptance that the Cadbury Report has raised standards. Its insistence on balance, its emphasis on independence, its clarification of roles, and its strengthening of audit committees have done nothing but good. We do not accept the thesis that all this was at the expense of enterprise—or is divisive. No director ever joined a company except to help it move forward to success. We agree very much with Cadbury and Hampel about the importance of nominating committees but more is needed to deal with appraisal. Directors should be chosen after an objective review of the board's needs and by a process that leaves them feeling their duty is to the company and is not coloured by the obligations of patronage. Their performance needs regular review. And shareholders should know that such a committee is in place, who is on it, and that appointees have actually emerged as a result of its work. We need a shift from reporting on board structure, to board dynamics.

THE SHAREHOLDERS' POSITIVE ROLE

Although the shareholders' role is sometimes presented in negative terms, we do not see it that way. Managing a business is often a lonely task, especially in difficult times. We see shareholders getting closer to the companies in which they invest not just to monitor them in an unhelpful way, but to support management and encourage it to invest and take risks. We deprecate any laws that inhibit such relationships, although we fully understand the need for them not to be abused. That is why we have made some suggestions about the insider trading laws and this explains our preference for a civil remedy rather than a criminal process, which in any case is rarely invoked.

WHAT IS THE ALTERNATIVE?

The background to our thinking is to set the company in its proper societal context. Shareholder value may be a king, but it is not a god. To us, the purpose of the company is to provide ethically and profitably the goods and services people need and want. Understanding this provides the context in which shareholders' interests are served. This is no easy task in a highly competitive world. It is right that the directors of companies should wield power; their competitive advantage depends on their doing so competently. We believe that those who are entrusted with power should be accountable for its use. The law provides that the people to whom they should be accountable are the shareholders. Our suggestions relate to their role, and critically, to ensure that shareholders assume the responsibilities that power confers. In the end we must all face up to one simple question: 'If not they, who else is there?'

APPENDIX 1

Report of the Committee on the Financial Aspects of Corporate Governance (Cadbury Code)

THE CODE OF BEST PRACTICE

1 The Board of Directors

1.1 The board should meet regularly, retain full and effective control over the company and monitor the executive management.

1.2 There should be a clearly accepted division of responsibilities at the head of a company, which will ensure a balance of power and authority, such that no one individual has unfettered powers of decision. Where the chairman is also the chief executive, it is essential that there should be a strong and independent element on the board, with a recognized senior member.

1.3 The board should include non-executive directors of sufficient calibre and number for their views to carry significant weight in the board's decisions.

1.4 The board should have a formal schedule of matters specifically reserved to it for decision to ensure that the direction and control of the company is firmly in its hands.

1.5 There should be an agreed procedure for directors in the furtherance of their duties to take independent professional advice if necessary, at the company's expense.

1.6 All directors should have access to the advice and services of the company secretary, who is responsible to the board for ensuring that board procedures are followed and that applicable rules and regulations are complied with. Any question of the removal of the company secretary should be a matter for the board as a whole.

2 Non-Executive Directors

2.1 Non-executive directors should bring an independent judgement to bear on issues of strategy, performance, resources, including key appointments, and standards of conduct.

2.2 The majority should be independent of management and free from any business or other relationship which could materially interfere with the exercise of their independent judgement, apart from their fees and shareholding. Their fees should reflect the time which they commit to the company.

2.3 Non-executive directors should be appointed for specified terms and reappointment should not be automatic.

2.4 Non-executive directors should be selected through a formal process and both this process and their appointment should be a matter for the board as a whole.

3 Executive Directors

3.1 Directors' service contracts should not exceed three years without shareholders' approval.

3.2 There should be full and clear disclosure of directors' total emoluments and those of the chairman and highest-paid UK director, including pension contributions and stock options. Separate figures should be given for salary and performance-related elements and the basis on which performance is measured should be explained.

3.3 Executive directors' pay should be subject to the recommendations of a remuneration committee made up wholly or mainly of non-executive directors.

4 Reporting and Controls

4.1 It is the board's duty to present a balanced and understandable assessment of the company's position.

4.2 The board should ensure that an objective and professional relationship is maintained with the auditors.

4.3 The board should establish an audit committee of at least three non-executive directors with written terms of reference which deal clearly with its authority and duties.

4.4 The directors should explain their responsibility for preparing the accounts next to a statement by the auditors about their reporting responsibilities.

4.5 The directors should report on the effectiveness of the company's system of internal control.

4.6 The directors should report that the business is a going concern, with supporting assumptions or qualifications as necessary.

THE COMMITTEE'S MEMBERSHIP AND TERMS OF REFERENCE

Appendix 1

Terms of Reference

The Committee was set up in May 1991 by the Financial Reporting Council, the London Stock Exchange, and the accountancy profession. It adopted as its terms of reference:

To consider the following issues in relation to financial reporting and account-ability and to make recommendations on good practice:

(a) the responsibilities of executive and non-executive directors for reviewing and reporting on performance to shareholders and other financially inter-ested parties; and the frequency, clarity, and form in which information should be provided;

(b) the case for audit committees of the board, including their composition and role;

(c) the principal responsibilities of auditors and the extent and value of the audit;

(d) the links between shareholders, boards, and auditors;

(e) any other relevant matters.

Membership

The committee's members were as follows:

Sir Adrian Cadbury (Chairman)
Ian Butler
   Council Member, CBI and former Chairman, CBI Companies Committee
Jim Butler
   Senior Partner, KPMG Peat Marwick
Jonathan Charkham
   Adviser to the Governor, Bank of England
Hugh Collum
   Chairman, Hundred Group of Finance Directors
Sir Ron Dearing
   Chairman, Financial Reporting Council
Andrew Likierman
   Professor of Accounting and Financial Control, London Business School
Nigel Macdonald
   Vice President, Institute of Chartered Accountants of Scotland
Mike Sandland
   Chairman, Institutional Shareholders' Committee
Mark Sheldon
   President, Law Society
Sir Andrew Hugh Smith
   Chairman, London Stock Exchange
Sir Dermot de Trafford, Bt
   Chairman, Institute of Directors

Observers: Mrs Sarah Brown (until October 1991), Mr Arthur Russell (from November 1991), *Head of Companies Division, DTI*

Secretary: Nigel Peace (*on secondment from DTI*)

Sir Christopher Hogg (*Chairman, Reuters Holdings PLC, Courtaulds plc, and Courtaulds Textiles plc*) acted as an adviser to the Committee.

APPENDIX 2

Directors' Remuneration
Report of a Study Group Chaired by Sir Richard Greenbury

2 CODE OF BEST PRACTICE

Introduction

2.1 The purpose of the accompanying Code is to set out best practice in determining and accounting for Directors' remuneration. The references at the end of each provision of the Code are to the fuller discussion in sections 4 to 7.

2.2 The detailed provisions have been prepared with large companies mainly in mind, but the principles apply equally to smaller companies.

2.3 We recommend that all listed companies registered in the UK should comply with the Code to the fullest extent practicable and include a statement about their compliance in the annual reports to shareholders by their remuneration committees or elsewhere in their annual reports and accounts. Any areas of non-compliance should be explained and justified.

2.4 We further recommend that the London Stock Exchange should introduce the following continuing obligations for listed companies:

- an obligation to include in their annual remuneration committee reports to shareholders or their annual reports a general statement about their compliance with section A of the Code which should also explain and justify any areas of non-compliance;
- a specific obligation to comply with the provisions in section B of the Code which are not already covered by existing obligations, and with provision C10 of the Code, subject to any changes of wording which may be desirable for legal or technical reasons.

2.5 Within section B, provision B3 requires remuneration committees to confirm that full consideration has been given to sections C and D of the Code.

The Code

A *The remuneration committee*

A1   To avoid potential conflicts of interest, Boards of Directors should set up remuneration committees of Non-Executive Directors to determine on their behalf, and on behalf of the shareholders, within agreed terms of reference, the company's policy on executive remuneration and specific remuneration packages for each of the Executive Directors, including pension rights and any compensation payments (paragraphs 4.3–4.7).

A2   Remuneration committee Chairmen should account directly to the shareholders through the means specified in this Code for the decisions their committees reach (paragraph 4.4).

A3   Where necessary, companies' Articles of Association should be amended to enable remuneration committees to discharge these functions on behalf of the Board (paragraph 4.3).

A4   Remuneration committees should consist exclusively of Non-Executive Directors with no personal financial interest other than as shareholders in the matters to be decided, no potential conflicts of interest arising from cross-directorships and no day-to-day involvement in running the business (paragraphs 4.8 and 4.11).

A5   The members of the remuneration committee should be listed each year in the committee's report to shareholders (B1 below). When they stand for re-election, the proxy cards should indicate their membership of the committee (paragraphs 4.12 and 5.25).

A6   The Board itself should determine the remuneration of the Non-Executive Directors, including members of the remuneration committee, within the limits set in the Articles of Association (paragraph 4.13).

A7   Remuneration committees should consult the company Chairman and/or Chief Executive about their proposals and have access to professional advice inside and outside the company (paragraphs 4.14–4.17).

A8   The remuneration committee Chairman should attend the company's Annual General Meeting (AGM) to answer shareholders' questions about Directors' remuneration and should ensure that the company maintains contact as required with its principal shareholders about remuneration in the same way as for other matters (paragraph 5.27).

A9   The committee's annual report to shareholders (B1 below) should not be a standard item of agenda for AGMs. But the committee should consider each year whether the circumstances are such that the AGM should be invited to approve the policy set out in their report and should minute their conclusions (paragraphs 5.28–5.32).

B *Disclosure and approval provisions*

B1   The remuneration committee should make a report each year to the shareholders on behalf of the Board. The report should form part of, or be annexed to, the company's Annual Report and Accounts. It should be the main vehicle through which the company accounts to shareholders for Directors' remuneration (paragraph 5.4).

B2   The report should set out the Company's policy on executive remuneration, including levels, comparator groups of companies, individual components, performance criteria and measurement, pension provision, contracts of service and compensation commitments on early termination (paragraphs 5.5–5.7).

B3   The report should state that, in framing its remuneration policy, the committee has given full consideration to the best practice provisions set out in sections C and D below (paragraph 5.25).

B4   The report should also include full details of all elements in the remuneration package of each individual Director by name, such as basic salary, benefits in kind, annual bonuses and long-term incentive schemes including share options (paragraphs 5.8–5.12).

B5   Information on share options, including SAYE options, should be given for each Director in accordance with the recommendations of the Accounting Standards Board's Urgent Issues Task Force Abstract 10 and its successors (paragraphs 5.13–5.16).

B6   If grants under executive share option or other long-term incentive schemes are awarded in one large block rather than phased, the report should explain and justify (paragraph 6.29).

B7   Also included in the report should be pension entitlements earned by each individual Director during the year, calculated on a basis to be recommended by the Faculty of Actuaries and the Institute of Actuaries (paragraphs 5.17–5.23).

B8   If annual bonuses or benefits in kind are pensionable the report should explain and justify (paragraph 6.44).

B9   The amounts received by, and commitments made to, each Director under B4, B5, and B7 should be subject to audit (paragraph 5.4).

B10 Any service contracts which provide for, or imply, notice periods in excess of one year (or any provisions for predetermined compensation on termination which exceed one year's salary and benefits) should be disclosed and the reasons for the longer notice periods explained (paragraph 7.13).

B11 Shareholdings and other relevant business interests and activities of the Directors should continue to be disclosed as required in the Companies Acts and London Stock Exchange Listing Rules (paragraph 5.24).

B12 Shareholders should be invited specifically to approve all new long-term incentive schemes (including share option schemes) whether payable in cash or shares in which Directors or senior executives will participate which potentially commit shareholders' funds over more than one year or dilute the equity (paragraph 5.33).

C Remuneration policy

C1   Remuneration committees must provide the packages needed to attract, retain, and motivate Directors of the quality required but should avoid paying more than is necessary for this purpose (paragraphs 6.5–6.7).

C2   Remuneration committees should judge where to position their company relative to other companies. They should be aware what other comparable companies are paying and should take account of relative performance (paragraphs 6.11–6.12).

C3 Remuneration committees should be sensitive to the wider scene, including pay and employment conditions elsewhere in the company, especially when determining annual salary increases (paragraph 6.13).

C4 The performance-related elements of remuneration should be designed to align the interests of Directors and shareholders and to give Directors keen incentives to perform at the highest levels (paragraph 6.16).

C5 Remuneration committees should consider whether their Directors should be eligible for annual bonuses. If so, performance conditions should be relevant, stretching and designed to enhance the business. Upper limits should always be considered. There may be a case for part-payment in shares to be held for a significant period (paragraphs 6.19–6.22).

C6 Remuneration committees should consider whether their Directors should be eligible for benefits under long-term incentive schemes. Traditional share option schemes should be weighed against other kinds of long-term incentive schemes. In normal circumstances, shares granted should not vest, and options should not be exercisable, in under three years. Directors should be encouraged to hold their shares for a further period after vesting or exercise subject to the need to finance any costs of acquisition and associated tax liability (paragraphs 6.23–6.34).

C7 Any new long-term incentive schemes which are proposed should preferably replace existing schemes or at least form part of a well-considered overall plan, incorporating existing schemes, which should be approved as a whole by shareholders. The total rewards potentially available should not be excessive (paragraph 6.35). (*See* also B12.)

C8 Grants under all incentive schemes, including new grants under existing share option schemes, should be subject to challenging performance criteria reflecting the company's objectives. Consideration should be given to criteria which reflect the company's performance relative to a group of comparator companies in some key variables such as total shareholder return (paragraphs 6.38–6.40).

C9 Grants under executive share option and other long-term incentive schemes should normally be phased rather than awarded in one large block (paragraph 6.29). (*See* B6.)

C10 Executive share options should never be issued at a discount (paragraph 6.29).

C11 Remuneration committees should consider the pension consequences and associated costs to the company of basic salary increases, especially for Directors close to retirement (paragraphs 6.42–6.45).

C12 In general, neither annual bonuses nor benefits in kind should be pensionable (paragraph 6.44). (*See* B8.)

D Service contracts and compensation

D1 Remuneration committees should consider what compensation commitments their Directors' contracts of service, if any, would entail in the event of early termination, particularly for unsatisfactory performance (paragraph 7.10).

D2 There is a strong case for setting notice or contract periods at, or reducing them to, one year or less (*see* B10). Remuneration committees should, however, be sensitive and flexible, especially over timing. In some cases notice or contract periods of up to two years may be acceptable. Longer periods should be avoided wherever possible (paragraphs 7.11–7.15).

D3 If it is necessary to offer longer notice or contract periods, such as three years, to new Directors recruited from outside, such periods should reduce after the initial period (paragraph 7.16).

D4 Within the legal constraints, remuneration committees should tailor their approach in individual early termination cases to the wide variety of circumstances. The broad aim should be to avoid rewarding poor performance while dealing fairly with cases where departure is not due to poor performance (paragraphs 7.17–7.18).

D5 Remuneration committees should take a robust line on payment of compensation where performance has been unsatisfactory and on reducing compensation to reflect departing Directors' obligations to mitigate damages by earning money elsewhere (paragraphs 7.17–7.20).

D6 Where appropriate, and in particular where notice or contract periods exceed one year, companies should consider paying all or part of compensation in instalments rather than one lump sum and reducing or stopping payment when the former Director takes on new employment (paragraph 7.20).

STUDY GROUP ON DIRECTORS' REMUNERATION

Chairman
SIR RICHARD GREENBURY   Chairman, Marks & Spencer plc.

Members
SIR MICHAEL ANGUS   Chairman, Whitbread PLC and
                                                           The Boots Company PLC
SIR DAVID CHAPMAN Bt   Wise Speke Limited (Stockbrokers) Newcastle
SIR DENYS HENDERSON   Chairman, Rank Organisation Plc
SIR DAVID LEES   Chairman, GKN plc (nominated by the Stock Exchange)
MR GEOFF LINDEY   Head of UK Institutional Investment
                                        JP Morgan Investment Management Inc.
          (nominated by the National Association of Pension Funds)
MR TIM MELVILLE-ROSS   Director-General, Institute of Directors
MR GEORGE METCALFE   Chairman and CEO, UMECO plc
SIR DAVID SIMON   Chairman, The British Petroleum Company plc
SIR IAIN VALLANCE   Chairman, British Telecommunications plc
MR ROBERT WALTHER   Group Chief Executive,
                                        Clerical Medical Investment Group
          (nominated by the Association of British Insurers)

Professional Advisers
MR ANDREW EDWARDS
MR JOHN GRIEVES   Freshfields
MR PETER JEFFCOTE   Freshfields

MR ANGUS MAITLAND	Maitland Consultancy
MR JOHN CARNEY	Towers Perrin

Secretariat
MR MATT LEWIS   KPMG, Secretary to the Group

APPENDIX 3

Committee on Corporate Governance

PRELIMINARY REPORT

2 Principles of Corporate Governance

2.1 We draw a distinction between principles of corporate governance and more detailed guidelines like the Cadbury and Greenbury codes. With guidelines, one asks 'How far are they *complied with*?'; with principles, the right question is 'How are they *applied* in practice?'. We recommend that companies should include in their annual report and accounts a narrative statement of how they apply the relevant principles to their particular circumstances. This should not be an additional regulatory requirement, nor do we prescribe the statement's content. But it could conveniently be linked with the compliance statement required by the Listing Rules. Given that the responsibility for good corporate governance rests with the board of directors, the written description of the way in which the board has applied the principles of corporate governance represents a key part of the process.

2.2 Against this background, we believe that the following principles can contribute to good corporate governance. They are developed further in later chapters.

A Directors

I.   *The Board.* **Every listed company should be headed by an effective board which should lead and control the company.**

2.3 This follows Cadbury (report, paragraph 4.1). It stresses the dual role of the board—leadership and control—and the need to be effective in both. It assumes the unitary board almost universal in UK companies.

II   *Chairman and CEO.* **There are two key tasks at the top of every public company—the running of the board and the executive responsibility for the** running of the company's business. How these tasks are carried out in each company should be publicly explained.

2.4 This makes clear that there are two distinct jobs, that of the chairman of the board and that of the chief executive officer. The wording leaves open whether the holders of the two posts need be different people, or whether one person can do both jobs. This is discussed below (3.17–3.19).

III *Board balance.* The board should include a balance of executive directors and non-executive directors (including independent non-executives) such that no individual or small group of individuals can dominate the board's decision taking.

2.5 Cadbury highlights the need to avoid the board being dominated by one individual (code 1.2). This risk is greatest where the roles of chairman and CEO are combined, though there may be cases where there are important offsetting advantages in combining the roles. But whether or not the two roles are separated, it is important that there should be a sufficient number of non-executive directors, a majority of them independent; and that these individuals should be able both to work co-operatively with their executive colleagues and to demonstrate robust independence of judgement and objectivity when necessary.

IV *Supply of Information.* The board should be supplied in a timely fashion with information in a form and of a quality appropriate to enable it to discharge its duties.

2.6 We endorse the view of the Cadbury committee (report, 4.14) that the effectiveness of non-executive directors (indeed, of all directors) turns to a considerable extent on the quality of the information they receive.

V *Appointments to the Board.* There should be a formal and transparent procedure for the appointment of new directors to the board.

2.7 The Cadbury committee commended the establishment of nomination committees but did not include them in the Code of Practice. In our view adoption of a formal procedure for appointments to the board, with a nomination committee making recommendations to the full board, should be recognized as good practice.

VI *Re-election.* All directors should be required to submit themselves for re-election at regular intervals and at least every three years.

2.8 We endorse the view that it is the board's responsibility to appoint new directors and the shareholders' responsibility to re-elect them. The 'insulation' of directors from re-election is dying out and we consider that it should now cease. This will promote effective boards and recognize shareholders' inherent rights.

B Directors' Remuneration

2.9 Directors' remuneration should be embraced in the corporate governance process; the way in which directors' remuneration is handled can have a damaging effect on a company's public reputation, and on morale within the company. We suggest the following broad principles.

I   *The Level and Make-up of Remuneration.* **Levels of remuneration should be sufficient to attract and retain the directors needed to run the company successfully. The component parts of remuneration should be structured so as to link rewards to corporate and individual performance.**

2.10   This wording makes clear that those responsible should consider the remuneration of each director individually, and should do so against the needs of the particular company for talent at board level at the particular time. The remuneration of executive directors should be linked to performance.

II   *Procedure.* **Companies should establish a formal and transparent procedure for developing policy on executive remuneration and for fixing the remuneration packages of individual directors. No director should be involved in fixing his or her own remuneration.**

2.11   Cadbury and Greenbury both favoured the establishment of remuneration committees, and made recommendations on their composition and on the scope of their remit. Like Cadbury, we think that the remuneration committee should operate by making recommendations to the board, rather than by discharging functions on behalf of the board. But we would expect the board to reject the committee's recommendations only very rarely.

III   *Disclosure.* **The company's annual report should contain a statement of remuneration policy and details of the remuneration of each director.**

2.12   This follows Greenbury (code, B.1) except that we do not specify that the statement should be in the name of the remuneration committee. This is in line with our view of the status of the committee.

C Shareholders

2.13   This section includes principles for application both by listed companies and by shareholders.

I   *Shareholder Voting.* **Institutional shareholders should adopt a considered policy on voting the shares which they control.**

2.14   Institutional shareholders include internally managed pension funds, insurance companies and professional fund managers. The wording does not make voting mandatory, i.e. abstention remains an option; but these shareholders must consider the merits of an active voting policy.

II   *Dialogue between companies and investors.* **Companies and institutional shareholders should each be ready, where practicable, to enter into a dialogue based on the mutual understanding of objectives.**

2.15   This gives general endorsement to the idea of dialogue between companies and major investors. In practice, both companies and institutions can only participate in a limited number of one-to-one dialogues.

III   *Evaluation and Governance Disclosures.* **When evaluating companies' governance arrangements, particularly those relating to board structure and composition, institutional investors and their advisers should give due weight to all relevant factors drawn to their attention.**

2.16 This follows from the discussion in Chapter 1, paragraphs 1.11–1.14 on the importance of considering disclosures on their individual merits, as opposed to 'box ticking'.

IV *The AGM.* **Companies should use the AGM to communicate with private investors and encourage their participation.**

2.17 Private investors hold about 20% of the shares in listed companies, but are able to make little contribution to corporate governance. The main way of achieving greater participation is through improved use of the AGM. We discuss a number of suggestions for this purpose later.

D Accountability and Audit

2.18 This section includes principles for application both by listed companies and by auditors.

I *Financial Reporting.* **The board should present a balanced and understandable assessment of the company's position and prospects.**

2.19 This follows the Cadbury code (4.1). It is not limited to the statutory obligation to produce financial statements. The wording refers mainly to the annual report to shareholders, but the principle also covers interim and other price sensitive public reports and reports to regulators.

II *Internal Control.* **The board should maintain a sound system of internal control to safeguard shareholders' investment and the company's assets.**

2.20 This covers not only financial controls but operational and compliance controls, and risk management, since there are potential threats to shareholders' investment in each of these areas.

III *Relationship with the Auditors.* **The board should establish formal and transparent arrangements for maintaining an appropriate relationship with the company's auditors.**

2.21 We support the Cadbury recommendation (report, 4.35(a)) that all listed companies should establish an audit committee, composed of non-executive directors, as a committee of, and responsible to, the board. The duties of the audit committee include keeping under review the scope and results of the audit and its cost effectiveness, and the independence and objectivity of the auditors.

IV *External Auditors.* **The external auditors should independently report to shareholders in accordance with statutory and professional requirements and independently assure the board on the discharge of their responsibilities under D.I and D.II above in accordance with professional guidance.**

2.22 This points up the dual responsibility of the auditors—the public report to shareholders on the statutory financial statement and on other matters as required by the Stock Exchange Listing Rules; and additional private reporting to directors on operational and other matters.

APPENDIX 4

List of IFMA Members, as at 1 July 1997

AMP Asset Management PLC
AXA Equity & Law Investment Managers Ltd.
Baillie Gifford & Co.
Barclays Asset Management Group
Baring Asset Management Ltd.
Britannia Investment Managers Ltd.
British Aerospace Pension Funds Investment Management Ltd.
BG Pension Funds Management Ltd.
CCLA Investment Management Ltd.
Capital International Ltd.
Cazenove Fund Management
Citibank Global Asset Management
Clerical Medical Investment Group
Commercial Union Investment Management Ltd.
Co-operative Insurance Society Ltd.
Crédit Suisse Asset Management Ltd.
Edinburgh Fund Managers PLC
Equitable Life Assurance Society
Fidelity Pensions Management
Fleming Investment Management Ltd.
Foreign & Colonial Management Ltd.
Framlington Group Ltd.
FP Asset Management
Gartmore Investment Management PLC
General Accident Managed Pension Funds Ltd.
Genesis Investment Management Ltd.
Goldman Sachs Asset Management
John Govett & Co. Ltd.
Guardian Asset Management Ltd.
Guinness Flight Hambro Asset Management Ltd.
HSBC Asset Management Ltd.

Henderson Investors
Hermes Pensions Management Ltd.
Hill Samuel Asset Management Group Ltd.
Imperial Investments Ltd.
INVESCO Asset Management Ltd.
Ivory & Sime PLC
Kleinwort Benson Investment Management Ltd.
Lazard Brothers Asset Management Ltd.
Legal & General Investment Management Ltd.
LGT Asset Management PLC
Lincoln Investment Management
Lucas Pensions Investment Management Ltd.
M. & G. Investment Management Ltd.
Martin Currie Ltd.
Mercury Asset Management Group PLC
Merrill Lynch Capital Management Group
Morgan Grenfell Asset Management Ltd.
Morgan Stanley Asset Management Ltd.
J. P. Morgan Investment Management Inc.
Murray Johnstone Ltd.
National Provident Institution
Newton Investment Management Ltd.
Norwich Union Investment Management Ltd.
Old Mutual Asset Managers (UK) Ltd.
PDFM Limited
Pension Services Ltd.
Perpetual Portfolio Management Ltd.
Prolific Asset Management Ltd.
Prudential Portfolio Managers Ltd.
Rothschild Asset Management Ltd.
Royal & Sun Alliance Investment Management Ltd.
RTZ Pension Investments Ltd.
Salomon Brothers Asset Management Ltd.
Schroder Investment Management Ltd.
Scottish Amicable Investment Managers Ltd.
Scottish Equitable PLC
Scottish Life Assurance Co.
Scottish Mutual Assurance PLC
Scottish Widows' Investment Management Ltd.
Shell Pensions Management Services Ltd.
Singer & Friedlander Investment Management Ltd.
SLC Asset Management
Standard Life Assurance Co.
State Street Global Advisors United Kingdom Ltd.
Stewart Ivory & Co. Ltd.
Sun Life Investment Management Ltd.
Templeton Investment Management Ltd.
Threadneedle Asset Management Ltd.
United Assurance Group PLCs
Zurich Investment Management Ltd.

APPENDIX 5

Extracts from IFMA Fund Management Survey 1997

Question 5 of the survey questionnaire sought data on the assets managed for institutional clients by main institutional type (pension funds, investment trusts, unit trusts, life funds, non-life insurance funds, and other). The responses are summarized in Table A1. (The results in this section are based upon seventy-four responses. The remaining one was omitted due to irreconcilable inconsistencies in the questionnaire answers.)

Table A1. Institutional client analysis (31 March 1997) (£bn.)

	Total assets	No. of non-zero returns	Mean	Max.
UK institutional clients				
Pension funds	495.8	69	7.2	53.5
Investment trusts	38.1	29	1.3	5.0
Unit trusts	71.9	55	1.3	6.0
Life funds	335.7	42	8.0	50.4
Non-life funds	41.8	27	1.5	8.3
Other	65.0	52	1.3	8.3
Total	1,048.3	73	14.2	69.9
Overseas institutional clients				
Pension funds	271.2	42	6.5	151.8
Investment trusts	2.9	9	0.3	0.7
Unit trusts	50.4	25	2.0	9.5
Life funds	71.2	17	4.2	29.1
Non-life funds	31.5	17	1.9	10.5
Other	207.3	39	5.3	29.5
Total	634.5	51	12.4	193.4

	Total assets	No. of non-zero returns	Mean	Max.
Total institutional clients				
Pension funds	767.0	71	10.8	182.1
Investment trusts	41.0	32	1.3	5.0
Unit trusts	122.3	58	2.1	12.0
Life funds	406.9	44	9.2	70.8
Non-life funds	73.3	33	2.2	15.1
Other	272.3	54	5.0	29.6
Total	1,682.8	74	22.7	235.7

Table A2. Fund management assets

	£bn.
Private clients	32.2
Institutional clients	1,067.0
of which:	
Pension funds	495.8
Investment trusts	38.1
Unit trusts	71.9
Life funds	335.7
Non-life funds	41.8

Select Bibliography and References

BAIN, N., and BAND, D. (1996), *Winning Ways through Corporate Governance*.

Bank of England (1665), *Tract on Appointments to the Court*.

—— (1997), *Fourth Report on Finance for Small Firms*, London: Bank of England.

Bankers' Digest, 27 March 1992.

BARCA, F. (1995), 'On Corporate Governance in Italy: Issues, Facts and Agenda'; paper presented to the OECD Conference, Paris, 23–4 Feb.

BERLE, A. A., and MEANS, G. C. (1932), *The Modern Corporation and Private Property* (rev. edn. 1967), New York: Harcourt, Brace & World.

BLAIR, M. (1996), *Ownership and Control: Rethinking Corporate Governance for the 21st Century*, Washington: Brookings Institution.

BOSWELL, J. (1823), *The Life of Johnson*.

BOWEN, W. G. (1994), *Inside the Boardroom*, New York: John Wiley & Sons.

BRANCATO, C. (1997), *Communicating Corporate Performance: A Delicate Balance*, The Conference Board.

BROWNE, G. (1866), *On Companies*, Jordan's, 44th edn.

BZW (1996), *Annual Equity Gilt Study*.

CADBURY, Sir A. (1995), *The Company Chairman*, Institute of Directors.

CAMERON, A. (1995), *Bank of Scotland*, Mainstream Publishing.

CAWSTON, G., and KEANE, K. H. (1896), *The Early Chartered Companies*, Edward Arnold.

Central Statistical Office (1996), *Financial Indicators*, London: CSO.

CHARKHAM, J. P. (1994), *Keeping Good Company: A Study of Corporate Governance in Five Companies*, Oxford: Oxford University Press.

COBBETT, W. (1826), *Rural Rides*, repr. Harmondsworth, Penguin, 1967.

Committee on Corporate Governance (1998), *Report*.

Committee on Private Share Ownership (1996), *Report*, Gee Publishing.

Committee on the Financial Aspects of Corporate Governance (Cadbury Committee) (1992), *Report*, London: Gee Publishing, Dec.

Cork Committee (1984), *Report on Solvency*.

CRYSTAL, GRAEF C. (1992), *In Search of Excess*, W. W. Norton.

DAVIES, R. (1996), *The Index of Nominees and their Beneficial Owners* (7th edn.), Fulcrum Research.

DEMB, A., and NEUBAUER, F. (1992), *The Corporate Board: Confronting the Paradoxes*, New York: Oxford University Press.

DENHAM, R., and PORTER, M. (1995), *Lifting All Boats*, report of the Capital Allocation Subcouncil to the Competitiveness Policy Council, Washington D.C.

DREW, C. (1995), 'The Director's Duties', *Law Society Gazette*, 1 March.

DTI (1996), *Shareholder Communication and the AGM*, London: DTI.

ELKINGTON, J. (1997), *Cannibals with Forks: The Triple Bottom Line of 21st Century Business*, Capstone.

European Stock Exchange Statistics (1995), *Annual Report*.

Extel (1997), *Annual Survey*.

Fabian Society (1996), 'Changing Work', report of inquiry chaired by John Jackson.

FELTON, R. F., HUDNUT, A., and HEEKEREN, J. V. (1996), 'Putting a Value on Board Governance', *McKinsey Quarterly*, 4.

Financial Services Authority (1997), preliminary documents.

FRANKS, J., and MEYER, C. (1993), 'Ownership and Control', inaugural lecture at the University of Warwick, 21 Feb.

GALSWORTHY, J. (1923), *The Forsyte Saga*, Heinemann.

GOYDER, M. (1998), *Sooner, Sharper, Simpler: A Lean Vision of an Inclusive Annual Report*, Tomorrow's Company.

GRAHAM, B., and DODD, D. L. (1934), *Security Analysis*, New York: McGraw Hill.

Greenbury Report (1995), *Directors' Remuneration: Report of a Study Group Chaired by Sir Richard Greenbury*, Gee Publishing, July.

HAWLEY, J. P., WILLIAMS, A. T., and MILLER, J. U. (1994), 'Getting the Herd to Run: Shareholder Activism', *Business and the Contemporary World*, 6/4.

HOWELL, P. (1991), 'Investment Dilemmas', speech to PIRC annual conference.

HUSON, M. R. (1997), *Does Governance Matter? Evidence from CalPERS Interventions*, University of Alberta Press/University of Texas Press.

HUTTON, W. (1995), *The State We're In*, Verso.

—— (1996), *The State to Come*, Verso.

ISC (1991a), *The Role of Directors*, IBS.

—— (1991b), *The Role and Responsibilities of Shareholders*, ISC.

ISAKSSON, M. GONEC (1997), background paper for the Business Sector Colloquium on Corporate Governance 'Institutional Modernisation for Effective and Adaptive Corporate Governance', June.

KEASEY, K., et al. (1997), *Corporate Governance: Economic, Management, and Financial Issues*, Oxford: Oxford University Press.

KEYNES, J. M. (1936), *The General Theory of Employment Interest and Money*.

KYNASTON, W. (1994), *The City of London*, 2 vols., Chatto & Windus.

LAPIDES, P. (1996), 'The Changing Role of the Audit Committee', *Directors' Monthly*.

L'HELIAS, S. (1997), *Le Retour de l'actionnaire: pratiques du corporate governance en France, aux États-Unis et en Grande Bretagne*, Gualino Éditeur.

The London Financial Guide (1998).

LOWENSTEIN, L. (1988), *What's Wrong with Wall Street?*, Reading, Mass.: Addison-Wesley.

—— (1996), *Columbia Law Review*, 96/5, June.

LOWENSTEIN, R. (1995), *Buffet*, Random House.

LSE Centre for Economic Performance (1996), *Study*, London: LSE.

MAIN, B. G. M., and JOHNSTON, J. (1992), *The Remuneration Committee as an Instrument of Corporate Governance*, Edinburgh: University of Edinburgh Press.

MILLSTEIN, I., et al. (1996), *Comparison of Materials on Board Guidelines*, Weil, Gotshal & Manges LLP.

MILLSTEIN, I., and MACAVOY, P. (1998), 'The Active Board of Directors and Improved Performance of the Large Publicly Traded Corporation', *Columbia Law Review*, June.

MONKS, R., and MINOW, N. (1995), *Corporate Governance*, Oxford: Blackwell Business.

—— —— (1996), *Power and Accountability: Watching the Watchers*, New York: Harper Collins.

MORTIMER, T. (1798), *Everyman his Own Broker, or A Guide to the Stock Exchange* (12th edn.), The Royal Exchange.

National Association of Corporate Directors (1996), *Report of the NACD Blue Ribbon Commission on Director Professionalism*, NACD.

NESBITT, S. L. (1994), 'Long Term Rewards from Shareholder Activism: A Study of the CalPERS Effect', *Journal of Applied Corporate Finance*.

O'BARR, W. M., and CONLEY, J. M. (1992), *Fortunes and Folly*, Homewood, Ill.: Business One Irwin.

Occupational Pensions Board (1997), *Guide for Pension Scheme Trustees*.

OECD (1997), 'Background and Issues Paper for the Meeting of the Steering Group on Corporate Governance and Disclosure', Oct.

Office of the American Workplace (1994), *The Road to High Performance Workplaces*, US DOL Report.

PARKINSON, J. E. (1994), *Corporate Power and Responsibility: Issues in the Theory of Company Law*, Oxford: Clarendon Press.

PIRC (1995), *A Corporate Governance Health Check: Annual Review*, PIRC.

—— (1996*a*), *Reform of the AGM: A Discussion Paper*, PIRC.

—— (1996*b*), *Rewarding the Board: Trends in Directors' Remuneration*, PIRC.

—— (1997*a*), *Proxy Voting Trends 1992–96*, PIRC.

—— (1997*b*), *A Guide to the Guidelines: Institutional Shareholder Corporate Governance Policies*, PIRC.

—— (1997*c*), *Fair Shares: Executive Share Schemes*, PIRC.

—— (1997*d*), *Nomination Committees*, PIRC, Nov.

—— (1997*e*), *Is Greenbury Working?*, PIRC.

—— (1998*a*), *Non-executive Directors: Assessing Independence*, PIRC.

—— (1998*b*), *Environmental and Social Reporting: Current Practice at FTSE 350 Companies*, PIRC.

—— (1998*c*), *Governance and Performance: Making the Link*, PIRC.

—— (1998*d*), *Proxy Voting Report 1998*, PIRC.

PLENDER, J. (1997), *A Stake in the Future: The Stakeholding Solution*, Nicholas Brealey.

—— (1998), 'Stakeholding', speech to RSA, Mar.

PRO SHARE (1996), *Annual Report*.

ProxInvest (1997), *Governance and Performance in French Companies*.

ROE, M. (1994), *Strong Managers, Weak Owners*, Princeton: Princeton University Press.

Royal Society of Arts, Commerce and Manufacture (1996), *Tomorrow's Company: Enquiry Report*, RSACM.

Scott Committee (1996), *Report*.

Shell UK (1998), *Shell UK Report to Society*.

SIMPSON, A. (1990), 'Institutional Investors', in J. Lufkin and D. Gallagher (eds.), *International Corporate Governance*, Euromoney Books.

—— (1991), *The Greening of Global Investment: How Politics, Environment and Ethics are Reshaping Strategies*, Economist Publications.

SMITH, M. P. (1996), 'Shareholder Activism by Institutional Investors: Evidence from CalPERS', *Journal of Finance*, 51.

SPINK, G. I. Grant (1977), *The Standard Catalogue of Provincial Banks and Bank Notes.*

STAPLEDON, G. P. (1996), *Institutional Shareholders and Corporate Governance*, Oxford: Clarendon Press.

SZYMANSKI, S. (1996), 'Gazza and Greenbury: Similarities and Differences', *Hume Papers on Public Policy*, 3/4.

THUROW, L. (1996), *The Future of Capitalism*, Nicholas Brealey.

Top Pay Research Group (1997), *Annual Survey*, Top Pay Research Group.

TREVELYAN, G.M. (1942), *English Social History*, 4 vols.

TRICKER, R. (1994), *International Corporate Governance*, Englewood Cliffs, NJ: Prentice Hall.

—— (1994–7), *Corporate Governance: An International Review*, vols. i–iii, Oxford: Blackwells Business.

TRUSKIE, S. D. (1996), *Director Survey*, Washington: National Association of Corporate Directors.

TUC (1998), *Pay Report*, London: TUC, Jan.

UBS Asset Management (1997), *Pension Fund Indicators: A Long Term Perspective on Pension Fund Investment*, London: UBS Asset Management.

University of Essex (1997), *Report on Takeovers*, University of Essex.

University of Northumbria at Newcastle, Newcastle Business School, Department of Accounting and Finance (1992), *Investor Relations Project: Survey Report and Results.*

Weinberg Committee (1996), *Private Share Ownership.*

WHEELER, D., and SILLANPAA, M. (1997), *The Stakeholder Corporation*, Pitman Publishing.

XUEREB, P. (1989), *The Rights of Shareholders*, BSP Professional Books.

Index